RODALE'S
SUCCESSFUL ORGANIC GARDENING®
HERBS

RODALE'S
SUCCESSFUL ORGANIC GARDENING®
HERBS

PATRICIA S. MICHALAK

Rodale Press, Emmaus, Pennsylvania

Copyright © 1993 by Weldon Russell Pty Ltd

If you have any questions or comments concerning this book, please write:

Rodale Press
Book Readers' Service
33 East Minor Street
Emmaus, PA 18098

Library of Congress Cataloging-in-Publication Data

Michalak, Patricia S.
   Herbs / Patricia S. Michalak.
      p.   cm.   —   (Rodale's successful organic gardening)
   Includes index.
   ISBN 0–87596–557–1 hardcover — ISBN 0–87596–558–X
   paperback
   1. Herb gardening. 2. Herbs. 3. Herbs — Utilization. 4. Organic
   Gardening. I. Title. II. Series.
   SB351.H5M48 1993
   635.7 — dc20   92–32758
                                            CIP

Printed in the United States of America on acid-free , recycled paper ♻

Rodale Press Staff:
   Executive Editor: Margaret Lydic Balitas
   Senior Editor: Barbara W. Ellis
   Editors: Nancy J. Ondra and Fern M. Bradley
   Copy Editor: Barbara M. Webb

Produced for Rodale Press by Weldon Russell Pty Ltd
107 Union Street, North Sydney NSW 2060, Australia
a member of the Weldon International Group of companies

   Publisher: Elaine Russell
   Publishing Manager: Susan Hurley
   Senior Editor: Ariana Klepac
   Editor: Margaret Whiskin
   Horticultural Consultants: Cheryl Maddocks, Tony Rodd
   Copy Editors: Bruce Semler, Yani Silvana, Dawn Titmus,
      Jill Wayment
   Designer: Rowena Sheppard
   Picture Researcher: Anne Nicol
   Photographer: David Wallace
   Illustrators: Barbara Rodanska, Kathie Smith
   Macintosh Layout Artists: Honor Morton, Edwina Ryan
   Indexer: Michael Wyatt
   Production Manager: Dianne Leddy

A KEVIN WELDON PRODUCTION

Distributed in the book trade by St. Martin's Press

       10   hardcover
       10 9   paperback

Opposite: Witch hazel
Half title: Bee balm
Opposite title page: Chamomile
Title page: Arnica
Opposite contents: Barberry
Contents page: Angelica (left), French sorrel (right)

CONTENTS

INTRODUCTION

Organic herb gardening offers just enough challenge to make it rewarding and fun. If you understand basic concepts of plant growth, you can easily grow and harvest an abundance of herbs using the organic method.

Gardening organically means following the advice of nature. In the wild, plants are provided with nutrients released as their ancestors decompose. You can think of this natural process as a circle in which one generation feeds the next and the foodstuffs remain within the circle. The same circle exists within your garden, with the exception that harvesting removes some nutrient material from the available pool. To compensate, you need to add compost and rock minerals.

The natural cycles in your garden also include the activity of insects and disease organisms. In a healthy garden, there is a balance between the pests that feed on your garden plants and the beneficial insects and micro-organisms that feed upon the pests. Some gardening practices upset this natural balance, and that's when the pests become most noticeable. The goal of the organic gardener is to keep all the natural cycles in balance.

The chapters that follow will describe the major cycles that occur in your garden. Begin by understanding how climate, sunlight, and soil control the growth of garden plants. Once you've learned these basic factors, you can select the herbs that are best suited to the conditions you have available and take advantage of your herbs' natural characteristics and growth requirements to create attractive and aromatic gardens.

Remember, there are differences among herbs when it comes to cultivation. Some have a reputation for slow growth, or being difficult to start from seed. Some adapt easily to one climate, others to another. Knowing about their differences and preferences will assure success.

When it's time to harvest, learn how to get the most from your herbs by following the advice on harvesting techniques. Many herbs will offer multiple harvests throughout the growing season. You can enjoy them fresh or preserve them to use later.

You can also include the herbs you've grown in your cosmetic routines. They have special properties to soothe irritation, protect skin, and enhance appearance. You can prepare your own natural cosmetics, or learn to look for them among commercial products.

Herbs also have a long history in pharmacy. Before the development of modern drugs, herbs provided the only medicines available to cure common ailments. In fact, they're still used in many medicines today. Although most are gentle and harmless in action, use them cautiously. Always identify a plant before ingesting it, and be sure it is edible. Keep in mind that excess quantities of certain plants, especially some herbs, can be dangerous.

Herbs may also contribute color, scent, and texture to home craft products. Many of the craft items included in this book are simple enough for a child to make, yet still offer opportunities for the experienced decorator.

There's more to herb gardening than you thought — more pleasure, more interest, more reward.

Opposite: A lavender-lined pathway is just one way to grow and enjoy herbs. Whether you want to soothe your sore throat, calm your nerves, cook with, or just simply look at your herbs, you will find one that is perfect.

HOW TO USE THIS BOOK

People have been growing herbs for thousands of years. In earlier times, herbal knowledge was passed along to each new generation through storytelling and lots of practical experience in the herb garden or time spent gathering wild plants. These days, not everyone is fortunate enough to have such personal guidance. We can't personally be at your side, so we've tried to provide in this book enough information to get you started and growing successfully.

Rodale's Successful Organic Gardening: Herbs is divided into two main sections. The first explains how to select, plant, maintain, harvest, and use herbs, without using synthetic fertilizers or pesticides. The second section, the "Plant by Plant Guide," starting on page 100, sets out in convenient reference form the requirements and characteristics of most herb species.

"Understanding Your Garden," starting on page 12, explains how the environment influences your garden. You can use the USDA Plant Hardiness Zone Map on page 154 to determine the climatic influences of temperature on your area. You'll also find out how climate affects your plants—what temperature ranges suit each type of herb and how frost and moisture play significant roles in the success or failure of your garden.

The topography of where you plant your herbs—be it on a hilltop or slope or in a valley—will also affect the growing conditions available in your garden. You'll also want to consider the amount of sun or shade your herbs will get. And understanding soils and plant nutrients helps you to fully appreciate the workings of nature and better manage your garden and its particular requirements.

When you are ready to select your plants, use the information in "Choosing Your Plants," starting on page 26. This is a guide to familiarize you with the life cycles of each type of herb—annuals, biennials, and perennials—and an analysis of the plant parts and the standard terms of classification. Tips on selecting the best plants for you are given to help you to make the right choice when you're confronted with a nursery full of stock. Also included in this section is a comprehensive species chart covering growth form and size, preferred climate, best soil conditions, propagation, pests and diseases, and primary uses for each herb. From this chapter, you will learn what to look for when buying herbs, where to plant them, and the many ways that herbs differ in their uses and their needs.

In "Cultivating and Planting," starting on page 40, you'll find out how to prepare your garden for planting, with methods of tilling, digging, and cultivating described in detail. Adding organic nutrients can supplement the fertility of your garden, and this chapter tells you how to go about understanding the needs of your soil. You'll learn what you can do, without chemicals, to ensure your plants have rich, fertile soil to grow in.

There are instructions here for making your own compost heap so that you can recycle waste from your kitchen and garden and, at the same time, have plenty of nutrient-rich material on hand to add to your soil when needed.

Once you have prepared your garden, you can move on to planting seeds with the aid of this chapter. You'll find information on choosing the right containers and growing medium, sowing, finding the right environment, thinning and potting-up, hardening off, and transplanting.

Once your herbs are up and growing, "Maintaining Your Garden," starting on page 54, offers advice on how to make sure they remain healthy and pest-free, using organic nutrients and pest-control measures.

You'll discover all sorts of practical information on watering and the conservation of water, weeding, propagating (including division and layering), overwintering, and mulching. Also included is a rundown of the most common pests and diseases you need to be aware of and tips on how to properly identify and deal with them.

The ultimate reward comes with harvesting and using your organically grown herbs. "Preserving, Storing, and Using Herbs," starting on page 72, leads you through the methods of harvesting and preserving, including air-drying, screen-drying, oven-drying, packing and storing, freezing, salting, and sugaring.

Then, with your herbs always at hand, you can find out how best to use them in the kitchen, for medicinal purposes, or for enchanting crafts and truly personal gifts. This chapter also includes a special double-page boxed section on herbal dyeing.

Plant by Plant Guide

This alphabetical listing, by common names, is an immensely practical and simple reference for a wide variety of herbs. (If you know an herb only by its botanical name, you can find its common-name cross-reference by referring to the Index.)

Each entry is accompanied by a color photograph for easy identification. You'll also find information on the best climate and site, ideal soil conditions, growing guidelines, growing habit, flowering time, pest and disease prevention, and harvesting and storing, as well as special tips, precautions, and other common names.

The "Plant by Plant Guide" is designed to help make organic gardening as easy and painless as possible by providing all the necessary information in a clear and concise way. The diagram below helps explain what to look for on these practical pages.

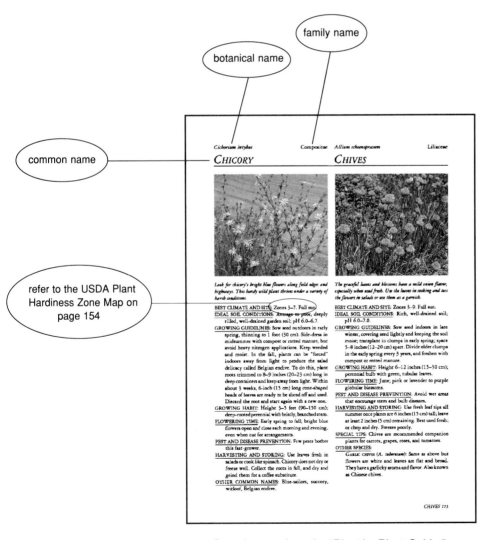

Sample page from the "Plant by Plant Guide."

UNDERSTANDING YOUR GARDEN

Learning about your local environment—including its climate, topography, sunlight, and soil —is critical for success with organic gardening. No matter what you plan to grow, you'll find that working with, rather than against, these factors will help you avoid many gardening problems.

The two most important natural resources to consider are your local climate and your soil. You might think there is nothing you can do to change your climate (short of moving), and this is almost true. What you can do is grow the right plants at the right time and in the right place. All plants have basic requirements for temperature, moisture, and light. Your gardening success depends on how well you understand these needs and the way plants interact with soil. If you understand how the environment works to make plants grow, you'll get the most rewards from gardening.

Good soil is like money in the bank. You'll have to make deposits (of organic matter and plant nutrients) before you can make withdrawals of plentiful harvests.

The "interest" that organic gardeners earn appears as healthy, pest-free plants and a soil that continues to improve each gardening season.

Garden planning is one step that too many gardeners take lightly. Especially if you're a beginner, you should take the time to decide exactly what you want to grow. Consider your future garden design plans as well. Most gardeners find that their landscape changes with each new growing season, simply because there's always something new to try. Make a rough garden plan and list the goals you'd like to accomplish each year. Gardens aren't made overnight, and rarely do they stop growing!

Keep track of new gardening developments by subscribing to horticultural magazines. Some specialize in herbs, some in organic gardening, and so on. The organic method is gaining more attention and a wider following all the time. Organic herb growers are increasing in numbers, so you'll have lots of company. Compare notes with other gardeners; their knowledge and experience is another valuable natural resource.

Opposite: When planning your herb garden, don't forget to take into consideration your local climate, topography, and soil conditions. Ask your neighbors what grows well in their garden—and what doesn't!

Climate

Climate is the way temperature, moisture, and wind interact in a particular region to produce local weather. Most important for gardeners, climate influences your choice of plants.

Before making your garden plans and selecting herbs to grow, you should consider the normal weather patterns of your climate. Since "normal" weather includes the unexpected, enthusiastic gardeners need to become avid weather watchers. You will have to monitor the weather in order to provide your plants with three basic, climate-dependent requirements: a suitable temperature range, a favorable frost-free period, and an adequate supply of moisture.

Temperature Range

The leafy green exterior of any plant gives no hint of the complex chemical processes occurring within. These processes are temperature-dependent, and different plants vary in their temperature requirements.

When it comes to air-temperature preference, most plants have upper and lower limits and are classified as cool-season, warm-season, or adaptable to both. Cool-season herbs, like mustard, continue growing even when the temperature drops as low as 40°F (4°C); they stop growing or die during the heat of summer. Warm-season herbs, like basil, are heat-lovers, and won't grow unless the temperature is 50°F (10°C) or above. Basil is very sensitive to cold and usually dies with the first cold snap in fall.

Hardy perennial herbs (those that live for more than 2 years) are cold-tolerant and will survive the extremes of winter in a dormant state. Dormancy means that the chemical processes normally occurring inside a plant slow down and the plant is in a resting stage. Likewise, any plant which is sensitive to heat will often become dormant in response to any high-temperature conditions.

Soil temperature also has an effect on plant growth. Roots

Borage, a hardy annual, tolerates light fall frosts.

Cool-climate Herbs

These herbs are adapted to cool climates, with winter temperatures commonly dropping below 10°F (-5°C). Nearly all these herbs can readily be grown in moderate climates, but in subtropical and tropical climates many of them will not thrive.

Angelica, anise, anise hyssop, arnica, barberry, bearberry, bee balm, betony, birch, borage, burdock, caraway, catnip, chamomile (Roman), chervil, chicory, chives, clary, comfrey, costmary, dandelion, dill, dock, elecampane, garlic, goldenrod, hop, horseradish, horsetail, hyssop, lady's bedstraw, lemon balm, lovage, marsh mallow, mugwort, mustard, nasturtium, nettle, New Jersey tea, pipsissewa, plantain, red clover, roses, saffron, sassafras, savory (winter), soapwort, sorrel, sweet cicely, sweet woodruff, tansy, tarragon (French), valerian, vervain (European), wormwood, yarrow.

---

tend to grow more slowly in cool soil, so your herbs may have trouble getting the nutrients they need for their flush of spring growth. An early spring application of compost will supply the nutrients your herbs need until their roots start spreading again. You'll also want to keep soil temperature in mind when planting your seeds. Some herb seeds, like caraway and chervil, germinate best at cooler temperatures, while others, like fenugreek and nasturtiums, prefer warmer soil. You'll find recommendations for the best time to sow each herb seed in the "Plant by Plant Guide," starting on page 100.

Frost-free Period

In most climates, the growing season begins after the last frost of the cold season and ends when frosts begin again in fall. If you live in a cool climate and want to use the flowers and seeds of your herbs, the plants you decide to grow will have to sprout, flower, and set seed within this period. Plants vary in the amount of time they require to reach maturity; seed and plant suppliers usually supply information as to the number of days needed by each variety. If you're growing herbs for their foliage, they won't need to flower and set seed, so the frost-free period is less important.

Frost occurs when the air temperature around plants falls to below 32°F (0°C) during the night, after dew has formed. The result is a lacy, white coating of water

The key to having a beautiful and productive herb garden is using herbs that are adapted to your climate.

Sweet basil will thrive in dry and warm climates.

crystals on your plants' leaves. Plants vary in their susceptibility to frost, but in those that are frost-sensitive, like basil, it injures internal structures and turns the foliage black. With sufficient damage, plants will die as a result of frost in spring or fall. Hardier annuals, like borage and dill, are able to tolerate light fall frosts. Most perennials are frost-tolerant.

If you're a new gardener, check with your neighbor or Cooperative Extension Service agent to find out the length of the growing season in your area.

Moisture

Plants are dependent on water. They cannot absorb nutrients and maintain essential processes unless they receive adequate moisture. As a general rule, your herb plants require the equivalent of 1 inch (25 mm) of rainfall each week. Rain is the best source of moisture during the growing season, but you will need to supplement this by irrigation or hand watering if rains fail. In some climates, snow contributes a great part of the annual water supply. Even though snow usually falls when most plants are dormant, it still contributes to the water reserves held in the soil below the surface.

Consistently inadequate moisture levels may cause irreparable damage to plants. The first sign is drooping and wilting foliage. Drought-sensitive plants grow slowly, become dormant, or die under dry conditions.

At the other extreme, too much water may flood the root system and prevent the plant from absorbing the oxygen and nutrients it requires. Plants susceptible to flooding may also wilt, drop their leaves, and die if the excess water is not quickly drained away.

Your herbs will require more water under windy conditions, as wind draws away moisture released through pores faster than normal. Wind shelter is important for your more sensitive herbs. To learn more about watering your herbs, see the section "Watering" on page 56.

Working with the natural landscape, simple terracing is used to create a level herb garden on a gentle slope.

Topography

Topography means the lay of the land. As hills and valleys dip and rise, small changes in altitude and slope and wind shelter create "microclimates" in particular areas. If your garden is on a hill or in a valley, you'll probably be faced with slightly different conditions from the average climate of your region.

Gardening in a Valley

Valleys tend to be cooler than the higher land around them. This happens because cool air is heavier than warm air. Cool air tends to drain towards lower ground. For this reason, gardens located at the bottoms of valleys suffer the latest frosts in the spring, the earliest frosts in fall, and the severest frosts in winter. The absence of wind in valleys increases susceptibility to frost.

Soil tends to be wetter in a valley, since water follows the path of least resistance and flows downward.

Where drainage is poor, water will puddle, creating spongy wet areas. Poor air circulation and high moisture levels in valleys create ideal conditions for fungal development, so fungal diseases of plants are more likely to occur.

You may find the best topsoil at the bottom of a valley. As water flows downhill, it washes away the slopes above and carries topsoil and organic matter away, depositing it lower down.

Gardening on a Hilltop

Air temperatures on hills tend to be lower than on flat land. You'll have greater protection from frost and plant disease on a hill, compared with a valley, since air movement is greater. Excessive winds, however, can damage plants, increase soil erosion, and speed the loss of moisture from the soil.

Since water drains from high ground, soil at the top of a hill will usually be drier than the land below. On

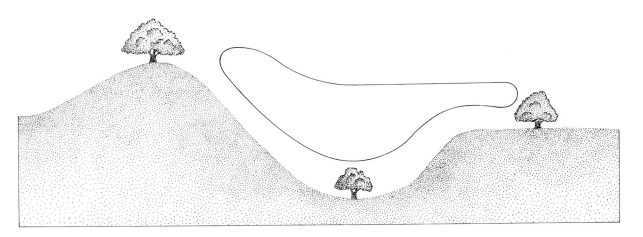

Above: Warm air rises over slopes and keeps frost away.
Below: Clary prefers sun and well-drained soil, so it is an
ideal herb for planting in hilltop gardens.

The Effect of Water

Large bodies of water like oceans and lakes
influence the climate of the land nearby. The
larger the body of water, the greater will be its
effect. Since water temperatures rise and fall
more slowly than land temperatures, they
modify the air temperatures of the
surrounding land. Coastal gardens, for
example, do not experience the same extreme
temperatures as inland gardens. Similarly, a
garden near a lake will experience less-extreme
air temperatures than one farther away. The
effect of the water on temperatures may be
enough to hold late and early frosts at bay,
giving you a longer growing season, and
temper the summer heat, making it possible
for you to grow a wider range of herbs.

hilltops, soil is generally thinner and nutrients will be
lost more easily through excessive drainage.

Gardening on a Slope

Gardening on a gentle slope can have advantages. Slopes
are often cooled by breezes in the afternoon or evening,
while warm air rising over them in the morning keeps
away frost. In cool northern climates, a slope with a
southern exposure warms more quickly in the spring,
and remains warm for a longer period at the end of the
growing season. This means a longer growing season
and potentially greater harvests.

Slopes, however, are subject to erosion from water
drainage and from wind unless they are sheltered by
natural or planted windbreaks and terraced where they
are steep. If drainage is excessive your plants may suffer
from lack of soil moisture, and you may find that topsoil
is thin on a slope due to soil erosion.

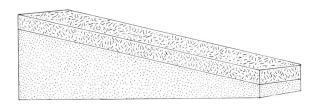

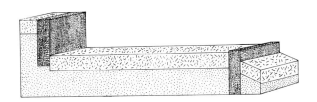

Leveling slopes by terracing makes a garden much more
manageable and prevents soil erosion. Terraces can
also guard against excessive drainage.

Even if your site is partly shaded, you can still have a beautiful herb garden.

Exposure

Exposure to sunlight is one of the factors you'll need to consider when adding herbs to your garden landscape. While most herbs prefer full sun, there are some that will grow in partial to full shade. The "Plant by Plant Guide," starting on page 100, will tell you about the light requirements of specific herbs. Quantity and duration of light are critical factors, especially for flowering and reproduction.

The quantity and duration of light in your garden affect the growth of your herbs. The intensity of the light influences photosynthesis, the plant's internal process that employs light energy to produce carbohydrates or sugar for food, using carbon dioxide and water. Photosynthetic activity generally increases with greater light intensity and decreases with less.

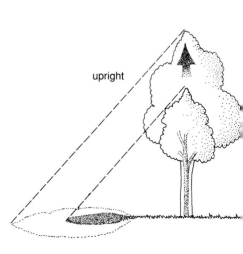

Common tree shapes include upright, pyramidal, and columnar. The shape of the tree determines how much shade it will cast.

upright

> ### Shade-tolerant Herbs
>
> The following herbs will tolerate shade (although dill, fennel, rosemary, and scented geraniums really prefer full sun).
> Agrimony, angelica, bay, bee balm, betony, catnip, chamomile, chervil, comfrey, coriander, costmary, feverfew, germander, ginger, horsetail, hyssop, lemon balm, lovage, Madagascar periwinkle, mint, parsley, pennyroyal, pipsissewa, plantain, sweet cicely, sweet woodruff, tansy, tarragon, thyme, valerian, violet, wormwood.

The intensity of sunlight varies with the season, the geographic location, and the atmosphere. During the winter, the sun is lower in the sky than it is during the summer. Sunlight travels a longer distance through the earth's atmosphere and strikes the earth's surface at a lower angle. As a result, it is less intense. In summer, sunlight reaches the surface more directly and is more intense. At any time of year sunlight is filtered through the atmosphere. When dust and other pollutants are in the air, less sunlight reaches your garden. Light is also usually less intense on a cloudy day than on a clear day.

To make sure your plants get the right amount of light, consider shade from trees, buildings, and hills when you're planning your garden. Space your plants correctly and weed regularly to reduce competition for sunlight. Some plants thrive in shade, others need full sun. When a plant receives too much sun, leaves may wilt, and it may develop a bleached, scalded appearance and grow poorly. With inadequate sunlight, plants become lanky and pale, flower poorly, and lack vigor.

Plants that need full sun are able to stand uninterrupted, unfiltered sunlight from sunrise to sunset.

Plants that prefer partial sun will usually be able to stand about 5 to 6 hours of direct sunlight, with shade or filtered sun the rest of the day. Place herbs that do best in partial shade in filtered, indirect light where trees provide dappled shade. Plants that require full shade need just that: solid and dense shade away from all direct sun.

The daily cycle of light and darkness influences several plant functions, including seed germination, root initiation, and the growth of blossoms, fruits, tubers, and bulbs.

In the tropics, the normal duration of sunlight is around 12 hours a day. North and south of the equator the day length varies with the season and the latitude, until the occurrence of day-long light in summer, and darkness in winter, near the poles.

Some plants, like chrysanthemums, require short days and longer nights to bloom and are called "short-day" plants. "Long-day" plants flower when the days are long and the nights short. Long-day herbs include most annuals. Other plants, like geraniums and roses, are unaffected by day length and are called "day-neutral."

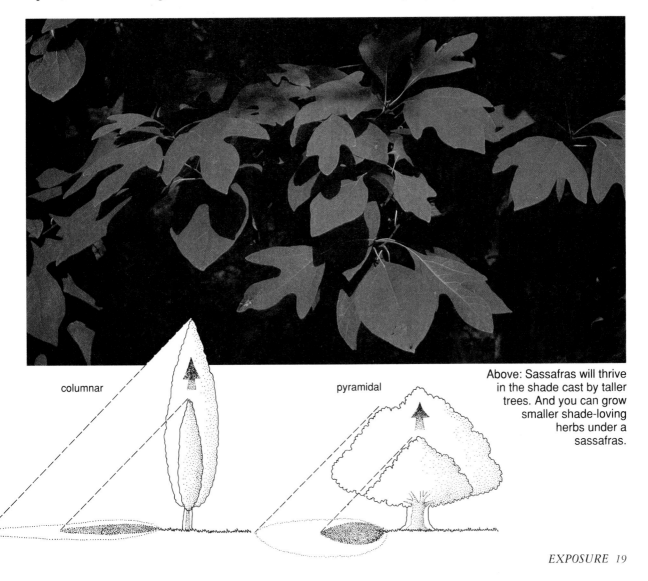

columnar

pyramidal

Above: Sassafras will thrive in the shade cast by taller trees. And you can grow smaller shade-loving herbs under a sassafras.

Soil

Good soil is the herb gardener's key to success. Besides providing physical support for plant roots, the soil provides the water and nutrients plants need to survive. A good soil is loose and well drained, but it also holds enough water and air for healthy root growth. If your soil is not ideal, there are things you can do to improve it; "Soil Preparation," on page 42, explains how to get your soil in good shape. But before you start digging, it's helpful to know about the physical characteristics of soil so you can choose a good site to start with.

Soil Composition

Soil is actually a mixture of mineral and organic matter, water, and air. In general, soil contains approximately 45 percent mineral matter, 5 percent organic matter, 25 percent water, and 25 percent air.

Organic matter is an essential part of the soil makeup because it supplies nutrients to the plants and can help to improve drainage.

Soil Texture

Soil texture is determined by the proportions of different-sized mineral particles in the soil. At one extreme are microscopic clay particles and at the other are coarse sand particles easily seen with the naked eye. Silt (the very fine soil often found in river banks) falls between these two extremes.

Soil texture can have a great effect on the growth of your plants. Roots will spread easily in open sandy soil, but water will drain away quickly, so your plants may need more frequent watering. In a "tight" clay soil roots will not penetrate so readily or widely and the soil will tend to become waterlogged. Also, in a clayey soil, water is so tightly held by the soil particles that it may not enter the roots freely.

You can easily check your soil's texture. Take a handful of your damp garden soil and squeeze it. If it crumbles slightly when you release your grip, its texture is probably satisfactory. If it runs through your fingers, it is too sandy; if it forms a sticky lump, it is too clayey. Loamy soils, which contain moderate amounts of clay, silt, and sand, often suit plants best.

Soil Structure

Soil structure refers to the way the sand, silt, and clay particles come together to form

The nitrogen cycle—animals feed on plants; animal manures add nitrogen to the soil; plants take up nitrogen; plants decompose and put nitrogen back into the soil. (Some nitrogen is lost to the air, but is returned with thunderstorms.)

clumps or aggregates. Most plants prefer a soil with a loose, granular structure. This type of structure has lots of open space (called pore space) that can hold air or water. The water forms a thin film around the granules and holds dissolved nutrients like calcium and potassium. Plants can take up these nutrients when tiny hairs on the tips of their roots enter the water film between the soil particles.

Unlike soil texture, structure can change depending on how you manage the soil. Working the soil when it is wet can break down the aggregates and destroy soil structure. Adding lots of organic matter is an easy and effective way to promote a good structure.

Organic Matter

Organic matter in the soil is made up of the remains of plants and animals at various stages of decomposition. Decaying organic matter adds minerals essential for plant growth, such as nitrogen and potassium, to the soil. It also helps improve soil structure—increase pore space—so roots can spread easily and water and air can move freely in the root zone.

Most plants thrive in soils rich in organic matter. Soils with a lot of organic matter are usually dark in color (often a rich brown) and open and light in texture. They crumble easily between your fingers. Add organic matter to your soil in the form of compost or green manure crops. To learn how to make compost and grow and use green manure crops, see "Adding Organic Nutrients" on page 44.

Air and Water

Your plants will require a good deal of water but they must also be able to take in air (for oxygen) through their roots. Most garden plants grow best

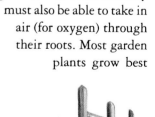

Soil should crumble slightly when squeezed.

Clayey soil forms a sticky lump when it is squeezed.

in well-drained soil. They don't like to have wet feet, since flooding cuts off the supply of oxygen. Plants obtain their oxygen from air-filled pores in the soil and take in carbon dioxide from the air. Oxygen they cannot use is given off from their leaves and *we* take that in.

Soil Nutrients

The availability of soil nutrients depends on the interaction of many factors, including soil texture, soil structure, moisture, organic matter, and pH. Fine texture, loose structure, ample moisture, high organic matter content, and near neutral pH are all conditions that make the most nutrients available to your plants.

One of the most important plant nutrients is nitrogen, which is found in soil in various chemical combinations plants can absorb. Keeping an adequate supply of nitrogen in the soil can be a challenge, since nitrogen is used up very quickly by plants. It also dissolves in water and leaches out of the soil. For plants to thrive, nitrogen must be resupplied. This is why heavy applications of nitrogen fertilizers are used in commercial agriculture. When they are washed out of the soil, their destination is often the groundwater, which may be the source of your drinking water. The best and most natural way to build up soil nitrogen is to grow green manure crops. See "Green Manures" on page 46 to learn how to grow and use them.

To check the nutrient content of your soil, it may be worthwhile to have a lab test your soil before you begin serious gardening. Even soils known to be highly fertile often lack specific nutrients or essential minerals. Private and government soil-testing agencies (including the Cooperative Extension Service)

will conduct tests on soil samples and provide you with a statement of your soil pH and the relative amounts of essential plant nutrients—nitrogen, phosphorus, potassium—in the soil. They will also indicate any other specific needs. This will show whether your soil is of high, medium, or low fertility. You can test again in a few years to monitor the results of your gardening practices and make adjustments if they're necessary. The testing agency will also recommend rates of application of fertilizing substances and lime based on the plants you've decided to grow, since crops vary in their requirements. Make sure you ask for recommendations for organic fertilizers.

Soil pH

It is helpful to know how acid or alkaline your soil is. If you have the soil tested, the results will include pH, which is the measure of acidity or alkalinity.

Soil pH is important because it influences soil chemistry. Plants can absorb most nutrients from the soil when the soil pH is in the neutral range. Plants cannot absorb nitrogen and sulfur, for example, if the soil pH drops far below 7, while iron and magnesium are less available as the pH moves above 7. See the "Soil pH Scale" above for the meaning of each pH level.

Most plants prefer a certain pH. Blueberries, for example, like an acid soil. Many herbs prefer a soil on the slightly acid side, with a pH around 6.

Plant nursery operators will know the approximate pH level that suits the plants they sell. Heavy, dense clay soils are often more acid than desirable. Lime or dolomite will not only make them less acid, but will also improve their structure. If your soil is too acid for the plants you plan to grow, the lab will be able to tell you how much lime to add. If you soil pH is high, you can lower it by adding sphagnum peat or sulfur. Don't add lime or sulfur unless recommended for your soil.

Garden Planning

If you're planning a new herb garden, you'll need to consider your garden's location, size, shape, and design. Start out simple. Seek inspiration from books and experienced gardeners. If you enjoy formal patterns, plan your garden along the lines of an Italian Renaissance garden or a knot garden, in which intertwining miniature hedges of different herbs create a knot-like shape. For something more informal, look for inspiration in a book about English cottage gardens. Perhaps you would prefer to specialize and grow a kitchen garden full of culinary herbs, a medicinal herb garden, a scented garden or simply a wild garden with herbs of many sorts.

The Garden Site

First decide where to locate your herb garden. You could reassign a section of your existing vegetable or flower garden, or perhaps create a whole new garden devoted to herbs. Of course, you may choose to place herbs in several different small sites. If you're starting from scratch, put as much thought as you can into site selection. You can avoid many problems by choosing a good location, especially if you plan to live in the same place for several years.

Your garden site has to suit the plants you will grow.

If your site is shady, choose herbs that will tolerate shade. If your site has wet conditions part of the year, choose plants that can tolerate this. If you have a range of possible sites, choose the one that provides as closely as possible the specific requirements of the plants you want to grow.

An ideal site will also correspond with your ideas of what a garden should be and where it should be. It may be most convenient for you to have your herb garden located near the kitchen door. Or perhaps you'll get most enjoyment from one that may be viewed from indoors through a window.

To choose a site, begin with a tour of your yard, keeping in mind the following considerations:
- If possible, choose a level site with good drainage, since it is easier to garden on flat surfaces, and soil erosion won't be a concern.
- Avoid hills that lose moisture quickly.
- Stay away from pockets of low-lying land, where poor drainage and inadequate air circulation could encourage related disease and pest problems.
- Garden across slopes, rather than in rows running up and down, to prevent erosion.
- Avoid areas where the soil is compacted and, therefore, hard to dig.
- Be sure that you have proper access to your garden site. You may only need room for a wheelbarrow to

Ideally, the well-organized garden will include culinary herbs which are positioned as close as possible to the kitchen.

Where your garden space is limited, a decorative and practical solution is a window box filled with herbs.

What Are Your Production Goals? How much you want to harvest will influence the size of garden you need. Perhaps you already know that you want to grow enough basil to make a batch of pesto sauce every week. Or you may want to have a variety of herbs available for drying to make potpourris. Your plans must allow space for the plants you want your garden to produce for you.

Matching Other Resources If soil moisture is limited, due to climate or soil type or topography, you will have to devise a way to supply water. A large garden will require more water than a small one. Mulching (see page 58) is an excellent way to control weeds and conserve soil moisture, but if you plan to mulch, how much material will you need and how much is available? If you are starting a new garden, how much of an investment can you afford to make in soil amendments, plants, seeds, watering equipment, tools, and structures during the first year? If you're unsure of the answers to these questions, it's probably best to keep it small and simple the first year and extend as you gain experience.

move between rows or beds, or you may need to provide access for a truck to deliver a load of soil.

- Clear rocks and brush from the site before you start your garden.
- Avoid planting in the root zones of trees, as tilling around the roots could injure the trees, and the trees will compete with your herbs for moisture and nutrients in the soil.
- Be sure you have access to an adequate water supply.
- Choose a site where your plants will get adequate light for at least part of the day.

Garden Size

The size of your herb garden will be determined by how much you want to grow and harvest, the suitable space available to you, the amount of time you have, and the availability of resources. If you're a beginner, it may be best to start with a small garden, and work with this until you gain experience.

The time any garden needs varies with climate and season, as do the tasks to be done. You'll need to prepare the soil by tilling and adding nutrients where necessary, plant your seeds or seedlings, and perform regular maintenance tasks including weeding, watering, pest control, and harvesting. The work will be slower and heavier if you're using hand tools than if you're using powered tools like a rotary tiller.

How much you want to harvest will influence the size of garden you need. One or two plants of an herb you have not grown before is usually enough, but you will soon develop favorites and learn which grow well in your garden. Parsley is a popular and nutritious herb with many culinary uses, so it is worthwhile to have a dozen plants at a time to ensure a good supply. A dozen basil plants would not be too many if you want to make pesto regularly. In the garden, a dozen parsley plants would require 2⅔ square feet (248 sq cm) of space, and a dozen basil would need 1½ square feet (139 sq cm). A larger plant like angelica would need about 12 square feet (1 sq m), while a barberry shrub would require 16 square feet (1.5 sq m). The spacing guidelines on the seed packet, or in the "Plant by Plant Guide," starting on page 100, will give you an idea how much space your herbs need.

In your planning, don't forget to make paths wide enough to accommodate the wheelbarrow.

Circular garden beds allow easy access to herbs and are attractive features in their own right.

Garden Style

Regardless of the size, shape, or location of your garden, its style is a reflection of your own tastes. At one extreme are the formal gardens with their angular knots and pruned hedges, and at the other are random groupings of whatever suits the season. The number of possible herb-garden styles is limited only by your imagination and creativity. You can plan one or more theme gardens to concentrate on a particular aspect.

Garden Shape

The simplest gardens to set out and manage are square or rectangular. If you must take advantage of every square inch of available space, it makes sense that you will follow the general outline of your property, and land is most often sold in box-like shapes. Laying out your herb garden with square or rectangular beds not only may be the most practical way, but can give the garden a formal look that appeals to many gardeners.

Of course, squares and rectangles aren't the only shapes. You may choose to lay your garden beds following the curve of a hill, stream, fence, or stone wall, or design them to accent the shape of a building. If you

The diagrams below show four practical approaches to designing an herb garden. Avoid circles and curves if space is limited.

want to be especially creative, garden within unusual boundaries like circles or ovals. You can make a garden in the shape of a spiral with one continuous bed beginning in the center and spiraling out in circles. A book or magazine on garden landscaping will offer you examples to follow in shaping your garden beds.

If you choose to garden in several small patches, position plants that need daily attention or frequent picking close to the house. If space is limited, take advantage of borders along paths and fences. At the least, you can dress your windows outdoors with boxes of luscious herbs close at hand.

Garden Design

Whatever design you choose, try it out on paper first. Use graph paper and do not draw to too small a scale. For example, you can let each square of the graph paper equal 1 square foot (9.3 sq cm) of your property. Keep it simple. Mark the outline of the garden first, then add other features of the location, including existing and future trees, shrubs, fences, paths, hills, and buildings. Make several photocopies of the base plan, and use the copies to draw out your different design ideas. Or simply lay tracing paper over the original plan and draw on that. That way, you'll always have a fresh base plan if you want to start over.

Paths are a necessity for work in your garden, and a garden stroll can also follow the paths you've planned. For both work and leisure, make garden paths 4 to 5 feet (1.2 to 1.5 m) wide.

If you're planting in beds, keep them under 5 feet (1.5 m) wide, not more than twice the distance you are able to reach from the side. You'll want to avoid walking on beds as you work.

Once you've located your paths, beds, or rows, begin selecting and arranging your plants. Prepare a list of the plants you want to grow, along with their growth habits, size at maturity, and special soil, space, or environmental requirements. Refer to the "Plant by Plant Guide," starting on page 100, for specific information about each herb's requirements. Remember that single plants tend to become lost in the crowd; it's more effective to plant in clumps. It's generally best to plant the tallest herbs at the back, the shortest in the front.

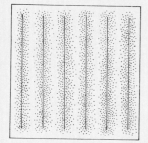

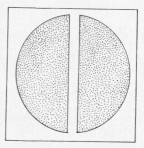
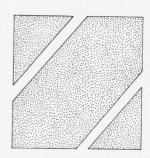

Keep the following in mind when you plan the design of your garden:

- Use your site's limitations to your advantage. If you're confined to gardening in the shade, use the opportunity to grow as many shade-loving herbs as possible. Include angelica, chervil, lemon balm, and sweet cicely. In wet areas, select from the wide assortment of plants in the mint family. Among the herbs, you'll find plants to fill just about every niche.
- Divide a large garden, or create several small gardens, by grouping herbs that serve particular purposes. Medicinal, dye, fragrance, and culinary gardens are some examples.
- Select herbs that flower at the same time or share the same color. Lavender and blue themes especially are easy to create with herbs. Or focus on foliage, and plant blue-green or silvery herbs mixed with darker greens for contrast.
- It's a good idea to group the perennials together since they tend to have similar requirements and this will help you avoid mistakes. If you're planning to grow invasive perennials like mint among other herbs, plant them in buried containers like clay drainage pipes or bottomless large cans that are at least 10 inches (25 cm) deep.

Above: Elaborate knot gardens first became popular in the fifteenth century in Europe.

Below: A classic design can fill the whole garden or, as in this garden, can become a feature that is part of a larger garden. The herb foliage is as important to the design as the flowers.

CHOOSING YOUR PLANTS

In the following chapter you will learn more about the different types of plants that are available, and what to look for in your herb plants and seeds when you go shopping.

You will learn about your herb plants' life cycles and the difference between annuals, biennials, and perennials. Although a lot of herbs are perennials, annuals and biennials are often the easiest to grow. Being well informed will help you to choose plants that will make your garden a success and fulfill your needs. For example, if you want your herb garden to be attractive all year round with minimal work, you may want to concentrate on perennials rather than annuals and biennials.

The number and variety of plants grown worldwide is enormous, and it is worthwhile to take a moment to teach yourself some basic botany. Learn about the variety of leaf size, shape, and color, and the different stem and root systems. Perhaps you would like to have herbs with attractive foliage, or it may be useful to grow herbs with taproots if watering resources are scarce. This section will help you to choose the right herb for your garden and your particular needs.

When you go to select and buy your herb plants, it will help to know a little about how they are classified into species, subspecies, varieties, and forms, and understand the relationship between a cultivar and a species. This will enable you to make sense of the labels attached to herbs in the shop!

And knowing the origins of your herbs will help you to understand how to care for them. Herbs that originated in a hot, tropical climate may require special treatment if you live in a cold climate. Take the following information into consideration when you visit your local garden center and you will be well rewarded.

Opposite: As you choose herb plants, consider what you want from them and what growing conditions you have available. If you keep these two things in mind, you'll buy herbs that will grow well and provide years of enjoyment.

Learning about Life Cycles

Knowing about the life cycles of your herbs can give you many clues to their needs and characteristics. "Life cycle" refers to the amount of time it takes for a plant to grow from seed, flower, set seed, and die. Annual herbs, like borage and calendula, complete their life cycle in one growing season. Biennials, like parsley and caraway, produce only leafy growth the first year, and complete their life cycle in the second growing season. Perennial herbs live for more than 2 years, producing leaves, flowers, and seeds each year. Herbaceous perennials, like bee balm and tarragon, have stems that usually die to the ground in winter and grow again in spring from a persistent rootstock. Woody perennials, including barberry and rosemary, have stems that expand each year as they build up woody growth.

As you plant and maintain your herb garden, though, it's not enough to know just what a plant's natural life cycle is: It also helps to know how the plant grows in your climate, and how you plan to use the herb. Some herbs that are normally perennial in warm climates, like marjoram and peppers, cannot survive the winter temperatures of colder climates. Gardeners in cold-climate areas must treat these warm-climate herbs as annuals, and grow them from seed each year. And how you grow a biennial herb depends on what you want to harvest from it. Parsley, for example, is commonly grown for its first-year foliage, not for its second-year flowers and seeds. So even though parsley is technically a biennial,

you'll need to start new plants each year if you want a good supply of foliage. If you are not sure what categories your herbs fit into, look them up in the "Plant by Plant Guide," starting on page 100.

Annuals

Annuals are generally easy to grow and offer the herb grower a wide range of plant sizes, colors, and shapes. In a new garden they are especially useful for filling spaces between perennials that are just newly planted. Many annuals bloom all season and then propagate themselves by producing lots of seeds. Some, like borage and coriander, will reseed before the end of the season and their offspring will germinate in the following gardening season.

Most annuals require full sun and are shallow-rooted. This means that they require plenty of water, since their roots remain near the surface. Many annual seedlings can be planted directly outdoors in garden soil, but others will require a warm start indoors.

coriander

It's easy to grow annual, biennial, and perennial herbs all together in one garden. Just start the annuals and biennials from seed as necessary and use them to fill in between the longer-lived perennials.

Biennials

Biennial herbs have a life span of 2 years. During their first year they produce plenty of foliage and strong root systems. Many biennials depend upon nutrients stored in their large roots to survive the period of dormancy in the cold season. Biennials flower and make seed in their second season just before they die. If you start biennials, like caraway and parsley, from seed indoors, sow them in peat pots that can be placed directly in the ground to avoid disturbing the sensitive taproot during transplanting. If your climate allows, sow biennials directly into the garden so you won't have to transplant them out later; this will help you avoid taproot damage.

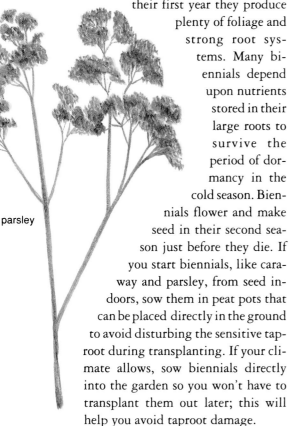

parsley

Perennials

Perennial herbs live for more than 2 years. Some, like clary and lavender, will reach their prime growth within 3 to 5 years. Growth then declines and the plants die unless they are resurrected by thinning and division. Other perennials, like tansy and mint, thrive and continue growing and spreading, unless you check their growth with thinning.

lavender

You can propagate a perennial vegetatively or from seed. Vegetative propagation involves plant division, layering, or taking cuttings, and it is the easiest and the quickest way to increase your stock of perennials. The seeds of perennials may be difficult to germinate, and others, like tarragon, don't make seed at all. While most perennials started from seed will flower during their second year, new plants started vegetatively often flower in the first year.

toothed

entire

lobed

toothed and lobed combination

Leaf edges are a good clue to help you identify unknown herbs.

Understanding Basic Botany

You can choose herbs for your garden for their attractive leaves, useful fruits, fragrant flowers, or perhaps deep taproots that cope better with poor water supply. Knowing about the functions and characteristics of the various plant parts will help you identify, select, and maintain your herbs most effectively.

Foliage

One of the main reasons gardeners grow herbs is for the flavorful or aromatic leaves. Among the herbs you will find every shape, texture, and color of leaf imaginable.

Leaves that are whole and undivided, like bee balm, are called simple. Leaves divided into two or more parts on the same stalk are called compound. The lacy, finely divided leaves of the carrot family, including dill, caraway, and parsley, are compound leaves.

Leaf shape ranges from the long, thin, linear leaves of lemongrass to the eye-shaped elliptical leaves of bay and the almost circular nasturtium.

Leaves vary in their edges as well as their shapes. A leaf like sweet bay with its smooth edge is called entire, those with jagged edges like lemon balm are toothed, and the wavy-edged parsley leaf is lobed. Once you become familiar with herbs, you'll depend on these differences for identification.

Growing for Flowers and Fruits

Tasty leaves aren't the only reason to grow herbs—many produce beautiful flowers as well. Most herb flowers are either single or clustered. A common clustered floral arrangement is the umbel, which is shaped like an upside-down umbrella, with clusters of dainty blossoms at the top. Members of the carrot or Umbelliferae family, like dill and caraway, have umbels. Flowers arranged along a tall stem, like lavender, are called spikes.

You can also grow herbs for their seeds or fruits. Some herbs, like dill and anise, produce an abundance of seeds that are easy to see and to collect. Others, like chives, hide their seeds within a capsule. Some herbs are cultivated for the fruit they produce. Certain roses produce a tart, berry-like hip that is high in Vitamin C. Bearberry's bright red berries appeal to bears, but not to people.

Herb leaves offer a tremendous variety of color. It's true that most leaves are green, but there are many shades of green! To vary your garden you can select the blue-grays of lavender and wormwood or the brilliant green of sweet basil. Basil is available in a deep purple cultivar, with occasional unpredictable streaks of green and purple mixed.

Leaves that are striped or blotched with different colors, like those of some types of geranium, are called variegated. Sage also has several variegated cultivars, including the yellow-and-green 'Aurea' and the cream-purple-and-green 'Tricolor'. Variegated herbs taste just as good as their green counterparts, and add color and interest to any planting.

From solid simple leaves to lacy dissected ones, herb foliage comes in a variety of types and textures to liven up your garden.

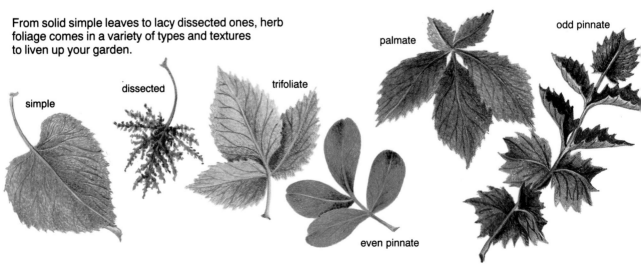

simple

dissected

trifoliate

palmate

odd pinnate

even pinnate

ovate · elliptical · oblong · linear · oblanceolate · obovate · lanceolate

Incorporating herbs with different leaf shapes into your garden will help to give it added interest.

Plant Stems

The stems of your herbs not only support the leaves, but also serve as pathways for movement of nutrients and water between roots and leaves. Like roots, stems are storage organs, too. Bulbs, like garlic and saffron, are actually specialized storage stems.

Some herbs have stems that are specially adapted for vegetative reproduction. Stolons (also called runners) are stems that travel horizontally along the soil surface. At certain intervals along the stolon, new shoots and roots will form, giving rise to new plants. Sweet woodruff and sweet violets are examples of plants that produce stolons.

Herbs like iris, mint, and tarragon form new plants from underground stems, called rhizomes. The creeping stems of mint spread quickly, traveling just below the surface of the soil and rooting as they go. For this reason you may want to grow them in containers, preferably large bottomless tubs or plastic pots. Otherwise build a wooden barrier about 12 to 14 inches (30 to 35 cm) deep around the mint patch to keep the plants under control.

Many herbs can be propagated by stem cuttings. Swollen buds, or nodes, located along the stems are the sites for new growth. When you take stem cuttings from your herbs to make new plants, the new root systems form underground at active nodes on the cutting. See "Cuttings" on page 62 for more information on how to take cuttings.

Root Systems

As a gardener, you probably select most plants for their aboveground appearance. But when selecting and planting herbs, you should also consider their root systems. In certain plants, like iris and ginger, the root may be the part that is used herbally.

Roots help to hold the plant firm in the soil and provide it with a system for absorbing water and nutrients. They may also act as storage organs, as in the carrot family, holding nutrients for use during times of vigorous growth or flowering.

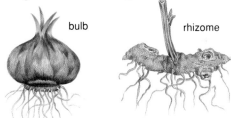

bulb · rhizome

Although it grows in the ground, a bulb is not a root, but a type of stem, compressed and covered with scale-like leaves. A rhizome is an underground runner or stem.

Most herbs have a fibrous root system, made up of many fine and branching roots. Annual herbs, in particular, tend to have shallow root systems. As fibrous roots do not penetrate particularly deeply, you'll need to pay special attention to the water requirements of such plants when rain is scarce.

Some herbs have strong central roots, called taproots, that travel straight down in search of water and nutrients. The taproot is a single, thick, and tapering organ (a carrot is actually an enlarged taproot) with thin side branch roots. Taprooted plants can more easily withstand fluctuating soil moisture conditions, but many, like parsley and lovage, are more difficult to transplant because their roots are so sensitive.

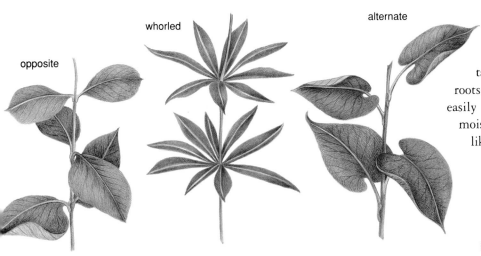

opposite · whorled · alternate

The way the leaves are placed on the stem is called the leaf arrangement.

Avoid buying plants with browned, curled, or insect-damaged leaves.

Choose plants that are healthy and have not outgrown their container.

Mustard is an herb you can confidently put in the hard-to-kill category.

Selecting and Buying Herbs

If you are a new herb grower, the easiest way to start will be to purchase your first plants in pots. You can find annual and perennial herbs in nurseries, markets, and garden-supply stores, and they are often listed in specialist nursery catalogs. Some local herb growers' associations sponsor annual plant sales that offer a wide assortment suitable for both new and experienced growers. Most herbs are prolific, so established herb growers often have plants they are willing to share or sell. If you buy a particular cultivar or other unfamiliar plant, make sure you get an identification tag.

The following sections will help you to learn about choosing herbs before you rush to the garden store.

Classification

If you've never grown an herb garden before, you may be confused by the large range of plants and their names.

Scientists name plants with a system that gives each plant two names. Every naturally occurring plant that is able to reproduce is called a species, and each species is given a two-part name, for example, *Mentha spicata,* or spearmint. The word *Mentha* indicates the genus (plural "genera") that includes all types of mint; *spicata* refers to the particular type of mint called spearmint.

Species may be divided further into subspecies, varieties, and forms. These terms refer to variants of a species that occur in nature. Cultivars, on the other hand, are distinct horticultural types that are selected or produced by breeding under cultivation. For example, *Lavandula angustifolia* 'Munstead' is a cultivar of English lavender. Cultivar names are always placed between single quotation marks. Cultivars are often mistakenly called varieties.

Sometimes plants from different species or genera will cross-pollinate, producing offspring that share the characteristics of both parents. These "new" plants are called hybrids. Hybrids may occur naturally or be man-made. An "x" in a plant's name (as in *Iris* x *germanica* var. *florentina*) indicates that the plant is a hybrid.

Plant Origins

Knowing the origins of your herbs can help you understand how to care for them.

Many of today's popular herbs are natives of the Mediterranean region, which has a sunny climate with low humidity and moderate rainfall. Mediterranean herbs include lavender, chamomile, thyme, borage, germander, and others. Since they developed on poor soils, they don't demand high soil fertility and, given the right environment, they're fairly easy to grow.

Many herbs that originated in warm or hot climates are widely grown in colder regions today. Pepper plants, for example, including hot and sweet peppers, are perennials in their native tropical America. They're usually grown as annuals in cooler climates because they cannot withstand frost. Basil is another cold-sensitive herb which originated in the warm, humid tropics. A favorite with herb growers everywhere for its profusion of fragrant leaves, basil is widely cultivated as an annual during the frost-free months.

The medicinal aloes and the scented geraniums both originated in Africa: the aloes in arid areas, the geraniums in the cooler and somewhat moister south. If you want to grow them in cold climates, you will have to bring them indoors during winter, or alternatively, use both of them as houseplants throughout the year.

The origins and history of herbs is a fascinating topic that you can explore further in many herb books found in well-stocked libraries.

Hardiness

Hardiness is the quality that enables plants to survive climatic extremes, especially cold, heat, and dryness. Hardy annuals and biennials, like dill and caraway, can be sown outdoors while spring or fall frosts still threaten. Hardy perennials, like tarragon and chives, can be left outdoors year round even in the extreme winter cold. Tansy is another hardy perennial that thrives in its native cold-climate winters.

Half-hardy annuals require a warm environment for successful germination but will withstand some frosts once they're established. Calendula is a half-hardy annual that benefits from an early start indoors and can be transferred outdoors fairly early.

Tender annuals and perennials are those that are quickly damaged by frost or cold. Tender perennials include rosemary and sweet bay, which must be potted and brought indoors during cold-climate winters. Basil is a tender annual that should be started and kept indoors in the spring until all danger of frost has passed.

Stocking Up

Before you shop, make a list of the herbs you want. Check the space requirements for each herb in the "Plant by Plant Guide," starting on page 100, and measure your growing space, then work out how many plants to buy. You may want to purchase several plants of various annuals, but don't take home more than one of each perennial; once they're established you can increase your stock by vegetative propagation. To learn how to do this, see "Propagating Herbs" on page 60.

Look for healthy, vigorous plants with bright, new growth. They should be free of insects and diseases. Without damaging the plant, check the undersides of leaves for insect pests and see that the stems are strong, with no signs of injury or rot.

In plants ready for transplanting, the root system should almost fill the pot. At the end of the growing season, you may find perennial plants offered at a reduced price because they have outgrown their pots. Take advantage of these if they are pest-free. If they are thickly bunched, you can slice the root ball into several sections with a knife. Plant these divisions as individual plants and water them well.

Annuals that need plenty of space, like basil, should be planted one per pot. If a pot contains several seedlings, you will find that it is difficult to separate them without damaging their root systems. Annuals, like dill and chives, which form clumps, may be sown thickly in the pot and can be successfully transplanted as a clump. If you prefer to start your own seedlings, "Planting Seeds" on page 50 will give you some useful tips. "Saving Seed" on page 62 tells you how to collect seeds. Consult "Propagating Herbs" to learn how to increase your perennial herb plants. Starting plants from seeds or cuttings is an easy and inexpensive way to fill a large herb garden with a selection of your favorite plants.

Easy-to-grow Herbs

The herbs listed below all fall into the "hard to kill" category and are thus good subjects for the beginning gardener.

Agrimony, angelica, barberry, basil (sweet), bee balm, borage, burdock, calendula, catnip, chamomile (Roman), chicory, chives, comfrey, coriander, dandelion, dill, dock, elecampane, fennel, feverfew, geranium (scented), goldenrod, horseradish, horsetail, lady's bedstraw, lavender (English), lemon balm, lovage, Madagascar periwinkle, marjoram, mint, mugwort, mustard, nasturtium, oregano, parsley (curled), pennyroyal (English), plantain, red clover, rosemary, rue, sage, santolina, savory (winter), soapwort, sorrel, southernwood, sweet woodruff, tansy, vervain (European).

Dill is a hardy plant that can be sown outdoors while spring or fall frosts still threaten. This is a very easy herb to grow.

Species Chart

The following alphabetical listing is intended as a quick gardening guide—a starting point for when you are trying to decide what to plant and assess how each herb will respond to your garden's unique climatic and topographic conditions.

In this instant reference, you will find the fundamen-tals that will put you on the right track to successful herb gardening. You can quickly and easily determine the growth patterns and approximate size of each plant, its preferred soil conditions, methods of propagation, and its primary uses. There is also a quick guide to any pests and diseases that might attack your plants, so you can be aware of potential problems and take preventive

Herb	Growth Form and Size	Preferred Climate (Coldest Zone)	Preferred Soil Conditions
Agrimony *Agrimonia eupatoria*	Perennial 2–5 feet (0.6–1.5 m)	Cool (Zone 6)	Most light soil, well drained
Aloe *Aloe vera*	Succulent evergreen perennial 1 foot (30 cm)	Warm (Zone 10); grow indoors in cooler Zones	Light sandy or gravelly soil, perfect drainage
Angelica *Angelica archangelica*	Perennial 5–8 feet (1.5–2.4 m)	Cool (Zone 4)	Cool, moist soil, slightly acid
Anise *Pimpinella anisum*	Annual 2 feet (60 cm)	Cool	Poor sandy soil, well drained
Anise hyssop *Agastache foeniculum*	Perennial 3 feet (90 cm)	Cool (Zone 5)	Rich soil, well drained
Arnica *Arnica montana*	Perennial 2 feet (60 cm)	Cool (Zone 6)	Dry, sandy, acid soil with humus, well drained
Barberry *Berberis vulgaris*	Deciduous shrub 6–8 feet (1.8–2.4 m)	Cool (Zone 4)	Average soil, well drained
Basil, sweet *Ocimum basilicum*	Annual 1–2 feet (30–60 cm)	Mild	Rich, loose soil, slightly acid
Bay, sweet *Laurus nobilis*	Evergreen shrub or tree 6–12 feet (1.8–3.6 m)	Mild (Zone 8)	Average soil, slightly acid
Bearberry *Arctostaphylos uva-ursi*	Creeping evergreen shrub to 3 inches (7.5 cm)	Cool (Zone 2)	Moist, peaty, acid soil, well drained
Bee balm *Monarda didyma*	Perennial 3–4 feet (90–120 cm)	Cool (Zone 4)	Rich, moist soil, slightly acid
Betony *Stachys officinalis*	Perennial 3 feet (90 cm)	Cool (Zone 4)	Average soil, well drained
Birch *Betula* spp.	Deciduous trees 40–90 feet (12–27 m)	Cool (Zone 4)	Fertile, well-drained, acid soil
Borage *Borago officinalis*	Annual 2–3 feet (60–90 cm)	Cool	Rich, moist, slightly acid soil, well drained
Burdock *Arctium lappa*	Biennial 3–10 feet (1–3 m)	Cool (Zone 3)	Deep, loose, moist soil
Calendula *Calendula officinalis*	Annual 1–2 feet (30–60 cm)	Mild or cool	Average soil, neutral to slightly acid, well drained
Caraway *Carum carvi*	Biennial 1–2 feet (30–60 cm)	Cool (Zone 3)	Light, fertile soil, slightly acid
Cascara sagrada *Rhamnus purshiana*	Deciduous shrub 5–25 feet (1.5–7.5 m)	Mild (Zone 7)	Moist, fertile soil, well drained
Catnip *Nepeta cataria*	Perennial 1–3 feet (30–90 cm)	Cool (Zone 4)	Drier sandy soil, slightly alkaline
Cayenne pepper *Capsicum annuum*	Annual or tender perennial 1–2 feet (30–60 cm)	Warm	Moist, fertile soil, neutral to slightly acid
Chamomile, Roman *Chamaemelum nobile*	Creeping perennial 6–9 inches (15–23 cm)	Cool (Zone 3)	Moist, light soil, neutral pH
Chervil *Anthriscus cerefolium*	Annual 1–2 feet (30–60 cm)	Cool	Moist soil, high in organic matter, slightly acid
Chicory *Cichorium intybus*	Perennial 3–5 feet (0.9–1.5 m)	Cool (Zone 3)	Deep, well-drained, poor to average soil, slightly acid
Chives *Allium schoenoprasum*	Perennial 6–12 inches (15–30 cm)	Cool (Zone 3)	Rich soil, well drained
Clary *Salvia sclarea*	Perennial 2–5 feet (0.6–1.5 m)	Cool (Zone 4)	Average soil, alkaline to acid, well drained
Coffee *Coffea arabica*	Evergreen shrub or small tree 15–40 feet (4.5–12 m)	Warm (Zone 10); grow indoors in cooler Zones	Moderately fertile soil with good organic content, well drained
Comfrey *Symphytum officinale*	Perennial 3–5 feet (0.9–1.5 m)	Cool (Zone 3)	Rich, moist soil, neutral pH
Coriander *Coriandrum sativum*	Annual 1–3 feet (30–90 cm)	Mild	Rich soil, well drained, slightly acid

measures. Included in this table is an explanation of each plant's preferred climate, as well as its coldest hardiness zone (for perennials). To work out which hardiness zone you live in, turn to the "USDA Plant Hardiness Zone Map" on page 154.

You should find this guide invaluable if you're new to gardening or have recently moved to a new area. Within a few minutes, you will be able to dismiss those herbs that are inappropriate for your intended use or for your particular soil, climate, and topography, and pull together a preliminary list of those worth investigating further. Then you can turn to the "Plant by Plant Guide," starting on page 100, for more complete information on each herb you are considering.

Propagation	Pests and Diseases	Primary Uses
Sow seed or divide early spring	Powdery mildew	Medicinal herb (dried foliage)
Remove and replant offshoots from parent plant in any season	Mealybugs	Medicinal herb, cosmetic preparation (peeled leaf or extracted mucilage)
Sow seed indoors early spring or outdoors late summer	Aphids, crown rot	Medicinal herb, confection, liqueur flavoring (dried roots or foliage, young stems)
Sow seed in spring	Few or none	Medicinal and flavoring herb (dried seeds, fresh leaves)
Sow seed in spring	Few or none	Herbal tea (fresh or dried foliage, dried flowers)
Sow seed indoors early spring; sow outdoors or plant divisions late spring	Aphids	Medicinal herb for external use (dried flowers, roots)
Plant cuttings or root suckers in fall or sow seed in spring or fall	Rust fungi	Medicinal herb, dyeing (berries, dried bark, dried root)
Sow seed late spring–early summer	Plant bugs	Culinary herb (fresh or dried foliage)
Sow from seed; take cuttings late spring or buy nursery-grown plants	Scale insects	Culinary herb (dried leaves)
Sow from seed; take cuttings in fall or layer branches any season	Few or none	Medicinal herb (dried leaves)
Sow seed in spring or divide clump in fall	Aphids, powdery mildew	Herbal tea, crafts, salad herb (dried leaves, fresh or dried flowers)
Sow seed early spring or divide in fall; take cuttings in late spring or summer	Few or none	Medicinal herb, dyeing (dried leaves)
Sow seed late summer or fall; buy nursery-grown plant late winter or early spring	Caterpillars, leafminers, borers	Beverages (dried leaves and bark)
Sow seed in spring	Japanese beetles, foliage rot	Culinary herb, flavoring drinks (fresh or pickled leaves, candied flowers)
Sow seed early spring	Few or none	Medicinal herb, vegetable (fresh or dried roots)
Sow seed early spring (cold climates) or fall (mild climates)	Powdery mildew, leafspot fungi, aphids, whiteflies, leafhoppers, slugs	Medicinal and culinary herb (fresh, dried, or preserved flowers)
Sow seed fall or early spring; take cuttings in fall	Few or none	Culinary, medicinal, and flavoring herb (dried seeds, fresh young leaves)
Sow seed or layer in spring or fall; take cuttings in summer	Few or none	Medicinal herb (dried bark)
Sow seed or take cuttings early spring	Few or none	Culinary and medicinal herb, cat attractant (fresh or dried foliage)
Sow seed late spring indoors (cold climates) or outdoors (warm climates); plant out after frost	Few or none	Culinary herb (fresh or dried fruits)
Sow seed late spring–early summer; divide in early spring	Few or none	Medicinal herb (dried flowers)
Sow seed in fall or early spring	Earwigs	Culinary herb (fresh or dried leaves)
Sow seed early spring	Snails, slugs	Culinary herb, vegetable, beverage (fresh leaves, dried roots)
Sow seed indoors late winter; plant seedlings or divide clumps early spring	Crown rot	Culinary herb (fresh or dried leaves)
Sow seed in spring; divide in early spring or fall	Few or none	Culinary herb, potpourri (fresh or dried leaves)
Sow seed in spring	Mealybugs	Beverage (dried and roasted seeds)
Sow seed or divide in spring or fall; take cuttings in spring	Japanese beetles, slugs, snails	Medicinal herb for external use (fresh or dried leaves, dried root)
Sow seed in spring or in fall	Few or none	Culinary herb, potpourri (fresh or dried leaves, seeds)

Herb	Growth Form and Size	Preferred Climate (Coldest Zone)	Preferred Soil Conditions
Costmary *Chrysanthemum balsamita*	Perennial 1–3 feet (30–90 cm)	Cool (Zone 4)	Drier soil, loose, fertile, slightly acid
Dandelion *Taraxacum officinale*	Perennial 6–12 inches (15–30 cm)	Cool (Zone 2)	Any loose-textured soil
Dill *Anethum graveolens*	Annual 3 feet (90 cm)	Cool	Rich soil, slightly acid, well drained
Dock *Rumex* spp.	Perennial 1–4 feet (30–120 cm)	Cool (Zone 5)	Average soil, moist, slightly acid
Elecampane *Inula helenium*	Perennial 4–6 feet (1.2–1.8 m)	Cool (Zone 4)	Moderately fertile, moist soil
Eucalypts *Eucalyptus* spp.	Evergreen trees 5–500 feet 1.5–150 m)	Mild (Zone 8)	Light-textured soil, well drained
Fennel *Foeniculum vulgare*	Perennial (grown as annual) 4 feet (1.2 m)	Mild (Zone 6)	Average soil, good organic content, well drained
Fenugreek *Trigonella foenum-graecum*	Annual 1–2 feet (30–60 cm)	Mild	Moist, rich soil, neutral to slightly alkaline
Feverfew *Tanacetum parthenium*	Perennial 2–3 feet (60–90 cm)	Mild (Zone 5)	Average soil, slightly acid
Garlic *Allium sativum*	Bulbous perennial to 2 feet (60 cm)	Cool (Zone 5)	Loose, well-drained soil, acid to slightly alkaline
Geranium, scented *Pelargonium* spp.	Evergreen shrub to 3 feet (90 cm)	Mild (Zone 10); annual in cooler Zones	Rich, loose soil, well drained, neutral to slightly acid
Germander *Teucrium chamaedrys*	Shrubby perennial to 2 feet (60 cm)	Mild (Zone 5)	Average soil, well drained, slightly acid
Ginger *Zingiber officinale*	Perennial 2–4 feet (60–120 cm)	Warm (Zone 9)	Moist, fertile soil, well drained
Goldenrod *Solidago* spp.	Perennial 3–7 feet (0.9–2.1 m)	Cool (Zone 4)	Average to poor soil, well drained
Hop *Humulus lupulus*	Climbing perennial 20–30 feet (6–9 m)	Cool (Zone 3)	Deep, rich soil, neutral to slightly acid
Horehound *Marrubium vulgare*	Perennial 2–3 feet (60–90 cm)	Mild (Zone 4)	Average soil, deep and well drained, fairly dry, neutral pH
Horseradish *Armoracia rusticana*	Perennial 2–3 feet (60–90 cm)	Cool (Zone 5)	Deep, moist soil, neutral to slightly acid
Horsetail *Equisetum* spp.	Perennial 4–18 inches (10–45 cm)	Cool (Zone 2)	Wet, peaty soil, acid to neutral
Hyssop *Hyssopus officinalis*	Shrubby perennial 1–2 feet (30–60 cm)	Cool (Zone 3)	Light soil, well drained, slightly acid
Lady's bedstraw *Galium verum*	Perennial to 3 feet (90 cm)	Cool (Zone 3)	Light soil, deep and well drained
Lavender, English *Lavandula angustifolia*	Shrubby perennial 2–3 feet (60–90 cm)	Mild (Zone 5)	Light soil, well drained, neutral to slightly alkaline
Lemon balm *Melissa officinalis*	Perennial 1–2 feet (30–60 cm)	Cool (Zone 4)	Light, sandy soil, well drained, neutral pH
Lemongrass *Cymbopogon citratus*	Perennial to 6 feet (1.8 m)	Warm (Zone 10)	Rich, loose, deep soil
Lemon verbena *Aloysia triphylla*	Evergreen shrub 5–10 feet (1.5–3 m)	Mild (Zone 9)	Rich, moist soil, slightly acid
Lovage *Levisticum officinale*	Perennial to 6 feet (1.8 m)	Cool (Zone 5)	Moist, fertile soil, well drained, slightly acid
Madagascar periwinkle *Catharanthus roseus*	Annual or short-lived perennial to 2 feet (60 cm)	Warm (Zone 9)	Average soil, well drained, fairly dry
Madder *Rubia tinctorum*	Trailing perennial to 4 feet (1.2 m)	Mild (Zone 7)	Deep soil, well drained, neutral pH
Marjoram *Origanum majorana*	Perennial to 2 feet (60 cm)	Mild (Zone 9)	Light soil, well drained, neutral pH
Marsh mallow *Althaea officinalis*	Perennial 4–5 feet (1.2–1.5 m)	Cool (Zone 3)	Light, moist soil, neutral pH
Mint *Mentha* spp.	Perennial to 30 inches (75 cm)	Mild (Zone 5)	Rich, moist soil, well drained, slightly acid
Mugwort *Artemisia vulgaris*	Perennial 3–6 feet (90–180 cm)	Cool (Zone 4)	Average soil, well drained, slightly acid
Mustard *Brassica* spp.	Annual 4–6 feet (1.2–1.8 m)	Cool	Rich soil, well drained, acid
Nasturtium *Tropaeolum majus*	Annual 1–2 feet (30–60 cm)	Cool	Average to poor, moist soil, well drained

Propagation	Pests and Diseases	Primary Uses
Divide clump in spring	Few or none	Culinary herb, potpourri (fresh or dried leaves)
Sow seed early spring	Few or none	Culinary and medicinal herb, beverages (fresh leaves, dried roots)
Sow seed early spring	Few or none	Culinary herb (fresh and dried leaves, dried seeds)
Sow seed in spring	Few or none	Medicinal herb (dried roots)
Sow seed in spring; take root cuttings in fall	Sap-sucking bugs, aphids	Culinary and medicinal herb (dried roots)
Purchase nursery-grown plant; plant out spring or fall	Scale insects, aphids	Medicinal herb (oil distilled from leaves), crafts
Sow seed in spring or fall	Few or none	Culinary herb (young leaves, bulbous leaf bases, seeds)
Sow seed late spring	Slugs, snails	Culinary and medicinal herb (dried seeds)
Sow seed indoors late winter; take cuttings or divide in spring or fall	Few or none	Crafts (dried flowers)
Plant cloves in fall	Bulb rot	Culinary herb (bulbs)
Sow seed indoors early spring; take cuttings spring, summer, or fall	Whiteflies	Potpourri, culinary herb (dried or fresh leaves)
Take cuttings spring or summer; divide or layer in fall	Few or none	Medicinal herb, ornamental (dried flowers and foliage)
Plant rhizome indoors any season; place pot outdoors in summer only in cooler climates	Few or none	Culinary herb (fresh or dried root)
Sow seed early spring; divide plants spring or fall	Few or none	Medicinal herb, crafts (dried leaves and flowers)
Take root cuttings in fall	Aphids, mites, fungal diseases	Medicinal herb, flavoring of beverages (dried female flowers)
Sow seed or divide plants early spring	Few or none	Medicinal herb, flavoring of beverages and candies (dried leaves)
Plant root pieces in fall	Few or none	Culinary herb
Divide plants in fall	Few or none	Ornamental, scouring of utensils (fresh or dried stems)
Sow seed early spring; take cuttings or divide plants spring or fall	Few or none	Medicinal and culinary herb (fresh or dried leaves)
Sow seed in spring; divide plants in spring or fall	Few or none	Ornamental, medicinal herb (dried flowering plant)
Take cuttings spring or fall	Stem rot, caterpillars	Crafts, potpourri (distilled oil, dried flowers)
Sow seed in spring; take cuttings or divide plants spring or fall	Powdery mildew	Culinary herb, herbal teas (fresh or dried leaves)
Divide plants late spring, place outdoors summer only in cooler climates	Basal rot	Culinary herb, potpourri, herbal tea (fresh inner leaves, distilled oil)
Take cuttings late spring–early summer or purchase nursery-grown plant	Mites	Culinary herb, potpourri (fresh or dried leaves)
Sow seed late summer–early fall	Leafminers	Culinary herb, vegetable (fresh young leaves and stalks, dried leaves and seeds)
Sow seed indoors winter or spring, plant out late spring–early summer	Few or none	Ornamental
Sow seed indoors early spring, plant out late spring–early fall	Few or none	Medicinal herb, dyeing (fresh or dried root)
Sow seed indoors early spring, plant out late spring; divide in fall	Few or none	Culinary herb (fresh or dried leaves)
Sow seed in spring; take cuttings or divide in fall	Few or none	Medicinal herb, vegetable (fresh leaves, dried flowers, fresh or dried roots)
Take cuttings or divide spring or fall	Aphids, plant bugs	Culinary herb, flavoring of beverages, confections, potpourri (fresh or dried leaves, distilled oil)
Sow seed indoors winter or early spring; divide plants spring or fall	Few or none	Crafts, insect repellent (dried leaves)
Sow seed early spring–fall	Caterpillars, slugs, snails, whiteflies	Culinary herb (dried seeds, seed oil)
Sow seed in spring after last frost	Aphids	Culinary herb (fresh leaves and flowers, pickled buds)

Herb	Growth Form and Size	Preferred Climate (Coldest Zone)	Preferred Soil Conditions
Nettle *Urtica dioica*	Perennial 2–6 feet (60–180 cm)	Cool (Zone 5)	Average soil
New Jersey tea *Ceanothus americanus*	Deciduous shrub 2–3 feet (60–90 cm)	Cool (Zone 4)	Light soil, well drained
Oregano *Origanum vuigare*	Perennial 12–30 inches (30–75 cm)	Mild (Zone 5)	Average soil, well drained, slightly acid
Orris *Iris* x *germanica*	Perennial to 30 inches (75 cm)	Mild (Zone 5)	Deep, rich soil, well drained, neutral pH
Parsley, curled *Petroselinum crispum*	Biennial 8–12 inches (20–30 cm)	Mild (Zone 5)	Moderately rich soil, well drained
Passionflower *Passiflora incarnata*	Climber (semi-woody) 25–30 feet (7.5–9 m)	Mild (Zone 7)	Deep, fertile soil, well drained
Pennyroyal, English *Mentha pulegium*	Perennial to 1 foot (30 cm)	Mild (Zone 5)	Moist, loamy soil, moderately acid
Pipsissewa *Chimaphila umbellata*	Evergreen perennial to 10 inches (25 cm)	Cool (Zone 4)	Rich but sandy soil, acid
Plantain *Plantago major*	Perennial 6–18 inches (15–45 cm)	Cool (Zone 2)	Any well-drained soil
Red clover *Trifolium pratense*	Perennial 1–2 feet (30–60 cm)	Cool (Zone 5)	Light, sandy soil, slightly acid
Rosemary *Rosmarinus officinalis*	Evergreen shrub 2–6 feet (60–180 cm)	Mild (Zone 8)	Light soil, well drained
Roses *Rosa* spp.	Deciduous shrubs or woody climbers 2–30 feet (0.6–9 m)	Cool (Zone 4)	Well-drained, neutral soil
Rue *Ruta graveolens*	Perennial 2–3 feet (60–90 cm)	Mild (Zone 4)	Average to poor soil, well drained, neutral pH
Safflower *Carthamus tinctorius*	Annual 2–3 feet (60–90 cm)	Cool	Average soil, dryish, well drained
Saffron *Crocus sativus*	Bulbous perennial to 12 inches (30 cm)	Cool (Zone 6)	Light soil, well drained
Sage *Salvia officinalis*	Perennial or subshrub 1–2 feet (30–60 cm)	Mild (Zone 4)	Light, sandy soil, well drained, slightly acid
Santolina *Santolina chamaecyparissus*	Perennial or subshrub to 2 feet (60 cm)	Mild (Zone 6)	Poor soil, well drained, neutral to slightly alkaline
Sassafras *Sassafras albidum*	Deciduous tree 20–60 feet (6–18 m)	Cool (Zone 5)	Average soil, well drained
Savory, winter *Satureja montana*	Perennial or subshrub 6–12 inches (15–30 cm)	Cool (Zone 6)	Poor soil, well drained
Soapwort *Saponaria officinalis*	Perennial 1–2 feet (30–60 cm)	Cool (Zone 3)	Average to poor soil, well drained
Sorrel *Rumex* spp.	Perennial 30–36 inches (75–90 cm)	Cool (Zone 5)	Rich, moist soil, acid
Southernwood *Artemisia abrotanum*	Perennial 3–6 feet (0.9–1.8 m)	Mild (Zone 4)	Average soil, well drained, slightly acid
Sweet cicely *Myrrhis odorata*	Perennial to 3 feet (90 cm)	Cool (Zone 3)	Humus-rich soil, well drained
Sweet woodruff *Galium odoratum*	Perennial 8–12 inches (20–30 cm)	Cool (Zone 3)	Moist, humus-rich soil, well drained, fairly acid
Tansy *Tanacetum vulgare*	Perennial 3–4 feet (90–120 cm)	Cool (Zone 4)	Average soil, well drained, slightly acid
Tarragon, French *Artemisia dracunculus*	Perennial to 2 feet (60 cm)	Cool (Zone 4)	Average soil, well drained, neutral pH
Thyme, garden *Thymus vulgaris*	Perennial or subshrub 6–15 inches (15–38 cm)	Mild (Zone 5)	Sandy soil, well drained, slightly acid
Valerian *Valeriana officinalis*	Perennial 3–5 feet (0.9–1.5 m)	Cool (Zone 4)	Rich, moist soil
Vervain, European *Verbena officinalis*	Perennial (grown as annual) 1–3 feet (30–90 cm)	Cool (Zone 5)	Rich, moist soil
Violet *Viola odorata*	Perennial 4–6 inches (10–15 cm)	Mild (Zone 5)	Rich, moist soil, neutral to acid
Witch hazel *Hamamelis virginiana*	Deciduous shrub 8–15 feet (2.4–4.5 m)	Mild (Zone 4)	Rich, moist soil, neutral to acid
Wormwood *Artemisia absinthium*	Perennial to 4 feet (1.2 m)	Cool (Zone 4)	Poor soil, well drained, slightly acid
Yarrow *Achillea millefolium*	Perennial to 3 feet (90 cm)	Cool (Zone 2)	Moderately rich, moist soil

Propagation	Pests and Diseases	Primary Uses
Sow seed early spring	Few or none	Medicinal herb, vegetable, fiber (fresh or dried foliage)
Take cuttings spring or fall	Few or none	Medicinal herb, herbal tea (fresh or dried leaves)
Sow seed indoors in winter or outdoors in spring; take cuttings or divide early spring	Mites, aphids	Culinary herb (fresh or dried foliage)
Plant rhizomes early spring; divide in late summer	Few or none	Potpourri (dried rhizome)
Sow seed early spring	Fungal diseases	Culinary herb (fresh or dried leaves)
Sow seed in spring; take cuttings in fall	Thrips, aphids, nematodes	Edible fruit
Sow seed or take cuttings early spring; divide in spring or fall	Few or none	Insect repellent, perfumery (fresh or dried shoots in bud, distilled oil)
Divide plants or take root cuttings spring or fall	Few or none	Medicinal and culinary herb (fresh or dried leaves)
Sow seed early spring or fall	Few or none	Medicinal herb, dyeing (fresh or dried leaves, dried roots)
Sow inoculated seed early spring	Few or none	Medicinal herb, herbal tea (fresh or dried flowerheads)
Sow seed indoors early spring; take cuttings in fall; layer branches in summer	Scale insects	Culinary and medicinal herb, potpourri (fresh or dried leaves, distilled oil)
Purchase nursery-grown plant, plant out fall or early spring	Fungal diseases, aphids, mites, caterpillars, beetles	Medicinal herb, herbal tea, perfumery (dried flower petals, fresh or dried fruit)
Sow seed indoors late winter; take cuttings in spring; divide plant in fall	Root rot	Ornamental, crafts (fresh or dried leaves and flowers)
Sow seed early spring	Few or none	Dyeing, vegetable oil (dried flowers, seeds)
Plant corms fall or spring	Few or none	Spice, dyeing (dried stigmas)
Sow seed late spring (or late winter indoors); take cuttings or divide plants spring or fall	Basal rot, slugs, snails	Culinary and medicinal herb (fresh or dried leaves)
Sow seed late spring; take cuttings, layer, or divide plants in spring	Basal rot	Insect repellent, perfumery, crafts (dried foliage and flowerheads)
Sow seed or take cuttings or root suckers in fall	Few or none	Ornamental, perfumery (dried root, distilled oil)
Sow seed late spring; take cuttings or divide plants spring or fall	Few or none	Culinary herb (fresh or dried leaves)
Sow seed indoors in winter, spring, or fall; divide in fall	Few or none	Soap substitute, medicinal herb (fresh leaves, fresh or dried roots)
Sow seed late spring; divide plants fall or early spring	Slugs, snails	Culinary herb, salad vegetable (fresh leaves)
Take cuttings or divide plants spring or fall	Few or none	Crafts, insect repellent, potpourri (dried foliage)
Sow seed late spring; divide plants spring or fall	Few or none	Culinary herb (fresh or dried leaves, dried seeds, dried roots)
Sow seed in fall; divide plants spring or fall	Few or none	Crafts, potpourri, insect repellent (dried foliage)
Sow seed indoors late winter; divide roots spring or fall	Aphids	Insect repellent, crafts, dyeing (fresh or dried flowering branches)
Take cuttings in fall; divide plants in spring	Fungal diseases	Culinary herb (fresh or dried foliage)
Take cuttings or divide plants in spring	Fungal diseases	Culinary and medicinal herb (fresh or dried foliage)
Sow seed in spring; divide plants spring or fall	Few or none	Ornamental, medicinal herb (dried roots)
Sow seed or take cuttings in spring	Few or none	Ornamental
Sow seed in fall; divide plants winter or early spring	Mites	Confectionery, perfumery (dried flowers, leaves, roots, candied flowers)
Sow seed outdoors in fall; take cuttings in summer; layer in fall	Few or none	Medicinal herb (bark, leaves, flowering twigs)
Sow seed outdoors in fall or indoors late winter	Few or none	Crafts, insect repellent (dried foliage and flowers)
Sow seed indoors late winter or outdoors late spring; divide plants fall or early spring	Powdery mildew	Crafts, dyeing (dried flowers)

CULTIVATING AND PLANTING

Before you begin to prepare your soil and plant your herbs, read "Understanding Your Garden," starting on page 12, to learn how to choose an appropriate site. Good soil preparation is one of the most important aspects of organic gardening. In the following chapter you will learn the steps to take for soil preparation as well as gardening techniques like double-digging and tillage. You'll also learn how green manures add organic matter and nutrients to the soil.

Knowing how and when to fertilize your herbs doesn't have to be a mystery. Whether you're starting a new herb bed or maintaining an established one, you'll find easy-to-follow advice on applying organic fertilizers and soil amendments to keep your garden healthy and productive. Composting kitchen scraps and garden wastes is a great way to recycle materials, and it's a free source of the nutrients and organic matter that your herbs will thrive on.

Once you've prepared the soil, you're ready to plant your herbs. You may be surprised to learn that many herbs are easy to grow from seed. If you want to try starting your own herbs, you'll find step-by-step directions for seed starting, as well as details on caring for young plants and transplanting them outdoors.

Opposite: Once you've chosen your herb plants and decided on a garden plan, learn how to prepare your soil and garden site. Simple cultivating techniques can make the difference between success and failure.

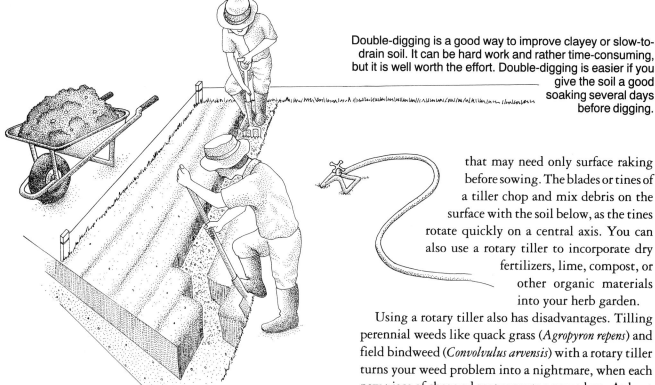

Double-digging is a good way to improve clayey or slow-to-drain soil. It can be hard work and rather time-consuming, but it is well worth the effort. Double-digging is easier if you give the soil a good soaking several days before digging.

Soil Preparation

Tilling, digging, or cultivating the soil to produce an open, even consistency prepares your garden soil for planting. A good seedbed will be finely crumbled and free of stones and hard clods so that tiny seeds have maximum contact with soil and can germinate easily. If you've raked out stones and other debris, the new roots will be able to spread quickly.

If you are growing only perennial herbs, or a mixture of annuals and perennials, you'll only have to consider the task of soil preparation once for each growing area. If you prepare the soil well before planting, your plants should thrive with a minimum of care. If you prefer to grow your annual herbs separately, you'll have an opportunity to prepare the soil before planting each year.

Digging or Tilling

If, like most people, you're growing herbs in small beds or borders, hand tools are all you need to work the soil. For hand-tilling you need only a spade or shovel for digging, and a spading fork to loosen the soil. To use a spading fork, thrust the tines of the fork into the soil, then twist or wiggle the fork to loosen the soil. Other hand tools include a trowel, a hand fork, a rake, a dutch hoe, and a tined cultivator. Your local hardware store or garden center will have these and other hand tools and will help you decide which ones you need.

On a small to medium scale, rotary tillers do the work of tilling and initial surface preparation in one pass. Tillers are fast and efficient, and leave a good seedbed that may need only surface raking before sowing. The blades or tines of a tiller chop and mix debris on the surface with the soil below, as the tines rotate quickly on a central axis. You can also use a rotary tiller to incorporate dry fertilizers, lime, compost, or other organic materials into your herb garden.

Using a rotary tiller also has disadvantages. Tilling perennial weeds like quack grass (*Agropyron repens*) and field bindweed (*Convolvulus arvensis*) with a rotary tiller turns your weed problem into a nightmare, when each new piece of chopped root sprouts a new plant. At least if you're tilling by hand, you can remove the weeds as you go. Rotary tillers don't remove rocks, either, so you'll have to do this by hand, too.

As mechanical tilling saves time and labor, it's tempting to till more frequently if you have a rotary tiller. This multiplies the disadvantages of tilling. Overtilling can damage the structure of your soil, depleting the organic matter content, and upsetting the balance of bacterial populations. Constant mechanical tilling can also create an impermeable layer of soil below the tilled layer, as you always cultivate to the same depth. The lower layer of soil can become compacted; water won't drain away and roots can't penetrate it. Tilling the soil when it is too wet can also destroy soil structure, which is often difficult to repair.

Working the soil modifies all of the factors related to plant growth, including soil oxygen, moisture, temperature, chemistry, and biological activity. For example, air is necessary in the soil, but the increased oxygen made available by cultivation speeds the decomposition of organic matter, and you may have to add more compost sooner than otherwise. Tilling the soil also exposes dormant weed seeds from deeper soil layers, and contact with light and oxygen at the surface triggers their germination.

Most gardeners use shallow cultivation to prepare their garden soil each year. Using a spade, spading fork, or rotary tiller, they mix and turn the soil to a depth of 3 to 6 inches (7.5 to 15 cm), or just enough to accommodate most plant roots. Some gardeners never till more than about 1 inch (2.5 cm) deep, in order to avoid exposing dormant weed seeds.

Once your garden bed is established, you can avoid further cultivation by covering the soil with a thick layer of organic mulch.

Mulch helps to keep weeds down and retain soil moisture. When you are ready to plant, push the mulch layer aside to expose the soil.

Double-digging

If your soil is on the clayey side and slow to drain, you may want to try a technique called double-digging. Double-digging penetrates the soil below the surface layer or topsoil, improves soil drainage, extends the depth of the root zone, and can result in greater productivity. This kind of tillage is usually performed only once, and is particularly helpful if your soil has been heavily compacted.

To double dig, you remove a layer of topsoil from your garden, loosen the layer below with a garden fork, and then replace the topsoil. The result is a loose, deep soil that plant roots find easy to penetrate. The main disadvantages are the time and labor required.

To use this method, mark a trench about 12 inches (30 cm) wide and as long as the finished bed is to be. A flat-bladed spade is best for removing the soil to a depth of about 12 inches (30 cm); place the soil in a wheelbarrow or on a tarp laid on the ground. Once you've reached the depth, use a spading fork to loosen and aerate the soil along the bottom of the trench, but do not turn the soil. Then spread a thin layer of compost on the broken surface.

Next, move back 12 inches (30 cm) and once again remove the soil to the same depth, but this time toss the soil into the first trench. When you've reached the bottom of the second trench, aerate with the fork and apply compost, then fill the second trench with soil from a third trench. You can add more compost or organic fertilizer to the topsoil as you work. Repeat the process until you've moved across the width of the new bed, filling the last trench with the soil saved from the first trench. As you work, avoid standing on the newly turned soil. From then on, avoid walking on the soil. Rake the tilled surface smooth to prepare for planting seeds or young plants.

Cultivating Established Gardens

If you're growing a conventional herb garden with a mixture of annuals and perennials, you'll need only a few hand tools to cultivate around them during the growing season. Basic tools include a trowel for transplanting and a hand fork for weeding and scratching in organic fertilizers. Other commonly used hand tools include rakes, hoes, and tined cultivators. Your local garden center or hardware store will have these or other tools and can help you decide which ones you need.

How to Determine Your Soil Texture

Soil texture is determined by the proportions of different-sized mineral particles in your soil. To determine your soil texture, simply fill a jar with soil and water. When the soil has settled, divide the height of each mineral layer by the height of total soil. Then multiply by 100 for the percentage of each mineral. In the illustrated example there is 50% sand, 25% silt and 25% clay.

(For more information on soil texture, see "Soil" on page 20.)

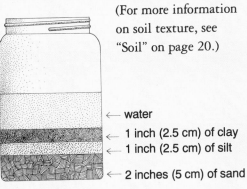

← water
← 1 inch (2.5 cm) of clay
← 1 inch (2.5 cm) of silt
← 2 inches (5 cm) of sand

Adding Organic Nutrients

Organic gardeners understand that it is almost impossible to overfertilize with organic matter. They make a common practice of simply applying a fresh batch of compost or well-rotted manure to the garden at the start of each season. In garden soil with an active microbial population and with nutrients in the proper ratios for plant use, a 1- to 2-inch (2.5 to 5 cm) application of compost or other organic matter will feed the soil adequately for most garden herbs throughout the season. The great advantage in using compost or well-rotted manure is that you're adding organic matter at the same time as fertilizing.

If plant production and health seem to be suffering, however, you will need to observe your plants closely and perhaps consult with your local extension agent, or have your soil tested by a soil-testing lab to determine what nutrients are missing, and to rule out environmental or disease problems. It might be necessary to apply one or more of the organic nutrients offered by garden centers and catalogs.

If you need to adjust your soil pH, follow the recommendations of the testing agency closely and make the changes at least 6 months before the season. Most liming materials need plenty of time to make a change in soil pH.

With a little calculation, you can substitute organic sources like homemade compost, organic fertilizers, or cover crops for chemicals recommended by the soil-test lab, or you can ask it to recommend organic amendments. You can use the

Applying a foliar spray of seaweed extract with a hand-held sprayer is an easy way to give your herb plants a light nutrient boost.

When you prepare a new site for an herb garden, work ample amounts of compost or composted manure into the site to build up soil fertility.

Avoid adding raw manure directly to garden soil—its high nitrogen content can burn plant roots. Compost the manure first, or use it to make manure tea.

Side-dressing is an easy way to fertilize herbs growing in rows. Apply a dry fertilizer in a band along the row, and scratch it into the soil with a hoe or rake.

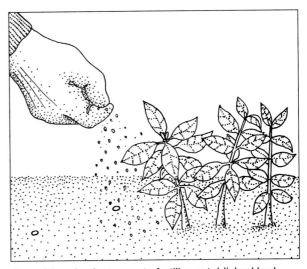

One of the simplest ways to fertilize established herb gardens is to lightly and evenly scatter a dry fertilizer over the soil surface.

To get the fertilizer closer to the roots, scratch it into the soil with a metal rake. Just work it in lightly to avoid damaging the plant roots with the rake.

information in the table "Building Up Soil Fertility with Organic Fertilizers" on page 47 to determine how much organic fertilizer to add to your soil before planting. This is especially simple when the crops are herbs, since herbs rarely are heavy feeders.

Plants need some essential elements—the so-called trace elements—in very minute quantities. Organic materials like compost usually supply sufficient amounts of trace minerals to the soil. If these elements are lacking, your plants may show deficiency symptoms such as yellowing between the leaf veins, brown and wilted shoot tips, or stunted growth. Applying a foliar spray of seaweed extract or side-dressing with kelp meal should help to provide your plants with the nutrients they need.

Most nutrients can be worked into the soil just before planting. If you're applying a nitrogen fertilizer, like bloodmeal, add it to the soil as you plant to avoid the loss of nitrogen. If plants aren't there to take it up, nitrogen tends to leach out of soil; that's why otherwise fertile soils in high-rainfall areas often lack nitrogen. You can broadcast dry organic fertilizers by hand (wear gloves and a dust mask) or with a spreader. Spread compost or well-rotted manure with a garden fork or a shovel, then either till it in or leave it on the surface as a mulch.

To feed perennial herbs, simply apply organic materials to the soil surface like a mulch. If you use a dry fertilizer, scratch it in to a shallow depth.

Green Manures

A green manure is a crop grown for the purpose of improving the soil. You turn the crop under before it matures, and it adds lots of organic matter and nutrients to the soil as it breaks down. Common green manures are buckwheat, rye, hairy vetch, and red clover. (Cover crops are similar to green manures, but their primary purpose is to cover the soil and protect it from erosion.)

Some green manures, such as clovers and vetches, are known as legumes. Legumes work together with certain soilborne bacteria to transform nitrogen into a form that plants can use. Different bacteria work with different legume crops. You can buy the appropriate bacteria in the form of a granulated mix called an inoculant. Mixing the inoculant with the seed before planting will ensure that the right bacteria will be there for your crop.

Dig or till to loosen the soil, break up the surface clods, and rake the surface smooth. Broadcast the seed by hand or with a mechanical spreader, then lightly till or rake it in. About 4 to 6 weeks before you are ready to plant your next crop of herbs, work the green manure crop into the ground. If the growth is heavy, you may have to mow it first or cut it down by hand.

Buckwheat This plant grows quickly, so use it to fill vacant garden space in the summer between your spring and fall crops. It's frost-sensitive, so sow in spring after the last frost or about 6 weeks before the first fall frost. Buckwheat is an annual that tolerates low fertility and acid soils. Sow at a rate of 2 to 3 pounds/ 1,000 square feet (100 to 150 g/10 sq m).

Winter Rye Sown in late summer or fall, rye will survive cold-climate winters and resume growing the following spring. It's a good choice where annual herbs leave the soil bare in winter. Sow at a rate of 2 to 3 pounds/1,000 square feet (100 to 150 g/10 sq m).

Hairy Vetch Sow in late summer or fall like rye, but be sure to add the proper inoculant to the seed. Ask the mail-order company or garden center, where you buy seed, which inoculant to use. Hairy vetch is an annual legume, so it adds nitrogen to the soil. It tolerates moist soils. Sow at a rate of 1 to 2 pounds/ 1,000 square feet (50 to 100 g/10 sq m).

Red Clover This plant is a biennial legume that can be left to grow for 1 to 2 years. As with hairy vetch, you'll need to add the proper inoculant. Red clover tolerates acid soils with poor drainage. Sow in spring or late summer at a rate of 4 to 8 ounces/1,000 square feet (10 to 25 g/10 sq m).

Right: To give your herbs an extra boost, apply organic fertilizers around the base of the plants in spring and summer.

Above: If you are growing annual herbs separate from the perennials, the soil in your annual beds may be bare between crops and during the winter. Take advantage of these times to protect and improve your soil with a green manure crop.

Below: Compost is an invaluable source of organic matter, as well as some plant nutrients. Spread compost evenly over the growing area at any time of year. Leave it on the surface as a mulch, or work it into the soil.

Building Up Soil Fertility with Organic Fertilizers

Use the results of your soil test to determine how much fertilizer to apply. If your soil is of low fertility, use the higher rate of application. If your soil is fairly fertile, you can use the lower rate or substitute a 1-inch (2.5 cm) layer of compost.

Fertilizer	Percent Nutrient			Application Rates
	Nitrogen (N)	Phosphate (P_2O_5)	Potash (K_2O)	lb/1,000 sq ft (kg/10 sq m)
Sources of Nitrogen				
Bat guano	10	3	1	10–30 (0.5–1.5)
Bloodmeal	11	0	0	10–30 (0.5–1.5)
Fish meal	5	3	3	10–30 (0.5–1.5)
Soybean meal	7	0.5	2.3	10–50 (0.5–2.5)
Sources of Phosphorus				
Bonemeal	1	11	0	10–30 (0.5–1.5)
Colloidal phosphate	0	2	2	10–60 (0.5–3)
Rock phosphate	0	3	0	10–60 (0.5–3)
Sources of Potassium				
Granite dust	0	0	4	25–100 (1.25–5)
Greensand	0	0	7	25–100 (1.25–5)
Ground kelp	1.5	0.5	2.5	5–20 (0.5–1)

Compost

Whether your garden is large or small, it's worth devoting some space to a compost pile to convert otherwise wasted products into the ultimate soil amendment. Worked into the soil or used as a mulch, compost can add nutrients, loosen up clay soils, and increase the water-holding capacity of dry, sandy soils.

Start saving any organic wastes you would normally discard, but avoid such waste products as oils and meat, since they will attract scavenging animals and slow the process of decomposition. Also avoid human or pet feces, pesticides, and pesticide-treated plant material,

Dig compost into a new garden to instantly enliven soil.

such as grass clippings from treated lawns. Don't add weeds or insect-infested or diseased plants unless you have a "hot" compost pile (see "Hot Compost" below). It's also not a good idea to add roots of perennial weeds, like Canada thistle, which may survive the composting process and be distributed throughout your garden as you spread the finished compost.

Compost can be in an open pile, but bins are helpful because they look neater and help keep animals out of the pile. You can choose from a variety of commercially sold containers made from timber or plastic, or you can make your own from timber, cement blocks, brick, or even chicken wire nailed to garden stakes. If you have the space, a multi-bin system is ideal, so when one part is full, you can start filling up the other side.

Whatever design you choose, it is best to stand it on a level, well-drained surface to prevent the pile from sitting in water. A coarse material, such as straw or sunflower stalks, is best as the bottom layer of the heap so that air can circulate freely.

If all the green material added to your compost is relatively moist, it will not be necessary to add extra water. If materials have been allowed to dry out, you may need to moisten them for effective breakdown.

Adding a few shovelsful of good garden soil or finished compost to the pile will add to the micro-organisms that help carry out the composting process.

Ideally, your pile should be at least 3 feet (90 cm) on each side, and no bigger than 5 to 6 feet (1.5 to 1.8 m) to break down properly.

There are two types of compost heaps: cold compost and hot compost. Cold compost is simpler and slower, while hot compost is more complex and faster.

Hot Compost

This type can be finished in 2 to 6 weeks or as soon as the temperature stabilizes and the individual materials you added at the beginning are no longer recognizable.

Waste material is stacked layer upon layer, or just jumbled together. Mix materials that are high in carbon with materials high in nitrogen. You can achieve a good balance with approximately equal volumes of dry materials such as leaves, straw, or paper, and green materials or manure. Too much carbon will mean the pile remains too cool. And excessive nitrogen creates odor problems. Sprinkle soil on top of alternate layers to inoculate the pile with the right decomposer organisms.

Wherever possible, break materials down before adding them to the pile. Woody prunings, tree bark, and newspaper should be shredded to fine pieces. Weeds or insect-infested or diseased materials should go in the center of the pile, where they will be exposed to the highest temperatures.

Your compost pile will be best at roughly 4 feet (1.2 m) on each side. Smaller piles won't heat as efficiently, and anything larger becomes a little unmanageable when turning the material over to redistribute and aerate.

Use a compost thermometer to monitor your pile's temperature.

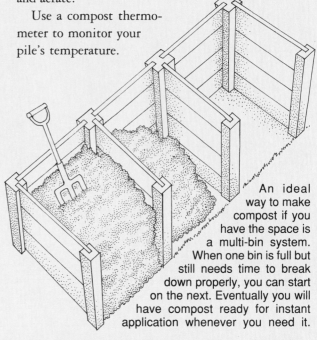

An ideal way to make compost if you have the space is a multi-bin system. When one bin is full but still needs time to break down properly, you can start on the next. Eventually you will have compost ready for instant application whenever you need it.

Keep the temperature below 160°F (71°C), since higher temperatures will kill important decomposer organisms. The turning process helps maintain a constant temperature. Regular turning will also help to increase the oxygen level in the pile and speed up microbial activity. If you are in a hurry for finished compost, turn the pile every few days until it stops heating up, and it will break down more quickly. Otherwise, turning the pile just once or twice after the initial heating is sufficient.

The heap should be kept moist, but not soggy. If it is drying out too much, simply moisten it with water from a watering can or hose. This may be necessary only around the edges. A tarp over the pile will help regulate moisture escaping and also prevent heavy rains from penetrating and washing nutrients out of the pile.

If odor is a problem with your hot compost, the pile needs to be turned and aerated; if it is too wet, mix in more dry materials and cover the pile with a tarp. If the breakdown is too slow, add more green or nitrogenous material or water the pile to keep it evenly damp.

Cold Compost

This is a much slower process of decomposition and requires no turning over with a garden fork. After piling together your waste material, simply wait 6 to 12 months. Don't add materials contaminated with pests, since temperatures won't be hot enough to kill them off.

Compost Tea

Compost tea adds nutrients to soil. Put compost or manure into a bag made of burlap (or other fabric) and tie the bag firmly at the top. Place the bag in a container of water; a shovelful of material will be suitable for a 5-gallon (23 l) container. Nutrients from the compost diffuse into the water from the bag. Dilute the tea to a light brown before using it on young plants, as strong tea can burn seedlings.

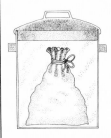

When your compost is fully decomposed, shake it through ½-inch (12 mm) mesh wire to screen out large particles. Each spring, spread 1 to 2 inches (2.5 to 5 cm) of compost over the surface of your garden. If soil tests indicate a nutrient imbalance, fertilize the soil appropriately first, then add the compost by digging it in or leaving it on the surface as a mulch. Use compost indoors as potting medium or for starting seeds. The screened compost can be used alone or mixed with vermiculite, perlite, or other potting ingredients.

Compost Ingredients

Material	Nitrogen	Carbon	Comments
Bread, cakes, etc. (stale or mildewed)	High	Low	May attract vermin; break into pieces and mix well into compost.
Coffee grounds	High	Low	Acidic; use in compost for acid-loving plants or mix in a little lime to raise pH.
Eggshells	Low	None	Slow to break down; crush before adding to compost; rich source of minerals.
Fallen leaves	Low	High	Also an excellent mulch for acid-loving plants.
Floor sweepings	Low	Low	Mainly inert material but may be high in minerals.
Garden prunings and clippings	Low	High	Woody materials are slow to break down; feed through a chipper or cut into short lengths.
Kitchen scraps (leaves, roots, stems, peelings)	Medium to low	Low to medium	Easy to compost.
Overripe or damaged fruit or vegetables	High	Low	Can attract fruit flies; best in a closed bin or tumbler at high temperatures.
Paper and cardboard	None	High	Wet thoroughly and mix with high-nitrogen ingredients; should not be more than 25% of the pile.
Potting mixes, used	Low	Low	Risk of transmitting plant diseases and pests; best composted at high temperatures.
Weeds	Medium	Medium	Compost at high temperatures to kill seeds and roots.

Planting Seeds

For most gardeners, spring planting is the ritual that marks the beginning of a new gardening year. If you're planting tender annual herbs like basil, you can get an early start by sowing seeds indoors. Other herbs, like safflower and sweet cicely, are easy to sow directly into the garden. The "Plant by Plant Guide," starting on page 100, lists the best way to sow specific herbs.

Starting Seeds Indoors

If you have the space, starting your seedlings indoors is by far the best way. You'll have more control over the environment than if you plant directly outdoors, which means that seeds will germinate faster and seedlings will grow more vigorously. It is much easier to give your seedlings the care they need when they are concentrated in one ideal location.

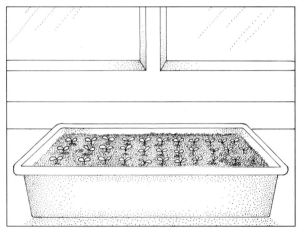

Once germinated, young plants may simply need a sunny windowsill position.

Sow your annual herb seeds indoors about 6 to 8 weeks before you plan to transplant them to the garden. Raising new perennials may require an additional 4 to 8 weeks if germination is slow.

Containers You can start seedlings in just about any container, provided you allow for drainage. Use small clay or plastic pots, or yogurt containers with holes punctured in their bottoms. If you are planting in large numbers, it may be more efficient to purchase the conventional ready-to-use short or long nursery flats with plastic inserts to hold a number of plants.

If you're reusing the previous year's flats and pots, either dip them in boiling water for several minutes or rinse them in a 10 percent bleach solution (1 part bleach to 9 parts water) to kill disease organisms before use.

Herbs that transplant poorly, like parsley, can be sown indoors in peat pots filled with growing medium, or in peat pellets, which are advertised in seed catalogs and may be bought in garden stores. Plant the whole pot or pellet containing the seedling in the ground at transplanting time.

Growing Medium New seedlings need a light growing medium for a quick start. Older seedlings need a medium with enough nourishment to last them until they're planted outdoors. There are plenty of recipes for growing mediums, and which one you use is a matter of personal taste and experience. Generally, a mix for starting seedlings will contain equal parts of fine compost or milled sphagnum peat moss and vermiculite or perlite. To provide the extra nutrients necessary for established seedlings, use a higher percentage of compost in the mix, or add a small quantity, ½ cup (4 fl oz/

The Right Environment

Most herb seeds will germinate successfully if kept at a temperature of 65 to 75°F (18 to 24°C) both day and night. In a cool house, you can achieve this by placing seedling containers on top of electric heating mats designed for that purpose, or on top of the refrigerator or a warm radiator.

Once your herbs have germinated, keep them near a sunny window or under some fluorescent plant lights. Most seedlings will need between 10 and 15 hours of light each day. Water them thoroughly, but let the surface dry out between soakings.

Many herb seeds germinate best in warm soil. Electric propagation units or heating mats help to keep the soil at an ideal temperature.

125 ml) or less, of a dry organic fertilizer to each 5-gallon (23 l) batch of medium.

Sowing The rate at which you sow will vary with the species and the expected seed germination rate (usually marked on the packet). Large seeds are fairly easy to sow and space evenly. When sowing tiny seeds, mix them with some clean white play sand before sowing, to get a more even distribution of seed.

Some gardeners recommend covering the flats with plastic or glass to keep them evenly moist. Damp newspaper is another good covering material, but only if your seeds don't need light to germinate. If you cover your flats with any of these materials, lift the covers each day to monitor germination. You will need to remove the covers as soon as the tiny seedlings begin popping through the surface.

Once the seeds have germinated, leave the surface open to air circulation to prevent disease, and water the containers with a mist spray as necessary to keep them moist but not soggy.

Sowing Seed

To help you to identify your seedlings at their various stages of development, prepare labels with the name of the seed and the date of sowing for each type of herb and use them to mark the rows as you sow. Either cluster seeds in the center of each small pot, or mark shallow furrows 2 inches (5 cm) apart in long flats and lightly sprinkle in the seeds.

Press any seeds that require light for germination into the surface and leave them uncovered by the mix. Lightly cover the seeds that germinate in the dark with ⅛ to ¼ inch (3 to 6 mm) of fine soil or sand.

1

4

5

1. Fill the container with a seed-raising mix.
2. Press the mix into the corners.
3. Level off the mix to ½ inch (12 mm) below the rim.
4. Scatter seeds and gently press in.
5. If the seeds do not need light, cover them with a fine layer of mix.
6. Water them with a fine mist spray.
7. Label the container.
8. Cover with plastic, glass, or damp newspaper.

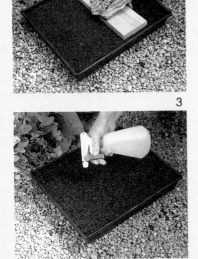

6

7

8

Step-by-step Potting Up

1. Place moist growing medium into new containers. Make a hole large enough so the root system of the transplanted seedling will not be crushed.
2. Remove one seedling at a time using a pencil or pointed stick.
3. Holding the seedling by its leaves, place it into its new container and gently firm the soil around it.

Left: Thin seedlings by clipping them off at soil level.

Thinning and Potting Up Seedlings need adequate space in which to grow and so will eventually need thinning out. Once seedlings have developed their first set of leaves, you can thin out with least disturbance by clipping some off at soil level with sharp scissors. If you've started them in a nutrient-free medium, you'll now have to supplement their diet with a liquid organic plant food like fish emulsion, seaweed extract, or compost tea (to learn how to make compost tea, see "Compost Tea" on page 49) until they're transferred to your garden.

If you plan to hold seedlings a while before transplanting them outdoors, it's a good idea to move them to their own small pots or individual cells in a tray. About 6 to 12 hours before potting them up, give the seedlings a thorough soaking to ensure that they are turgid and that the roots will retain plenty of soil when the plants are lifted. Also moisten the growing medium in the pots or cells before planting. Using a pencil, plant label, or other pointed stick, make a hole in the medium in the new pot. The hole should be large enough to accept the root system of the transplanted seedling without crushing the roots together. Then use the stick to carefully dig one seedling at a time from the original container. Lift each seedling by one of its leaves (not the fragile stem), and move it to its new container. Gently firm the soil around the roots of the seedling, and water it to settle it into the new container.

Hardening Off As planting time approaches, harden off your tender seedlings by gradually introducing them to the great outdoors. Begin by placing them outdoors each day for a short period, gradually lengthening the exposure over a 7- to 14-day period. Begin with 1 to 2 hours of exposure, slowly working up to 24 hours. Watch the weather forecasts, and bring seedlings indoors if there's a chance of a late frost. Gradually reduce watering, so that the soil is noticeably drier; plants can withstand transplanting more successfully if they are used to slightly less water. Reduce applications of fertilizer (particularly nitrogen) by half at the same time, because this will allow plants to develop more roots in proportion to the rest of the plant, and hence help the plant to transplant successfully.

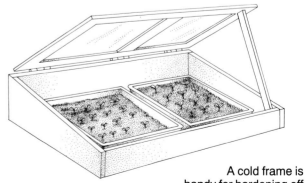

A cold frame is handy for hardening off seedlings. Open the frame during the day to avoid excessive heat buildup.

Transplanting Once your seedlings have adjusted to the outdoors you can plant them out. If they're frost-sensitive, wait until the danger of frost has passed. If they're hardy annuals or perennials, the hardening-off period should have prepared them for the garden. Follow the spacing guidelines on the seed packet or in the "Plant by Plant Guide," starting on page 100.

Make a hole with your trowel, pop the small plant out of its container, and insert the plant. You can plant slightly deeper than in the pot, especially if the young plant has grown tall. Firm the soil around the roots and water it gently. Some herb growers water with a diluted solution of fish emulsion or compost tea. Give your seedlings a good start by transplanting on a cloudy day or in the evening to avoid the sun's drying effect.

Starting Seeds Outdoors

Hardy annuals can be sown directly outdoors in early spring. If you're planting seeds of frost-sensitive plants, wait until the frost season has ended. You can sow seeds directly in rows, or start them in a separate seedbed from which you can transplant later.

Preparing the Seedbed If you're sowing directly outdoors, clear all weeds from your planting site first and destroy them. Prepare the soil, digging if necessary to remove clods, stones, weeds, and roots. Rake it smooth to create a fine-textured surface.

Transplanting requires a minimum of tools: Just a simple trowel or hand fork will do the job. You'll also need a watering can for irrigating your seedlings.

Sowing Sow the seeds in shallow trenches. If the seed packet doesn't recommend a sowing depth, a good rule of thumb is to plant the seed to a depth of three times its thickness. Completely cover the seeds by gently raking the soil over them and firming it down well. Keep the soil moist to encourage the best germination. Avoid watering with a strong spray that may wash the seeds out. Plant each herb species at the time and soil temperature recommended for best success (you'll find this information in the "Plant by Plant Guide").

Thinning Once your seedlings are strong and growing well, thin them to the proper spacing. You can clip or pinch out extras at soil level, or dig them out carefully and move to new positions.

Step-by-step Transplanting

1. Make a hole for the transplanted seedling wide enough so the roots won't be crushed.
2. Plant the seedling in the soil and gently firm the soil around the plant.
3. Gently water the seedling.

MAINTAINING YOUR GARDEN

To achieve the best results and conserve your gardening time and energy, you'll need to fine-tune your gardening skills. Like all plants, herbs show symptoms that tell you when they're under stress from insect pests and diseases. They'll also let you know when it's time to water. Good gardeners walk through the garden at least once daily, morning or afternoon, just to be sure not to miss a distress signal, such as discolored leaves or wilting stems. If you are familiar with your plants when they are healthy, you will soon notice if they are distressed. Wilting could be caused by incorrect watering (too much or too little) or it could be caused by root damage. Curled leaves or those with holes in them could indicate insect damage, and those that have turned a strange color could be diseased or suffering from a nutrient deficiency.

When you patrol your plants, watch for the beginning signs of insect and disease damage. The least disruptive pest-control methods, like handpicking, spraying with water, or pruning, are most effective when used at the first sign of damage. If you have to resort to an organically acceptable insecticide, pick the product formulated specifically for the pest on your plants—consult a book on garden pests and learn to identify particular pests before you use any control method.

Most of the insects you will discover among your herb plants won't be doing any damage at all. More likely, they're just passing through. If you're lucky, beneficial insects, like tiny parasitic wasps, and bugs and beetles with voracious appetites for harmful insects, will live among the foliage. Biological controls are nature's defense against pest attack.

Proper watering is a critical part of garden maintenance. While the amount of water required varies from plant to plant, most herbs thrive in evenly moist soil. If the weather is dry, keep an eye on your herbs and water them when necessary; if the weather is wet, try removing the mulch from around the plants to let the soil dry out. And don't allow weeds to compete with your herbs. Weeds are specially adapted to grow and reproduce quickly, and will soon crowd your herb plants.

If you want to increase your herb crops, learn how to propagate them. Once you master techniques like plant division and rooting cuttings, described in "Propagating Herbs" on page 60, you'll find that your hobby will become popular among your friends as you distribute the extra plants.

By growing herbs outdoors you can surround yourself with fresh herbs almost year round. Growing them indoors in winter will keep your kitchen supplied and make winter meals more appetizing.

Opposite: Garden maintenance is essential if you want to continue to enjoy your herbs. Make sure you properly identify the pests and diseases that are causing you problems—this will enable you to find an appropriate solution.

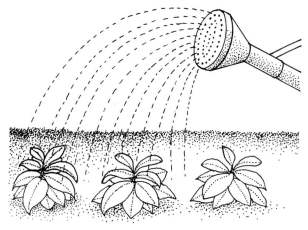

Using a sprinkling can helps conserve water because it allows you to provide water to herbs only where it is needed.

If natural rainfall is inadequate, water your herbs regularly to promote healthy, vigorous growth.

Watering

Water makes up from 85 to 95 percent of the weight of living plants. It's not surprising that when water is lacking, a plant stops growing and wilts. After wilting comes collapse of the cell structure in the wilted leaves and stems. After that, if much of the plant is affected, comes the death of young or delicate plants! Your goal is to water *before* wilting occurs.

Garden plants require about the equivalent of 1 inch (25 mm) of rainfall each week under average soil and climate conditions. Gardens in hot, dry climates will lose moisture faster and may need the equivalent of up to 2 inches (50 mm) each week. In cool and wet climates, plants lose less moisture and less water evaporates from the soil, so you may not have to water at all.

To monitor rainfall, purchase a rain gauge (available at most hardware stores) and set it in or near your garden. Check it immediately after rain storms, before water in the gauge is lost to evaporation. If natural rainfall is inadequate, you should plan to water regularly to maintain plant health and growth. Checking your soil for moisture is also a good idea.

There are several methods of checking soil moisture. Move the surface soil or mulch and look at the soil in the root zone. Most plant roots are in the top 12 inches (30 cm) of soil. If the soil is cool and moist and there are no signs of stress—wilting—you can probably hold off on the hose. A daily check is a good idea in dry weather, particularly if it is also hot.

Or take a soil sample from the root zone and examine it. Dry, sandy soils will flow freely through your fingers but will stick together slightly with adequate moisture. Heavier clay soils will appear hard and crumbly when dry, and feel slick when adequately moist.

How Much to Water

You should water sufficiently to keep your plants growing, but not so much that the roots become oxygen-starved. In most soils, one good soaking is better than several shallow waterings because it encourages roots to spread in search of water that is farther away.

Hand Watering

Rain barrels, sprinkling cans, and hand-held hoses work well if you have a small garden and plenty of time. You'll know just how much water you are actually applying and where it is going. If you're tending a large garden, though, you'll probably choose overhead sprinklers or drip irrigation.

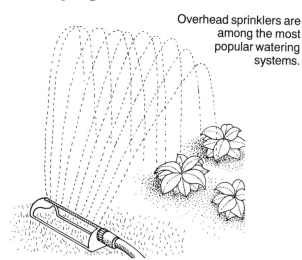

Overhead sprinklers are among the most popular watering systems.

Overhead Sprinklers

Although popular and inexpensive, overhead watering systems have two main disadvantages. First, they assume a plentiful, even extravagant, water supply. In the time it takes water to reach the soil, 30 to 50 percent of the water used may be lost to evaporation on a hot, windy day. Secondly, sprinklers take longer to wet the soil, especially if the water must first penetrate a mulch. Fungal diseases that thrive in moist conditions spread easily and quickly when the foliage is wet. The advantage is that an overhead watering system requires only an inexpensive sprinkler unit and enough hose to reach the garden.

While watering, monitor the rate of application by placing one or several rain gauges in your garden under the overhead sprinkler. Water for 20 to 40 minutes and check the soil again. You'll want to water until the roots receive some relief. The time required to water sufficiently will depend on your water pressure, the size of the nozzles, the distance from the pump, the diameter of your hose, your soil type, and the drying effect of wind and sun. You may need to water two or three times each week or even daily in hot, dry periods. Check the soil at root depth to be sure you're watering enough.

How to Conserve Water

The following list gives ideas on how you can conserve water in your herb garden.

- Designate separate parts of the garden for herbs with low, medium, or high water requirements and water them individually. Annual herbs will need more water than the deep-rooted, established perennials.
- Insulate the soil surface with a thick layer of organic mulch. To learn how to use mulch, see "Mulching" on page 66.
- Maintain your soil's organic matter by working in plenty of compost. Organic matter holds water in the soil like a sponge.
- Eliminate weeds as they appear.
- In dry climates, select herbs that are drought-tolerant, such as burdock and germander.
- If paths are included in your garden design, use crushed gravel or sawdust to pave them. A living cover like grass will compete with your herbs for moisture.

Drought-tolerant Herbs

While herbs generally grow best with an even supply of moisture, the ones listed below can tolerate drier soil.

Arnica, burdock, catnip, chicory, costmary, elecampane, germander, goldenrod, hyssop, marjoram, New Jersey tea, oregano, pennyroyal (American), pipsissewa, rue, safflower, santolina, savory (winter), southernwood, thyme, wormwood.

Drip Irrigation

Drip irrigation eliminates some of the problems encountered with overhead systems. It is the most economical system in terms of water volume used. Drip lines use less water, since they apply water directly to the soil where plants need it. Less water runs off and more water sinks in. Cool water helps to keep the soil temperature low, especially if you mulch. And since foliage remains dry, fungal diseases are not encouraged. The disadvantage is that drip systems require more expensive installation. Once installed, however, you need only turn on the water and your herbs are irrigated most efficiently.

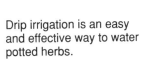

Drip irrigation is an easy and effective way to water potted herbs.

If you are unsure about the moisture content of your soil, check below the soil surface. If the root zone is dry, it's time to water.

A thick layer of grass clippings or another organic mulch will help keep weed problems to a minimum.

Weeding

Your nongardening friends may sometimes mistake your herbs for weeds, but *you* must know the difference. Weeds are often the most visible and persistent problem in the home herb garden.

Weeds are simply plants growing in the wrong place at the wrong time. Most of them are aggressive, wild plants that know a good opportunity when they find it. They usually grow rapidly and reproduce freely.

The Role of Weeds

Weeds, however, have their own importance in the plant world. Maybe you've noticed the resemblance of certain weeds to some of your herbs. Perhaps you're growing as herbs some plants that other gardeners would pull as weeds, like burdock or dandelion. Many of the plants we call weeds have culinary or medicinal uses that were discovered long ago. The tender leaves of dandelion and lamb's-quarters, for example, are often found in salad bowls along with lettuce. Wild comfrey was used medicinally long before modern herb growers added it to their gardens.

Weeds hold the soil in place, break up compacted soil with their vigorous root systems, and help to conserve nutrients that leach away when the soil is left bare. Some plants that are considered to be weeds, like clover and vetch, are also legumes and can be grown to fix nitrogen in the soil. Many beneficial insects that pollinate flowers or help to control garden pests spend part of their lives on wild plants. Queen Anne's lace and goldenrod are dependable bloomers that provide nectar for the beneficial wasps that prey on aphids.

The presence of certain weeds indicates soil imbalances. Dandelions and quack grass, for example, prefer soil that is compacted and low in oxygen—think of

Organic Weed-control Techniques

Mulching with organic or synthetic materials is one of the easiest ways to keep weeds under control. Organic mulches, like straw, compost, and shredded leaves, help to keep weeds down while adding organic matter to your soil. Apply a layer 3 to 7 inches (7.5 to 17.5 cm) deep, since it will settle to a thin layer over time. Black plastic can also be used, but it requires annual replacement, and it can be difficult to apply in a mixed planting of annuals and perennials. For more complete information on choosing and using mulches, see "Mulching" on page 66.

Other weed-control techniques include tilling or cultivating, and cover crops. When tilling or cultivating, try to work as shallowly as possible. This will avoid bringing dormant weed seeds to the surface, where they will germinate when exposed to light. If you are starting a new garden area, or if you have one that you use only for annual herbs, you can try controlling weeds with a cover crop or green manure. Cover crops and green manures grow quickly and out-compete native weed populations. Crops like buckwheat grow best when it's warm; rye, vetch, and clover prefer cooler weather. To learn more on growing and using these crops, see "Green Manures" on page 46.

If a garden bed has a serious weed problem, you may just want to start over in that area. Dig out any herbs you want to save, and then use a process called soil solarization to destroy weed seeds that are close to the surface. Solarize your garden soil by laying a sheet of clear plastic over moist soil. Tuck the edges of the plastic into a shallow trench, and cover them with soil. As solarizing only works when the weather is consistently clear and fairly hot, it's best to solarize from mid-June to mid-August. The soil under the plastic will heat, and this will kill most of the weed seeds (as well as insects and disease organisms) in the top layer of soil. Avoid turning over the soil after you solarize it, or you'll just bring up a new crop of weed seeds.

Some weeds indicate soil imbalances. Dandelions, for example, may mean more organic material is needed.

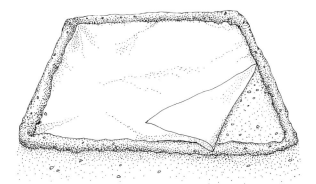
Solarizing the soil by laying a sheet of clear plastic over it during hot weather is an effective method of eradicating weeds. The weed seeds die as the soil heats up.

them as red flags for areas that need extra organic matter. Mustards and sorrel flourish in acidic soil, indicating it's time to have the soil pH tested.

On the negative side, weeds are major garden pests when they compete with your garden herbs for nutrients, moisture, and light. They often harbor diseases or insect pests that can easily find their way to your herb plants. Some weeds, like poison ivy, horsenettles, and nightshade, are contact or internal poisons. Other, nonpoisonous weeds, can cause an allergic reaction in sensitive people.

Controlling Weeds

Your first step in the battle against weeds is to identify the ones you need to control. Learn to recognize the annuals and perennials so you'll know whether you can till them in (the annuals) or must pull them out (the perennials). You also need to learn to recognize juvenile weeds; otherwise, you may end up weeding out your herb seedlings by mistake.

Annual weeds live only one season, but this is long enough for them to produce lots of seeds that can sprout next spring. The seeds can also remain dormant in your garden soil as long as 100 years, coming to life when you till a new garden patch. Pulling, hoeing, and cultivating are often sufficient to control annual weeds. The summer annuals begin life in the spring and die in fall. Winter annuals, like chickweed and yellow rocket, sprout in late summer and survive severe winters in a dormant state, flowering and reseeding themselves the following spring before they die.

Biennials like Queen Anne's lace live for two seasons, flowering and dying during their second year. You'll need to control them before they flower.

Perennial weeds live more than 2 years, and are especially troublesome because they can reproduce sexually by seed, or spread vegetatively with their specialized root and stem structures. Perennials, like quack grass and field bindweed, shouldn't be tilled in, since this chops and distributes their hardy root pieces, each of which will sprout into new plants.

To eliminate weed seedlings, scrape the soil surface with a hoe each week. Choose any blade, but to avoid straining your back, make sure the handle is long enough to allow you to stand straight. Your motion should be more like sweeping, rather than chopping. Use a hand fork to dig out older weeds that escape the hoe, before they have a chance to flower and set seed.

Clean, weed-free straw makes a great garden mulch.

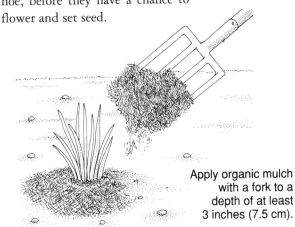
Apply organic mulch with a fork to a depth of at least 3 inches (7.5 cm).

Propagating Herbs

Many perennial herbs are difficult to grow from seed; some take 4 to 8 weeks to germinate, while others may need special treatment, like chilling. For this reason, it's best to buy vegetatively propagated perennial herbs sold as transplants. Once you have established perennials, however, you can use the following vegetative propagation methods to produce more plants.

Division

Dividing is a way to start new plants as well as clean up and rejuvenate old ones. Most perennial herbs spread underground as well as aboveground. The plants usually increase in size each new growing season, perhaps taking up more space than you wish, so it's a good idea to divide them every few years.

Early spring and fall are good times to divide perennials, when the air temperature is low and soil moisture is usually high. Herbs easily propagated by division include chives, germander, horehound, marjoram, mint, sorrel, tansy, tarragon, thyme, woodruff, and many others.

Start by slicing with a spade or shovel around the perimeter of the plant's root system. With the last slice, push the blade under the base of the plant and lift it up: soil, roots, and all. Set the clump on the ground and begin dividing it into smaller clumps. Divide small clumps by hand or with a trowel. Pry apart larger clumps or very old clumps using garden forks: Stick two garden forks back to back in the center of the clump and force it apart. Remove the young shoots from the outer side of the clump by breaking or cutting them off. Cut all the leaves back to within 1 inch (2.5 cm) of the roots and replant immediately, or put the clumps in pots in a shady area until you can replant them.

Plants that send out underground runners, like mint, are just as easily divided without digging up the whole plant. If you follow the underground stems that sprout new plants, you can simply lift out each new plant with a trowel or shovel.

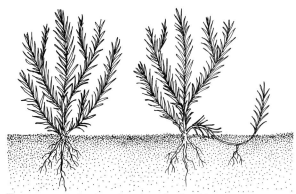

To propagate by layering, bend a healthy stem over and bury it in the ground in spring or fall. Roots form on the buried part of the shoot, near the bend.

Once you've reduced the large clump to several smaller plants, replant them in holes lined with fresh compost. Follow the proper spacing guidelines for each herb in the "Plant by Plant Guide," starting on page 100. Firm the soil around the new plants, water generously, and mulch with organic materials. Pot up any extras, and give them away or sell them to your green-thumbed friends.

Layering

Layering is a simple method for propagating garden herbs with stems that root easily, including tarragon, rosemary, thyme, and sage. Select a long and flexible stem, and bend and lightly bury a section of it in the soil around the parent plant. You can make a small wound along the stem first, by nicking the soft wood with a knife, to encourage fast rooting. Some horticulturists recommend removing the leaves along the section of stem to be buried. Mound soil on top of the buried stem, holding it in place with stakes or pins made from a forked stick or bent wire.

New roots will form underground if the soil is kept moist. Wait 3 to 4 weeks, until the new plant has produced some growth and you can be sure that it has taken root. Then sever the stem connecting the old and new plants by pushing a shovel or trowel into the soil between the new plant and the old. Wait several more weeks before digging up the new plant. Plant it in a hole lined with fresh compost, or pot it up to grow indoors or on the patio.

"Stool" layering is another method you can use to make new plants. This method works best with plants that have plenty of sprawling stems like tansy, santolina, winter savory, and sage. Simply mound the soil around and over the base of already established plants. Wait 4 to 6 weeks, then slice away the new plants that have developed their own root systems.

Dividing perennial herbs every few years increases your collection while at the same time rejuvenating the parent plant. Early spring and fall are the best times to divide perennials.

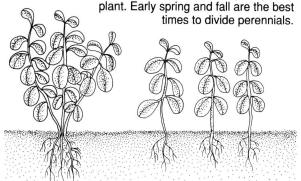

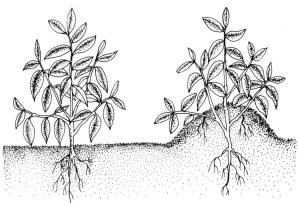

Stool layering is a simple method of propagating herbs. Mound soil over the base of the parent plant. Remove new plants that grow after 4 to 6 weeks and replant.

Step-by-step Division

1. Dig around the clump.
2. Shake off as much soil as possible. Separate good shoots with roots from the parent plant.
3. Cut back ragged tops and shorten the stems.
4. Place some well-rotted compost into the planting hole and position the plant at the same depth as it was growing before.
5. Water the plant with a soluble organic fertilizer to minimize transplanting shock.

Clump-forming herbs, such as chives, are easy to propagate by division in spring or fall.

1

2

3

4

5

Some herbs, such as scented geraniums and wormwood, become straggly after a few years and new plants should be started. Use the spring or fall prunings to start new plants.

Cuttings

You can make new plants from the prunings of perennial herbs like scented geranium, bay, lavender, oregano, and wormwood, to name just a few. Most herbs are easily propagated from fresh cuttings. The best time to take cuttings is in early spring or fall, when the plants are growing vigorously and there are plenty of new tips to choose from.

The best cuttings are from fresh, green growth. Cut 3 to 5 inches (7.5 to 12.5 cm) of stem, cut just below a leaf joint (node). Remove the lower leaves. To promote root formation on slow-to-root plants like rosemary and bay, dip the base of the cutting into rooting hormone.

Insert the cut end of the cutting in a moist, light soilless mix like perlite or vermiculite, making certain that several nodes have contact with the moist medium. Use small pots or any containers with good drainage. Some herb growers enclose the pots in plastic bags or upside-down glass jars to maintain humidity around the top growth while the stems form new roots underground. Keep the pots indoors and away from direct sun. After 4 to 6 weeks, check for rooting by gently tugging on the cuttings: If you can feel resistance, new roots have formed and the cuttings should be ready to transplant to individual pots. Place your new plants in the shade for several days before planting out in the herb garden.

Step-by-step Cuttings

1. Select healthy green growth.
2. Cut stem below the leaf node.
3. Remove the lower leaves.
4. Insert cutting firmly into mix.
5. Cover the cuttings with a glass jar to maintain humidity.

To propagate garlic, choose the largest bulbs, divide them into individual cloves, and plant these root-side down. Avoid overhandling the bulbs if you can to ensure healthy new growth.

Growing from Bulbs

Some herbs, like chives, saffron, and garlic, grow from bulbs or similar structures. To propagate chives and saffron, lift the clumps out of the soil and divide them as you would any other plant.

To propagate garlic, harvest the bulbs as usual, allowing them to dry. Save the largest bulbs with the largest cloves for replanting and use the rest in the kitchen. There's no need to clean the bulbs you plan to replant. The more they're handled and peeled, the more likely they'll rot in storage. Store them in a dark, cool location until planting time.

To plant, divide the bulbs into individual cloves. Plant only the outer, large cloves; small, inner cloves will yield small bulbs, if any. Keep the small cloves in the kitchen to use soon—once separated from the bulb, they won't store well. Plant the individual cloves root-side down, approximately 1 inch (2.5 cm) deep and 6 inches (15 cm) apart in a deep bed with loosened soil. Work in plenty of organic materials like compost, but go easy on the nitrogen.

Saving Seed

Although most perennial herbs are easy to propagate vegetatively—by division, layering, or cuttings—you can grow many herbs from seed if you have the patience.

Annuals and biennials, like coriander, dill, fennel, borage, and even some types of basil, will reseed themselves before the season ends. All that's required next season is patience while you leave the soil undisturbed to see which herb seedlings volunteer. Resist the temptation to till or hoe in areas that were heavily seeded naturally the previous season.

When the new plants are established, dig them up while the weather is cool and move them as needed. Leave them in clumps or divide them up into individual plants.

To save seed for planting next spring, wait until they've matured on the plant before collecting them. Hold the seed heads over a container and gently tap to release the seeds. Alternatively, you can harvest the seed heads and then hang them in paper bags to dry. It is important that the seeds are thoroughly dried before storing in air-tight containers. For more information on growing herbs from seed, see "Planting Seeds" on page 50.

Bulbs

Growing your own garlic is easy and rewarding. Mid-fall is the best time for planting. The bulbs will produce roots and small shoots before the ground freezes. When the weather warms in spring, the shoots will start growing actively.

1. Save large, healthy garlic bulbs for replanting. Store them in a dark, cool place.
2. Divide the bulbs into individual cloves.
3. Plant the cloves about 1 inch (2.5 cm) deep and 6 inches (15 cm) apart. Cover the cloves with soil rich in organic matter.

1

2

3

Overwintering

If you live in a cold climate, you may find the most difficult part of winter is giving up the summer's harvest. Organic vegetables are available most of the year in many markets, but the fresh herbs to accompany them at mealtime are more expensive and harder to find in winter. Growing your own herbs indoors during winter is an alternative.

There are other reasons to bring your herb plants indoors for the winter. Tender perennials, like rosemary and bay, won't survive when exposed to cold-climate winters. Cuttings that you take in fall will be ready to move to the garden in spring if you nurture them indoors all winter. You can also pot up annuals and bring them indoors for winter use, or start fresh ones from seed.

Perennials

You have several methods to choose from when raising a winter supply of herbs. Perennials can be grown in the garden soil in summer, then potted up for winter indoors. At the beginning and end of the season, leave the plants in their pots in a shady spot outdoors for at least 1 week before moving them to their new home.

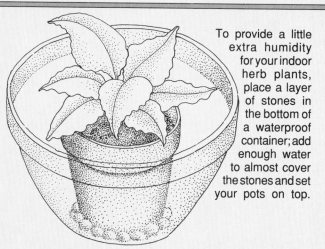

To provide a little extra humidity for your indoor herb plants, place a layer of stones in the bottom of a waterproof container; add enough water to almost cover the stones and set your pots on top.

This helps them adjust to the change in light from bright to moderate and vice versa. Be sure you choose a pot large enough to accommodate the root system. When digging up the plant from the garden, cut all the way around it with a shovel, then gently lift the whole root ball into a pot lined with fresh potting soil.

Perennials like sage, chives, and rosemary also make good container plants year round—just move the pots outdoors in the summer, near the water supply so you won't forget to water them.

You can also start new plants for the winter from cuttings. To grow the largest winter plants, take 4-inch

Parsley is often difficult to transplant, due to its deep taproot. If you want to grow parsley for indoor use, either start seeds indoors or pot up very small self-sown plants from the garden.

Indoor herbs need plenty of light for good growth. Set them on a sunny windowsill with at least 5 hours of direct natural light, or provide 14 to 16 hours of fluorescent light each day.

(10 cm) cuttings in midsummer and root them singly in pots of sterilized potting soil left in the shade. Keep them moist to encourage root formation. You can take cuttings from established plants outdoors well into fall, as long as there is new growth to choose from and the plants have not become dormant.

Annuals

Annual herbs for winter growing are best started fresh from seed in fall. Sow them the same way you start your spring seedlings indoors. Grow them in 3- to 4-inch (7.5 to 10 cm) pots so they will have enough room to grow all winter. Sow hard-to-transplant herbs like parsley directly into deep pots.

Light

Your indoor herbs will need plenty of light each day for strong, vigorous growth. A sunny window is ideal, but keep the pots well away from cold windows and drafts.

Once your potted herbs have filled the windows, take a step up and purchase one or more sets of fluorescent light fixtures. Use a mixture of cool white bulbs and the red or blue lights designed for plants, in order to imitate sunlight. You can hang the light fixtures below a shelf and set the plants with their tops 6 to 8 inches (15 to 20 cm) away from the lights on shelves or plant stands, using bricks to raise or lower individual pots as needed.

Temperature

Most herbs appreciate daytime temperatures of 60 to 70°F (15 to 21°C), with cooler temperatures of 50 to 65°F (10 to 18°C) at night. Most important is a day–night change of about 10°F (5.5°C), although most herbs will survive at a constant temperature. Annual herbs like basil prefer to be kept warm, while perennials and biennials do better if kept cool.

Moisture

Water thoroughly, then allow the soil to dry a little before watering again. Don't overwater. Evaporation may be less indoors, or more if your house is heated in winter. Excess moisture encourages fungal diseases, and prevents roots from getting the oxygen they need. If humidity is low, spray plants several times a day with a light mist. Grouping plants together also helps to retain humidity.

Overwintering Outdoors

The success of overwintering your perennials outdoors in the garden depends on your climate. Hardy perennials like sage will survive a cold winter in perfect condition, ready to bloom when temperatures rise in spring. Some of the less hardy herbs, like lavender and oregano, may need help getting through a cold winter.

The best protection is a blanket of snow. If snowfall is minimal or absent, protect perennials from the drying effects of winter winds by covering them with evergreen boughs or surrounding them with burlap-covered frames. To overwinter small perennials, wait until the soil has frozen, then mulch heavily with straw or leaves. Remove the mulch gradually in spring.

If there is little or no snow, you may want to surround your perennial herbs with a burlap screen to block the harsh winter winds.

Many organic materials are useful for mulching, including straw and grass clippings (above left); whole leaves (left); and shredded leaves, compost, and bark chips (above).

Mulching

Mulching simply means covering the surface of your garden soil with a layer of organic or inorganic material. Mulching helps keep the soil warmer in winter and cooler in summer, helps retain soil moisture thereby reducing the need for you to water, keeps dirt off you and your plants, and protects soil from erosion. A layer of mulch applied after the soil freezes in late fall will prevent the soil from thawing and refreezing, which can damage tender roots. Mulches can also inhibit the germination of weed seeds, and it's easy to pull out any weed seedlings that do sprout up in a loose organic mulch. Mulching will save you time and labor.

Mulching Tips

If you are planting in early spring, wait until the soil warms up before mulching. If you are planting in fall, apply the mulch right after planting. Mulch earlier in dry climates to trap the moisture from spring rains. In wet climates, mulch a bit later in the season to give the soil a chance to dry out. If you've kept your perennials mulched throughout the winter, pull the mulch away from them in the spring to allow the soil to warm and to promote growth. A light-colored mulch such as straw will keep soil cool, which can promote the growth of plants like mint that prefer cooler temperatures. A

dark-colored mulch, like black plastic, will keep the soil warmer for heat-loving plants like basil. Always weed the soil before mulching, and provide a 3- to 7-inch (7.5 to 17.5 cm) layer of mulch to keep weeds down. Shady areas are less conducive to weeds and will require less mulch. Don't mulch around new plants until they are tall enough so that the mulch won't smother them. Organic mulches can harbor snails and slugs and promote rot when wet, so keep mulch away from the stems of your plants.

Organic Mulches

Organic mulches, like compost, grass clippings, shredded leaves, straw, and hay, are a good choice for mulching, since they'll improve your soil while providing all the other benefits of a mulch. They will add organic matter and nutrients to the soil as they decompose, enhancing soil productivity. Use whatever organic materials are most easily available to you. You can make your own compost following the directions in "Compost" on page 48. The beneficial organisms in compost help control soilborne plant disease, and there's no need to remove the mulch at the end of the season since the compost decomposes naturally.

Shredded leaves also make a nutrient-rich mulch. Prepare them with a leaf-shredding machine, or simply run over piles of leaves with a lawn mower. Don't use the leaves unshredded, as they can blow away when dry or create an impenetrable mat when wet, preventing moisture reaching your plants' roots.

Straw is preferable to hay, as hay tends to carry weed seeds and provide a habitat for rodents, snails, and slugs. Bark and wood chips work well to keep down weeds in plantings of perennial herbs.

Inorganic Mulches

The most common and practical inorganic mulching materials are black plastic and landscaping fabrics. Though you may find them expensive, if you purchase good-quality materials, you can remove and store them at the end of the growing season and reuse them for several years.

Black plastic helps soil retain the warmth from the sun into the night. It prevents weed growth and retains soil moisture. You can apply black plastic several weeks before planting to warm the soil. Buy sheets of plastic at least 1 foot (30 cm) wider than your row or bed. Lay out the plastic and anchor the sides with rocks or soil. Make slits or holes for planting, and to allow water to penetrate. Don't use black plastic under shrubs, as it can cause the roots to grow very close to the surface of the soil, undermining the health of the plant.

Landscaping fabrics allow water and air to penetrate and can be walked on. Roots of some shrubs may grow up into the fabric, making removal difficult. Some weeds may also survive and grow through the fabric. Some landscaping fabrics degrade in light, so you may have to cover them with a second mulch, like straw or wood chips, to protect them.

Fallen leaves should not be thrown out. Shred them with your mower, then distribute them as a mulch on your beds.

Choose Your Mulch	
The following are some of the best mulches to consider for your garden.	
Material	**How to apply**
Chopped leaves	Apply in 3-inch (7.5 cm) layers; best if chopped, composted, and allowed to sit outside for several months.
Compost	Spread 1 or more inches (2.5 or more cm) as a topdressing around plants or along rows.
Grass clippings	Apply a 1–4 inch (2.5–10 cm) layer around plantings. Make sure clippings are herbicide-free. May burn tender seedlings if placed too close.
Newspaper	Lay down whole sections of the paper and anchor with soil or stones, or shred paper and apply 4–6 inch (10–15 cm) layers. Good to use under more attractive mulches. Do not use colored newspaper; some inks can be toxic.
Pine needles	Apply in 2–4 inch (5–10 cm) layers. Needles tend to acidify soil; don't use around non-acid-loving plants.
Shredded bark chips	Apply a 2–4 inch (5–10 cm) layer around established plantings of trees or perennials. Can tie up nitrogen in soil, so don't apply to vegetable garden. Composted bark or wood chips are best.
Straw	Lay down 8-inch (20 cm) layers of material around but not touching plants. Mulch heavily between rows to keep weeds at bay. May tie up nitrogen; oat straw is best.

Preventing Pests and Diseases

Herbs are rarely bothered by pests, especially when they are grown in an appropriate site. If your plants are healthy, they attract fewer pests and are less susceptible to diseases. To grow healthy, trouble-free plants, take good care of your soil—provide plenty of organic nutrients and make sure you keep the pH at an appropriate level. Remove and destroy any diseased leaves or insect-infested stalks as soon as you find them, and keep your tools clean to avoid spreading diseases. To check the individual requirements of each herb, refer to the "Plant by Plant Guide," starting on page 100.

Some herbs are even planted in the garden specifically for their insect-repellent properties. Pennyroyal, rue, and wormwood are just a few herbs that may be used to discourage insects from converging on neighboring plants. Many of the small-flowered herbs, like fennel, dill, and thyme, attract insects that help the gardener by preying upon or parasitizing their pernicious cousins.

If your herbs do occasionally fall prey to insects or diseases, you can choose from several organically acceptable control options.

Preventing Insect Pests

Get into the habit of checking your plants for pests at least once a week. Don't worry if you find a few. In an organic garden, as in nature, the life cycles of beneficial predators and parasites are usually closely synchronized with those of the pests. When the pests increase, so do the predators.

If nature's controls aren't doing their job quickly enough, handpick the pests from plants and drop them into a can of soapy water. Or suck up insects from plants with a portable, hand-held vacuum cleaner. You can also use a forceful spray of water from the hose to knock pests, like aphids and mites, from foliage. If pests are limited to one plant or stem, prune away the infested parts and destroy them along with the invaders.

If insects are a serious problem, try covering your plants with a floating row-cover fabric.

Adult whiteflies are about ¹⁄₁₂ inch (2 mm) long, white, and covered in a powdery substance. Nymphs are green and translucent. Both forms suck the juices from new growth on the host plant.

These light gardening fabrics keep flying and crawling pests away from your plants. Remember to cover the rows as soon as you've planted seeds or transplants, anchoring the material with soil, stones, or boards. As your plants grow, the lightweight fabric will rise with them. You can leave the covers on all summer as long as temperatures don't exceed 75°F (24°C). If you are growing herbs for their seeds, you'll need to remove the covers so that insects can pollinate the flowers.

Rotating your annual and biennial herb plants is a good idea, especially before you encounter any pest problems. Crop rotation, which means avoiding planting the same crop in the same place 2 years running, is common practice in organic gardening. If you usually grow several large annual crops, it makes sense to work out a rotation based on the same number of growing plots. The result will be that a given area will repeat a

Adult Japanese beetles are ½ inch (12 mm) long, and are metallic blue or green with coppery wing covers. Adults skeletonize leaves and eat the flowers of host plants.

for signs of disease and reject any that look suspicious or unhealthy. Remember that symptoms like off-color leaves or stunted growth *could* be due to poor growing conditions, but they could also indicate another problem like disease.

If it is likely that you've been handling soil or plants that may be sources of infection, clean your boots and hands with a 5 percent solution of household bleach, or wipe them with rubbing alcohol. And if wet weather prevails, stay away from the garden until the weather is fine again. Many disease organisms require moisture for reproduction or mobility, and they're easily spread on films of water you may carry from plant to plant.

Regularly inspect your plants for signs of disease, and pull and remove unhealthy specimens. It's best to burn them, since some pathogens are sufficiently hardy to survive the hottest compost piles. However, if burning is prohibited in your area, put diseased plant materials in sealed bags for disposal with the household trash. Mulch your perennials with regular applications of compost. Not only does it act as a barrier between foliage and soilborne pathogens, but beneficial microbes in the compost suppress the development of many disease organisms.

Adult mites are reddish-brown or pale, spiderlike, and about ⅟₅₀ inch (0.5 mm) long. They feed on leaves and roots. Leaves become silvery and curled, and may be covered by a fine web.

particular crop only every third or fourth year. There's no need to have an elaborate rotation scheme unless your herb garden is large. Simply avoid planting the same herbs in the same location each year, so that potential pests won't build up to the point of causing noticeable damage. Rotation also helps avoid the danger of exhausting the supply of plant nutrients especially favored by particular crops.

Preventing Plant Diseases

Plant diseases are frustrating to deal with. Symptoms like leaf wilting, or yellowing, stunted growth, or misshapen leaves are often the only clues you'll have when trying to diagnose the problem. The pathogens that cause disease, including fungi, bacteria, viruses, and nematodes, are minute organisms that you can see only with the aid of a microscope. They can spend the winter in soil or clinging to the garden tools, and they're often unknowingly transported indoors on pots or in contaminated soil.

Your best defense against disease organisms is prevention. Good sanitation practices are essential in the garden and greenhouse. When purchasing new plants, inspect them carefully

Organically Acceptable Insecticides

If prevention fails to stop the pests, you may have to use an organic insecticide as a last resort. If so, make sure you properly identify the pest, and then start with the most specific and least disruptive insecticide, to avoid killing the beneficial insects that are also sure to be there.

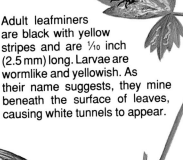

Adult leafminers are black with yellow stripes and are ⅟₁₀ inch (2.5 mm) long. Larvae are wormlike and yellowish. As their name suggests, they mine beneath the surface of leaves, causing white tunnels to appear.

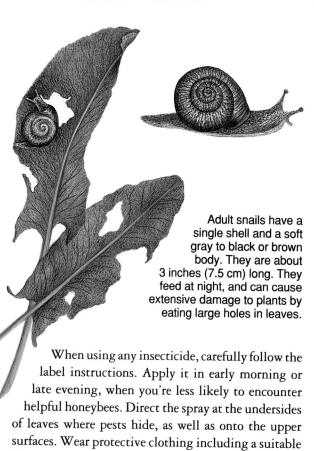

Adult snails have a single shell and a soft gray to black or brown body. They are about 3 inches (7.5 cm) long. They feed at night, and can cause extensive damage to plants by eating large holes in leaves.

Adult earwigs are thin and brownish with short forewings, and are about ¾ inch (19 mm) long. They have pincers on the tips of their abdomens. Nymphs feed on new plant shoots and eat holes in flowers and foliage.

When using any insecticide, carefully follow the label instructions. Apply it in early morning or late evening, when you're less likely to encounter helpful honeybees. Direct the spray at the undersides of leaves where pests hide, as well as onto the upper surfaces. Wear protective clothing including a suitable face mask and gloves. It's preferable never to spray botanical insecticides on herbs you plan to ingest. However, if you must, check the recommended interval between spraying and harvest. Wash well any herbs that have been sprayed with rotenone, in case any residues remain on the plants.

To control aphids and mites, the most common pests found on herbs, use commercial insecticidal soap products, whose active ingredients are of organic origin and break down quickly once applied. Aphids are soft-bodied insects with six legs and two thorn-like projections on their backs. Mites usually look like dark dots on webbing. Through a magnifying glass you can see that mites are tiny, eight-legged creatures that resemble spiders. Both aphids and mites are often found on the undersides of leaves, or they may be clustered on unopened blossoms.

Microbial insecticides are naturally occurring insect diseases that you can buy and use as pest-control agents. If caterpillars are your problem, you may use one of several brands of *Bacillus thuringiensis,* also known as "BT." This microbial insecticide halts the process of digestion in caterpillars, permanently discouraging them from eating. It acts only against the immature stages of moths and butterflies.

If all of these means to control insects fail, you can select one of several commercial brands of botanical

Slugs are similar to snails except that they don't have a shell. They are gray to black or brown in color, and are 3 inches (7.5 cm) long. They feed at night and, like snails, can cause great damage to plants.

insecticides that contain rotenone or pyrethrin. These naturally derived insecticides share with most synthetic poisons the disadvantage of killing the good with the bad, so use them only as a last resort. Refer to the "Plant by Plant Guide," starting on page 100, for specific suggestions for using botanical insecticides and other control methods to fight pests on your herbs.

Organically Acceptable Fungicides

Organically acceptable fungicides, such as sulfur and copper sprays, will protect your plants from fungal disease only if they're in place before infection. You can dust plants with copper or sulfur preparations if you suspect fungal disease is a problem in your garden, but do it before or during bouts of wet weather, when plants are most likely to be infected, and before the pathogens penetrate the leaf.

You can easily make your own fungicides at home. Household baking soda can reduce the spread of some fungal diseases. Just mix together 1 teaspoon of baking soda and 1 quart (1 l) of water. Use a spray bottle to drench your plants thoroughly with the mixture at the first sign of disease.

You can also use some of your own herbs to control disease problems. Garlic has fungicidal as well as insecticidal properties. Prepare an oil extract by mixing 3 ounces (85 g) of finely minced garlic with 2 teaspoons of mineral oil. Allow it to stand 24 hours, then add 16 fluid ounces (500 ml) of water. Mix and strain into a glass jar for storage. Combine 1–2 tablespoons of this concentrate with 16 fluid ounces (500 ml) of water before spraying on your plants. Adding a few drops of liquid dish detergent as a wetting agent will help the solution stick to plant leaves.

Adult aphids are about 1/12 inch (2 mm) long and either winged or wingless. They feed on leaves and flowers. Affected foliage turns yellow and may pucker.

About 2 inches (5 cm) long, the parsleyworm larvae are brown with a white-spotted back; later they become green with white-spotted black bands. They chew leaves and stems.

Some herbs, like pennyroyal, are planted in the garden for their ability to repel insect pests. They help to protect your herb crop by deterring insects from settling on neighboring plants. Other herbs, like fennel, are useful because they attract beneficials.

Preserving, Storing, and Using Herbs

Herbs are so versatile that you can surround yourself with herbal products every day of the year. Make herbal potpourris to perfume your bureau drawers, add a few drops of aromatic herbal oil to your bath, decorate and perfume your house with dried herb arrangements, and sleep well at night with a soothing, herb-scented pillow.

Use herbs in the kitchen when you're cooking or baking. You'll find few recipes that don't call for a pinch of this or that herb. And when you sit down to relax at the end of the day, brew a hot cup of herbal tea to enjoy with a friend.

Express yourself creatively with herbs and invite your friends to share your enthusiasm. Pass around gifts of your own homemade herbal soaps and candles. Or exchange jars of homemade herbal jelly, honey, or vinegar with other herb growers. For special gifts, arrange dried herbs into wreaths or baskets that smell as good as they look.

Herbs were among the first traditional medicines used to treat simple aches, pains, and infections. However, this is one area in which you should proceed with caution, since many herbs are potent drugs. Carefully check the properties of any herbs you intend to use medicinally and be sure that you have correctly identified them before use. If you have a severe medical problem, consult your physician before trying *any* home remedy.

However you use your herbs, you will have the satisfaction that comes of having grown them yourself.

Opposite: Herbs are very satisfying plants to grow. They are wonderful in the garden and they have a thousand-and-one uses in the home, not only in the kitchen, but also as decorations, perfumes, and medicines.

Harvesting

One of the first rules to learn about growing herbs is to harvest them early in the morning. The best picking time is just after the morning dew has dried, but before the sun has had a chance to warm them. The reason is that essential oils, those mysterious components that give herbs their flavor and fragrance, lose their quality when exposed to heat.

There's nothing wrong with morning dew, but wet leaves require a longer drying period before you can store them. For the same reason, refrain from harvesting on rainy days. A cool, dry, sunny morning is best. You need not be so fussy if you plan to use fresh herbs immediately. You may pick and use these whenever you need them.

The intended use of your herbs, maturity of the plant, and climate all influence the time of harvesting. Cold-climate gardeners will have fewer chances to harvest; they're happy to get their herbs up and growing before the frosts return. Gardeners in warmer climates have the advantage of a longer growing season, and the chance to harvest more often.

Perennials

Avoid heavy harvests of perennial herbs during the first year of growth, to allow them to establish themselves in their new surroundings and to encourage root growth. You may trim them lightly to promote bushiness.

Once they're established, you can harvest up to two-thirds of the foliage of a hardy perennial at one time in the spring and again in summer. In colder climates, take only a third of the growth in fall and stop cutting 40 to 60 days before you expect the first frost. During winter, perennials will subsist mainly on foods they've stored in their roots. Plenty of foliage and lots of fall sun will let perennials manufacture and store adequate food for winter and the following spring's new growth. If food reserves are low, they're less likely to make it through a stressful winter. In warmer climates, plants will suffer little winter stress and the plants' dormant period may be only a few weeks long. In these areas gardeners can harvest lightly right into late fall.

lavender

When harvesting lavender, cut the whole stem with the flower heads attached, just before the blooms open fully.

Harvesting for the Kitchen

For the best flavor, harvest herbs just before the buds open, when the concentration of essential oils is greatest. Follow this rule if you are harvesting a large quantity to dry or freeze for winter. To learn how to dry and freeze herbs, see "Drying Herbs" on page 76 and "Freezing Herbs" on page 78.

Herbs grown for their seeds should be harvested after the seeds have turned from green to brown—but make sure you harvest them before they begin to fall from the plant. For garnish or flavor, harvest fresh blossoms like chives, borage, or calendula at full bloom or just before. If you're picking chamomile flowers for tea, pinch them off when they are fully open.

Harvest herbs grown for their roots when the roots are fully developed in fall. Carefully scrape the soil away from the base of the plant, and use a sharp knife to harvest some of the largest roots. Or you could use a spading fork to lift the whole plant out of the ground for an easier harvest. Either way, make sure that you leave some roots so the plant can re-establish itself and provide future harvests. Replant or backfill with the soil you removed, and water the plant to settle it back into the soil. Scrub the harvested roots well before using or drying. You can slice or grate them to speed drying.

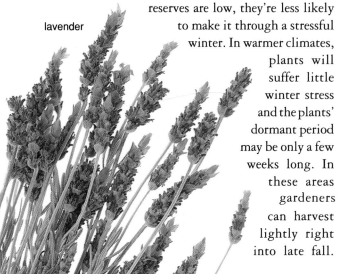

Nettles can be used to make a soothing tea, but wear gloves when harvesting them because they sting!

a mulch that limits their contact with soil, you may not have to wash them. If they are gritty with soil, however, you can swish them through cold water and pat them dry, or hang them in shade to drip.

If you plan to dry your herbs, bunching them as you collect them saves handling time later. Collect enough stems to make a 1-inch (2.5 cm) thick bundle, then wrap a rubber band over the cut ends. When harvesting annuals in fall, simply pull and hang the whole plant, after first cutting away the roots and soil.

oregano

Annuals

Since annuals are limited to one season of growth, your only concern in cold climates is harvesting as much as you can before the killing fall frosts. The same is true if you are growing biennial herbs, like parsley, for their foliage. During the growing season, harvest annuals and biennials for foliage so that at least 4 to 5 inches (10 to 12.5 cm) of growth remains. A good general rule is to harvest no more than the top half of the plant at one cutting. Most annuals and biennials may be harvested several times each season. Before the first frosts, you can cut annual plants to the ground, or pull them for drying. If you are growing biennial plants, like caraway, for their seeds, avoid harvesting the foliage the first year. The more energy the plants can make and store, the more seeds they can set the following year.

How to Harvest

Use sharp scissors or a garden knife when harvesting your herbs. If you're collecting leaves, cut the whole stem before stripping away the foliage. With small-leaved perennials, like rosemary and thyme, save only the leaves and discard the stems—or use them for potpourris. When harvesting herbs that spread from a central growing point, like parsley and sorrel, harvest the outer stems or leaves first. If you're collecting leaves or flowers from bushy plants, do so from the top of the plant; new growth will come from below.

Of course, you can harvest foliage and flowers from both perennials and annuals continuously if you're just snipping a few leaves and blooms here and there to collect the ingredients for a recipe.

Herbs retain their best qualities if they're left unwashed until it's time to use them. Some growers advise sprinkling the plants the day before harvesting, to wash away the dust. If your plants are surrounded by

---

Harvesting for Crafts

Most of the fragrant herbs commonly used as wreath backing, or as the base of dried arrangements, should be cut when they're flowering. Southernwood may be cut back by a third after its first flush of spring growth, then again in late summer. If you're collecting flowers like yarrow for dried arrangements, wait until full bloom or just before. Cut them with plenty of stem.

Collect rose petals at full bloom, after the morning dew has dried. When cutting lavender, harvest the whole stem with the attached flower heads, just before the blooms are fully opened.

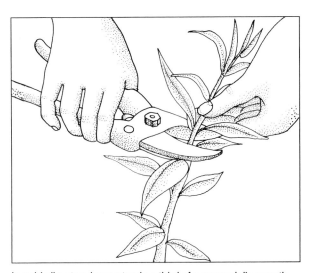
In cold climates, harvest only a third of a perennial's growth.

Drying Herbs

Some growers claim that dried, summer-grown herbs have better flavor than herbs grown indoors in winter. If you enjoy cooking with herbs, you may want to try preserving some of the summer garden's bounty for use in winter recipes. Most herbs dry easily, and under the proper conditions they will retain their characteristic aroma and flavor.

Where to Dry Herbs

The best place for drying herbs is someplace dry and dark, with good ventilation. Depending on what the weather is like, you may find it necessary to speed the process with fans, dehumidifiers, or an air conditioner. The best weather conditions for air drying are low humidity and soft breezes.

Drying screens and bunches can be placed in a dry attic, around the hot-water heater, on top of the refrigerator, or in a gas oven with a pilot light. Barns make excellent drying sheds as long as they are shady and well ventilated. In summer some gardeners dry their herbs on small screens placed inside the car. Cover the herbs with paper toweling and park the car in light shade.

If the weather hasn't cooperated and the drying process seems painfully slow, you can speed the action in your oven. Just place your herbs on baking sheets and set the oven temperature at its lowest setting. Monitor progress until leaves are crispy dry.

Drying in Bunches

Long-stemmed herbs like lavender, mint, and yarrow are easy to dry in bunches. Select only the highest-quality foliage and blossoms, removing any dead or wilted leaves. Make bunches about 1 inch (2.5 cm) in diameter for quick drying; the number of stems in each bunch will naturally vary. You can tie the bunches with string, leaving a loop for hanging, but small rubber bands are easier to use.

Fasten the bunches on wire clothes hangers. Hold the bunched stems along one side of the horizontal wire of the hanger, then pull a loop of the rubber band down and then up over the wire. Pull the band over the stems and release it. Hanging one full hanger in one spot is easier than hanging separate bunches all over the place. Each herb species or cultivar gets its own hanger, making organization easy. You can label each bunch or each hanger. When you're ready to use the herbs, simply pull the bunch down to release it.

Hang your herbs where you have plenty of space, and where you can leave them undisturbed until they're dry. If your house has exposed ceiling rafters, arrange wooden dowels along them and hang the herbs from the dowels. Single bunches may be hung from conveniently placed hooks or nails. When the bunches are crispy dry, remove the leaves from the stems.

Brown Bag Method If dust is a problem, place the bunches inside paper bags, lantern style. Punch a hole in the base of the bag, pull the stems through this hole, and fasten them with string or a rubber band. Hang the bag in a cool, dry place. To increase air circulation, cut flaps in the side of the bag. After 1 week, look inside a few bags to make sure the herbs are drying and free of mold. They may take up to 2 weeks to become crisp and crumbly. (Seeds can be dried in the same way by placing seed heads, with stems up, in an unpunched paper bag.) When the herbs are dry, remove the stems and spread the leaves on a baking sheet. Then place the baking sheet in an oven, set at about 100°F (40°C), for several minutes to complete the drying process.

For very simple storage, hang your herb bunches from clothes hangers. First, wrap each bunch with a rubber band. Then take one loop under the bottom of the hanger. Bring it up over the wire and the top of the stems to secure the bunch.

Lavender flowers retain their fragrance after drying.

Drying on Screens

Herbs with short stems and small leaves, like thyme, are difficult to bunch. The best drying method is simply to snip off the foliage with scissors and spread it on a screen in a single layer. You can dry large-leaved herbs on screens, but first strip the foliage from the stems. Hold the stems upside down in one hand while running the other hand down the stem. Loose herb blossoms and flower petals can also be dried on screens. Remember to stir the herbs once a day on the screens for even drying.

You can construct your own screens with scrap lumber and window screening, then set them on bricks or wooden blocks so that air circulates freely. If the herbs are fine, spread a paper towel or sheet of paper on the screen first. Your herbs should be dry in 7 to 10 days.

Drying in the Oven

Oven-drying is the best method, since the herbs dry quickly and retain their aromatic oils. In a conventional oven, spread herbs one layer deep on paper toweling set on baking sheets, set the temperature at 80 to 100°F (25 to 38°C). If you smell the herbs immediately, lower the temperature to avoid losing essential oils. Stir once every half hour. Drying should be complete in 3 to 6 hours. Herbs with fleshy leaves will take longer than those with tiny or thin leaves, so it is wise not to mix

Dried herbs store best in cool, dark places. If you like the look of the bunches, it's fine to hang some around your home for decoration. But store the herbs you plan to use for cooking in air-tight jars.

different leaf types in one batch. Remove the herbs when they are crispy dry, and before they turn brown.

Food dehydrators are good for drying herbs, too. Follow the same instructions as for regular oven-drying.

You can also dry herbs in a microwave oven. Sandwich the herbs between sheets of microwave-safe paper towels. Put a cup of water in the microwave while drying the herbs. Leave the herbs in the oven for about 1 minute on a low setting. Remove them and check for dryness. If they're still moist, repeat the process for a few seconds. Watch the herbs carefully during drying, and stop the process if any sparks appear. If your herbs turn brown or black, try heating for shorter periods.

Drying Herb Seeds

Many of the herbs you'll grow are used for their seeds. If you're collecting coriander, dill, caraway, or other herb seeds for the kitchen, snip off the seed heads when they've turned brown. You'll have to blanch them in order to destroy the seemingly invisible insect pests that can hide inside. Gather the seeds in cheesecloth and dip them in boiling water, or place the seeds in a sieve and pour boiling water over them. Spread them on paper or a fine-mesh screen to dry in the sun.

If you plan to sow the seeds you've saved, skip the blanching. Dry them in the sun several days before transferring them to a cool, dry location.

If dust is a problem, you can dry long-stemmed herbs in paper bags. Punch a hole in the bottom of the bag, secure the stems, and hang to dry. Cut flaps in the bag to increase air circulation.

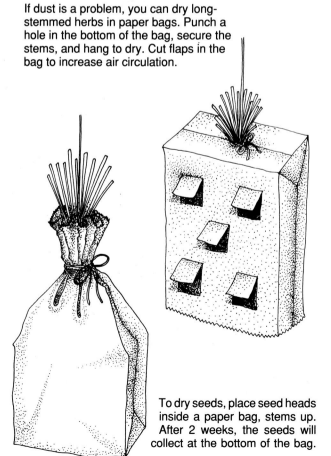

To dry seeds, place seed heads inside a paper bag, stems up. After 2 weeks, the seeds will collect at the bottom of the bag.

Preserving and Storing Herbs

When your herbs have dried thoroughly, strip the leaves from their stems or remove them from the drying screens. Discard stems or save them to add to potpourris. If you're saving herbs for culinary use, crush them or push them through a coarse strainer. Leaves and blossoms saved for tea can be left whole. Crumble dried roots to sizes that will fit their use.

Store dried herb foliage, blossoms, roots, or seeds in air-tight containers away from bright light. Tins or canning jars with rubber seals work best. Or pack the dried materials into resealable plastic bags, squeezing out the air before you seal them. Label your containers, since all dried herbs tend to look the same.

It's fine to dry your herbs on top of the refrigerator, but don't store them there. Ideally, dried herbs should be kept cool and dry. If you like the look of herb bunches and arrangements hanging about the kitchen, make them especially decorative with added ribbons or lace and decorative jars, and use them as ornaments, but keep culinary herbs in air-tight containers.

If your herbs were grown, harvested, dried, and stored properly, they will remain green and fragrant for a long time. If you're in doubt, just crush a few leaves and sniff—scentless, brown herbs will have little flavor. Toss them in your compost pile.

Freezing Herbs

If you have more freezer space than cupboard space, you may want to freeze your herbs instead of drying them. Chervil, dill, fennel, marjoram, mint, parsley, and tarragon freeze very well. Herb growers report mixed results with coriander and chives—it seems they freeze

Braided garlic bulbs can look decorative in the kitchen.

very well or very poorly! You'll have to experiment, and keep records of what works best for you.

Harvest the herbs at their peak and wash them gently but thoroughly, then pat dry. You can chop the herbs by hand, of course, but the simplest method is to chop them in the food processor until the pieces are the right size to add to soups or other recipes. Pack them in freezer bags, squeezing out the air until you have a flat layer of herbs, and seal. Be sure to label the bags, since most frozen herbs look alike in the middle of winter. When you're ready to use them, simply break off a corner, or as much as you need, and return the bag to the freezer.

Some herb savers purée fresh herbs with water or oil. They pour the purée into ice-cube trays and, when the cubes are solid, move them to labeled freezer bags. Herb cubes are easy to use—just toss

Once your herbs have dried, strip the leaves from the stems. Crush the herbs that will be stored for culinary use. Leaves and blossoms that will be used for tea should be left whole, while dried roots should be crumbled. Store your herbs in air-tight containers in a cool, dark place.

Bunches of herbs add a touch of summer to the kitchen.

them into soups or stews. Basil retains the best quality when frozen in an olive oil purée. It's easy to prepare winter pesto—mix in the cheese, pine nuts, and garlic as the basil thaws.

Salting Herbs

Salting is an old method of culinary herb preservation, and it works especially well with basil, chives, garlic, marjoram, oregano, rosemary, savory, tarragon, and thyme. Cooking with herb salt will add flavor to your meals and encourage you to reduce actual salt use. Harvest the herbs at their peak and wash and dry thoroughly. Then pack alternate layers of fresh leaves and salt in a glass jar. Make the first and last layers of salt thicker than the middle layers, which should be quite thin and just cover the herbs. Store the tightly sealed jar on a cool, dry shelf in the kitchen. Pick out the salted herbs for use in stews and sauces. Use the remaining flavored salt for salad dressings, roast meat, or wherever the flavor of herbs is needed.

Herb Salt for the Table

1 cup (8 oz/250 g) non-iodized sea salt or kosher salt
1 cup (1½ oz/45 g) packed fresh herbs, washed, dried, and minced, *or* 2 tablespoons dried herbs

Grind the salt and herbs together in a blender, or finely crumble the herbs by hand and mix them into the salt. Place the mixture in a shaker, and use it to add flavor to your meals. You can make different mixtures to accompany vegetables or meat. For ideas on what herbs to combine, see "Cooking with Herbs" on page 84.

Herbs in the Kitchen

Herbs are a welcome addition to any kitchen. A pantry well stocked with special herbal treats will enable you to have what you need for that extra something. Sprinkle herbal vinegars and oils on salads all year round for a quick alternative to bottled dressing. Herbal jellies and honeys are simple to prepare and can be used in a surprising number of ways, as well as making ideal gifts. And don't overlook the delights of candied flowers—these delicacies will last for months.

Herbal Vinegars

You can use herbal vinegars in most recipes that call for vinegar, including sauces, marinades, and stews. If you don't have much kitchen experience, follow the simple instructions in the recipe below. With experience, you'll learn how much of each herb to use for the best flavor. Some herb growers simply pack the jar with fresh herbs, then fill with vinegar (no measuring necessary!), or you can heat the vinegar almost to a boil—warm vinegar releases the essential oils faster.

Wine-based vinegars are ideal as a base for herbal vinegars, since their flavor is mild and blends well with the herbs. Use white-wine vinegar with chive blossoms, lavender, marjoram, nasturtium flowers and leaves, dark opal and lemon basil, tarragon, and thyme. Use red-wine vinegar with bay leaves, dill, fennel, garlic, lovage, mint, sweet basil, and thyme.

Try combining several herbs to create your own special vinegars. Garlic and chives combine well with most of the strongly flavored herbs, such as basil, dill, and thyme. Mix equal parts of parsley, thyme, and rosemary for a special blend.

Once your herb vinegar has aged, transfer it to decorative bottles that you can buy from cooking-supply stores or through catalogs. Or use recycled bottles from salad dressing, ketchup, sauce, and wine.

For a special effect, seal the bottle caps with scented wax. Melt 1 cup (8 fl oz/250 ml) of paraffin with ¼ cup (¾ oz/20 g) of mixed spices (try cinnamon, nutmeg, cloves, or allspice) in a tall can placed in 1 inch (2.5 cm) of water in a saucepan. Melt the mixture slowly (paraffin ignites easily). Make sure your vinegar bottles are capped tightly, then turn them over and dip the top of each bottle (just past the cap) into the melted wax. Dip them several times, allowing the wax to dry (less than 30 seconds) between dips. Add more wax and spices as needed. You can store any leftover wax in the same can. Let the bottles cool before handling them. To open, lightly score the wax just under the end of the cap.

Herbal Vinegar

1–2 cups (1½–3 oz/45–90 g) packed fresh herbs, washed and dried well *or* 2–3 tablespoons herb seeds, *or* 10 cloves garlic
4 cups (1 qt/1 l) vinegar (5 percent acidity)

Wash and dry the herbs (water will turn the vinegar cloudy), then pack them into hot, sterilized glass jars using a wooden spoon. Fill with vinegar, leaving 1 inch (2.5 cm) at the top. With the spoon, push the herbs down and lightly bruise them. If you're using seeds or garlic, first bruise them using a mortar and pestle. Cover the top of the jars with plastic before putting on the metal lids, to prevent chemical reactions between the vinegar and metal, then screw the seal tight. Let the herbs steep in a warm, dark place for 3 to 6 weeks, then strain the flavored vinegar through a paper coffee filter. Pour the clear vinegar into hot, sterilized jars or decorative bottles, add a few sprigs of fresh herbs, and cap.

Herbal oils add flavor to salads, sauces, and marinades.

Use wine-based vinegars as a base for herbal vinegars. Try combining several herbs to create your own special blend.

Herb-flavored Oils

Flavored oils go well with herbal vinegars in salads. You can also use them in sauces and marinades, or wherever you want an extra touch of flavor.

Herbal Oil

¼ cup (¼ oz/10 g) packed fresh herbs, washed and dried well, *or* 3 cloves garlic
1 cup (8 fl oz/250 ml) olive or vegetable oil

Place the herbs in the bottom of a hot, sterilized jar. Heat the oil in a saucepan until just warm, then pour it into the jar. Let the flavored oil cool, then cover tightly, and store in the refrigerator.

Take Care!

Be careful when preparing garlic-flavored oils, as botulism was recently traced to garlic butter prepared from a minced-garlic-and-oil preparation that had not been refrigerated. When preparing garlic-flavored oils, it's safest to first soak the garlic in vinegar overnight. Then strain out the garlic, place it in a sterile container, cover it with oil, and refrigerate.

Herbal Jellies

Herbal jellies are simple to prepare and make attractive and useful gifts. You can use herbal jellies just like fruit jellies, but that is only the beginning. Glaze roast or broiled meat, fish, and chicken with herb jellies. Spread them on peanut-butter sandwiches, or dab them into thumbprint cookies. Spread them with cream cheese on crackers, or on herbal rolls hot from the oven.

While most jelly recipes you'll find require large quantities of sugar, it is also possible to create attractive, great-tasting jellies with honey as a healthier alternative. Honey-sweetened herb jellies do require longer cooking times than traditional jellies. If you are used to making sugar-based jellies, be sure to follow the instructions in this recipe closely for best results.

As you prepare your jelly, you'll want to boil it until it is ready to set properly. You can check this during the cooking process by doing a jelly test. When you are ready to test, remove the syrup from the heat, and try one of the methods discussed below.

Sheet Test To use the sheet test, scoop up a small amount of the boiling jelly with a cold metal spoon. Raise it about 1 foot (30 cm) above the pot, away from the steam, and wait about 20 seconds. Then turn the spoon so the syrup flows off the side and watch carefully. If the syrup forms two drops that flow together and slide off the spoon in one sheet, the jelly should be done. If the syrup slides from the spoon in several separate drops, cook the syrup a little longer and then test again.

Freezer Test   Put a spoonful of boiling syrup on a cold plate, and chill it in the freezer compartment of your refrigerator for a few minutes. If the mixture gels, it is done. If not, keep cooking and try again.

Metal Bowl Test   Float a light metal mixing bowl in a larger bowl filled with ice water. Drop a spoonful of syrup into the bottom of the smaller bowl, wait a few seconds, and then run your finger through the jelly. If the syrup doesn't run together, your jelly is ready. Otherwise, return the syrup to the heat for a few minutes and then test again.

Once your jelly is finished, pour it into glass canning jars. If you plan to use the jelly immediately, unsealed, covered jars will keep in the refrigerator. Try pouring hot jelly into lightly buttered molds and place them in the refrigerator, then invert them on a decorative plate garnished with fresh herbs for a special meal. If you want to store your jelly for any length of time, you'll need to process the jars in a boiling-water bath. Follow the instructions that come with your canner.

Making the Jelly

Take the following steps to ensure success when making your jelly.

- Harvest your herbs, then make sure you wash and dry them thoroughly.
- Sterilize your jars and lids, and prepare the ingredients and utensils you'll need. Keep the jars and lids hot while you prepare the recipe. You can use paraffin to seal the jars, but recent research suggests that rings with rubber seals are safer.
- Skim off any foam that forms during the cooking process. It will detract from the appearance of the finished product.
- Follow the recipe. Pour the jelly into the hot jars, screw the lid on tightly, then invert to coat the lid and create a seal. Leave the jars upright until they're cool. Store in a cool, dark place.

Mint is delicious in jelly or when used to flavor honey.

Mint Jelly

4½ pounds (2.25 kg) apples
Water
Honey
Fresh mint leaves, washed and dried well

Wash the apples, and remove the stems and dark spots. Quarter the fruit, but do not pare or core it. Place the pieces in a medium-sized stainless steel or enamel pot, and add just enough water to half cover the fruit. Cook over low heat until the fruit is soft (about 1 hour). Place the cooked apples in a jelly bag and drain out the liquid. (You'll get more juice if you squeeze the bag, but it will make a cloudy jelly.) Measure the juice, and add ½ cup (4 fl oz/125 ml) of honey for every 1 cup (8 fl oz/250 ml) of juice. Boil until a good jelly test is obtained.

Just before removing the apple jelly from the heat, add ¼ cup (⅜ oz/10 g) packed mint leaves for every quart (liter) of juice. Stir, remove the leaves, and ladle the jelly into hot, sterilized jars. Seal the jars, and process them for 5 minutes in a boiling-water bath before storing.

Herb-flavored Honeys

Herb-flavored honey makes a comforting addition to hot tea, as well as an attractive gift. Use it to sweeten hot and cold drinks, substitute it for sugar in recipes, or combine it with an equal part of butter or margarine for a sweet spread.

Use any herb singly, or combine several. Good herbs to use include anise seed, coriander, fennel seed, lavender, lemon verbena, marjoram, mint, rose-scented geranium, rosemary, sage, and thyme.

Coriander is one of the many herbs that go well with honey.

Herbal Honey

1 tablespoon fresh herbs, washed and dried well, *or*
   1½ teaspoons dried herbs, *or* ½ teaspoon herb seeds
2 cups (16 fl oz/500 ml) honey

Bruise the herbs lightly, and place them in a cheesecloth bag or directly into the bottom of a saucepan. Pour the honey into the pan, over the bag or the loose herbs, and heat until just warm; high heat will spoil the honey. Pour the mixture into hot, sterilized glass jars and seal tightly. Store at room temperature for about 1 week, then rewarm the flavored honey and strain out the loose herbs or remove the bag. Alternatively, you can leave the fresh chopped herb leaves in the honey, for texture and color. Return the honey to hot, sterilized jars and seal.

Candied Flowers

Edible herb blossoms are a treat normally limited to the growing season. However, you can preserve blossoms, like borage and violets, with sugar, and they'll last for 4 to 6 months under the right conditions. Pick the blossoms just after they've opened, and leave enough stem attached to the flower to hold as you work. Try using rose petals, mint leaves, lavender flowers, or scented geranium leaves.

Candied Herb Blossoms

1 egg white, beaten until frothy
Fresh blossoms, washed and drained well
Superfine sugar

Paint the blossoms with egg white, using a soft brush; make sure you cover them completely. Hold the blossoms over a bowl of sugar while you sprinkle them with sugar, being sure to coat all surfaces. Line up the coated blossoms on waxed paper and dry them in a warm place for 2 days. When they're dry, store the candied blossoms in a tightly sealed glass jar with waxed paper placed between the layers.

Candied Flowers

1. Assemble the ingredients and utensils you'll need, and wash and dry the fresh blossoms.
2. and 3. Beat the egg white until it is frothy. Using a soft brush, coat the blossoms with the egg white. Sprinkle them with superfine sugar.
4. Let them dry for 2 days, and then place the candied blossoms between layers of waxed paper in a tightly sealed glass jar.

Cooking with Herbs

If you want to learn how to use the culinary herbs, grow them! A bushy, fragrant herb plant just outside the kitchen door is the best inspiration for culinary success. If you've never used herbs before, start by following simple recipes that appeal to you. Most cookbooks offer a variety of dishes that require herbs for flavoring. Try something you've enjoyed in a restaurant but never made at home.

Another way to become familiar with herbs is to add them to foods you already make. Add snips of fresh herbs to scrambled eggs or omelets on the weekend, trying a new herb each time. Or add them to bland foods like cottage cheese, cream cheese, or rice. Once you've developed preferences for certain herbs, try combining them with others in the same foods.

When using herbs, a little bit goes a long way. Culinary herbs should be used sparingly, to enhance the natural flavors of other ingredients in your recipes. Most herbs should be added at the end of the recipe. Their flavors are released with gentle heat, but are quickly lost if cooked longer than 30 minutes. An exception is bay leaf, which stands up to a long stewing time.

Herbs go just as well in cold foods. Add them to butter or sour cream and refrigerate for several hours or overnight. The addition of lemon juice or vinegar speeds up the flavor development.

When using fresh herbs in recipes, save the leaves, flowers, or seeds and discard the stems. For small quantities, snip leaves with kitchen shears right over the pot. If you need larger quantities, bunch the leaves

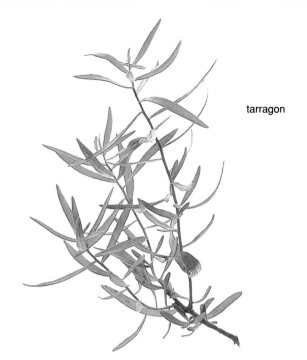

tarragon

on a cutting board and mince the pile with a sharp knife. Food processors are handy tools for chopping large batches of herbs for recipes like pesto or tabbouleh.

Many cooks rub fresh and dried herbs between their hands before adding them to the pot, in order to crush the herbs and release their essential oils. If your recipe calls for a fine powder, grind dried herbs with a mortar and pestle, or purchase a special spice grinder. A coffee grinder works well, but be sure to carefully wipe it clean after use. Ground herbs should be used immediately for the best flavor. You can freeze the leftovers in airtight containers. Remember, though, that it's very important to wash and dry herbs thoroughly before using them in the kitchen.

Saffron threads are harvested for their rich flavor.

Chop herb bunches with a sharp knife on a cutting board.

Using Fresh Herbs

You can substitute fresh for dried herbs in most recipes. Since fresh herbs contain more water than dried ones, use two to three times more fresh herbs than the dried measurement to get the same amount of essential oil.

Fresh herbs are great salad additions. Add chopped or whole sprigs of basil, chervil, chives, dill, oregano, thyme, tarragon, or whatever flavors or blends you enjoy. Use herb blossoms from chives, borage, and nasturtium to garnish the finished salad. Or use fresh herb leaves like nasturtiums as a wrapping for pâté or softened cream cheese, rolled into bundles.

Fresh herbs are delightful in all kinds of cooking.

Herb Butters

Herb butters are colorful and fragrant spreads for warm biscuits, vegetables, poultry, fish, or meat. Add a dab to pasta or rice, or use an herb butter to baste grilled or broiled fish. Most herb butter recipes call for sweet, unsalted butter. To reduce cholesterol, use margarine instead. Let it soften at room temperature, then beat in the herbs and other seasonings by hand or with an electric mixer. For the best flavor, chill for at least 3 hours before serving. Pack the flavored butter into molds or crocks; form balls with a melon-baller; or shave curls from chilled butter with a sharp knife. Store herb butter wrapped tightly in plastic for up to 1 month in the refrigerator, or keep frozen for up to 3 months.

Make up your own recipes to suit the menu, or follow the ones below. For 1 tablespoon of fresh herbs, you may substitute 1½ teaspoons of dried herbs or, if you prefer, ½ teaspoon of seeds.

Simple Herb Butter

1 tablespoon minced fresh herbs, washed and dried well
½ cup (4 oz/125 g) sweet (unsalted) butter or margarine, softened

Mix ingredients together. Use herbs singly or in combinations. Try mint with dill, dill with garlic, chives with lovage, or marjoram with garlic.

Culinary Terms

The following terms describe different culinary uses for herbs.

Bouquet Garni Add this "herb bouquet" to soups, stews, and sauces, but remove it before serving. The essential oils provide a subtle flavor and aroma. Traditional *bouquet garni* includes a bay leaf, thyme, and parsley or chervil, all bunched together with string, or in a cheesecloth bag. Tie the string to the pot handle to make removal easy. You may add other seasonings to suit your taste.

Fines Herbes Unlike *bouquet garni, fines herbes* are left in the food to add color as well as flavor. Mince together fresh herbs like basil, chervil, chives, marjoram, tarragon, and thyme, and add them to sauces and omelets at the end of cooking.

Infusion An infusion is made in the same way as a tea, but it is used as an ingredient in recipes. For instructions on making infusions, see "Herbal Infusion" on page 88.

Marinade A marinade tenderizes and flavors the foods that soak in it. Refrigerate pieces of meat or poultry in a marinade containing wine, vinegar, and herbs for several hours or overnight, turning the pieces several times.

Ravigote Ravigote is a sauce of mixed and chopped herbs like tarragon, chives, and parsley, with shallots and wine vinegar.

Tisane This term usually refers to a tea made from fresh or dried herbs steeped for a few minutes in boiled water.

Parsley Butter

⅓ cup (½ oz/15 g) minced, fresh, curled parsley tops, washed and dried well
1 tablespoon lemon juice
1 teaspoon Worcestershire sauce
1 cup (8 oz/250 g) sweet (unsalted) butter or margarine, softened

Mix all ingredients together.

Garlic Butter

4–6 cloves garlic, finely minced
1 cup (8 oz/250 g) sweet (unsalted) butter or margarine, softened

Mix all ingredients together.

Mixed Herb Butter 1

1 teaspoon each minced fresh marjoram, thyme, and rosemary
¼ teaspoon each minced fresh garlic, basil, and sage
½ cup (4 oz/125 g) sweet (unsalted) butter or margarine, softened

Wash and dry all herbs thoroughly. Mix all ingredients together.

Mixed Herb Butter 2

½ cup (¾ oz/20 g) each minced fresh parsley and lovage
1½ teaspoons minced fresh thyme
½ teaspoon each minced fresh sage, marjoram, and garlic
¼ teaspoon freshly ground pepper
1 cup (8 oz/250 g) sweet (unsalted) butter or margarine, softened

Wash and dry all herbs thoroughly. Mix all ingredients together.

Spread herb butter on fresh, crusty bread for a tasty treat. Or use it to baste fish and poultry.

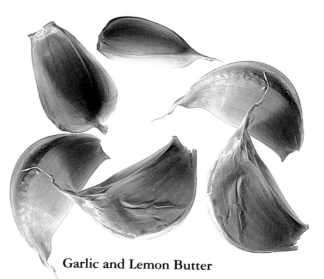

Garlic and Lemon Butter

2 teaspoons minced fresh garlic
2 tablespoons lemon juice
½ cup (4 oz/125 g) sweet (unsalted) butter or margarine, softened

Mix all ingredients together.

Salad Dressings

Homemade salad dressings are far superior to the commercial versions. Make them yourself and cut the oil in half to limit calories. Shake the ingredients together 30 minutes before serving. Use any single herb or combination that suits your menu.

French Dressing

2 tablespoons minced fresh herbs, washed and dried well
¾ cup (6 fl oz/185 ml) olive oil
¼ cup (2 fl oz/60 ml) vinegar

Shake all ingredients together.

Herb and Yogurt Dressing

2 tablespoons minced fresh herbs, washed and dried well
1 cup (8 fl oz/250 ml) plain yogurt

Shake all ingredients together.

Mixed Herb Dressing

1 cup (3 oz/90 g) dried parsley
½ cup (1½ oz/45 g) each dried basil, thyme, savory, and marjoram
¾ cup (6 fl oz/185 ml) olive oil
¼ cup (2 fl oz/60 ml) vinegar

Mix together the dry ingredients and store in an air-tight container. Each time you need a dressing, shake together 1 tablespoon of the dry herb mix with the oil and vinegar.

Herb Bread and Biscuits

When baking bread or biscuits at home, knead in about 1 teaspoon of fresh minced herbs per loaf or dozen biscuits. Use parsley, dill, oregano, or rosemary fresh from your garden. For an added treat, top off with garlic-flavored butter before serving.

Bay, thyme, parsley, chives, mint, and sage are all useful herbs in the kitchen.

Handy Hints for Herbal Cooking

Here are some hints to help you incorporate herbs into your cooking.

- Rub fresh herbs like marjoram or lemon basil into fish before grilling.
- Add 1 teaspoon fresh basil or dill to 1 cup (8 fl oz/250 ml) of mayonnaise for a special spread.
- Sprinkle omelets with fresh minced herbs before folding. Try cheese-and-herb combinations like feta and marjoram or Parmesan and basil.
- Mix together ½ cup (4 oz/125 g) of butter or margarine, 1 teaspoon each of fresh oregano and parsley, and ½ teaspoon each of fresh basil, onion powder, and garlic powder. Toss with hot popcorn.
- Stir together 1 packet of oyster or other snack crackers with ¼ cup (2 fl oz/60 ml) of melted butter or margarine and 3 teaspoons of fresh minced herbs.

Salt Substitutes

If you're trying to cut down on salt, use your dried herbs and spices to make salt substitutes. Grind the dry ingredients together and fill the salt shaker. Experiment with combinations of dried herb leaves and seeds, orange peel, and spices like ground cloves or ginger. Add ground pepper if you like.

Herb Seasoning

¼ cup (¾ oz/20 g) each of dried parsley, savory, and thyme
2 tablespoons dried marjoram

Grind ingredients together.

Spicy Herb Seasoning

3 tablespoons each dried basil, marjoram, parsley, and thyme
4½ teaspoons dried chives
2½ teaspoons each dried paprika, rosemary, and onion powder

Grind ingredients together.

Herb Teas

Herb teas don't have to be medicinal for you to enjoy them. After a stressful day, a soothing cup of herbal tea is relaxing and satisfying. Use ½ to 1 teaspoon fresh herb leaves for each cup (8 fl oz/250 ml) of boiling water, make herbal tea by pouring boiling water over the herb in a china or glass pot. (Metals, including stainless steel, can change the flavor of some herbs.) Herb tea should be lightly colored and mild. Steep for only 5 to 10 minutes for the best flavor. A strong tea will be bitter, and might cause unexpected side effects if the herb has medicinal properties.

Brew herbal teas in a china, earthenware, or glass pot.

Medicinal Herbs

Compared with the precision of modern diagnosis and prescription medicine, herbal remedies can seem out of place and rather old-fashioned. Wild and homegrown herbal preparations were once the only medications used, but they've been largely replaced by synthetic drugs today.

Modern physicians argue that synthetic medicines are superior since they are free of impurities, are of known strength and effects, and are more stable. Herbal practitioners claim that when used properly, herbal remedies have an important role even today. In many countries, herbal remedies remain the only readily available treatment. And, of course, many of today's medicines are derived from naturally occurring plants.

Herbal Remedy Precautions

Use all herbal remedies cautiously and follow these guidelines:

- Always consult a physician if you have painful or chronic symptoms.
- Don't mix herbal medicines with medical prescriptions.
- Always identify wild plants accurately and be aware of their properties and dangers.
- Check the "Plant by Plant Guide," starting on page 100, for poisonous herbs.
- Avoid large doses of any herb.
- Grow your own herbal medications for the best purity and quality, label and store them, and refresh the supply each season.
- Follow the instructions for harvesting and storing herbs properly.
- Stop using any herbal medicine if you notice any side effects, such as headaches, dizziness, or an upset stomach.
- Avoid using herbal medicines if you are pregnant or nursing, unless you have the consent and supervision of an obstetrician.
- Do not give herbal medicines to children less than 2 years old without the consent of your pediatrician.

How to Prepare Herbal Remedies

Prepare herbal remedies, such as infusions, decoctions, syrups, compresses, poultices, and ointments, from your herb harvest to treat a number of common ailments. Refer to the "Quick Guide to Medicinal Herbs" on page 90 for the appropriate herb to use.

Herbal Infusion

2 tablespoons dried herbs, *or* 1½ cups (2½ oz/75 g) packed fresh herb leaves or flowers, washed and dried well

2 cups (16 fl oz/500 ml) boiling water

Pour the boiling water over the herb, allowing it to brew for 15 minutes to several hours. Use a glass or ceramic pot and fresh spring, well, or distilled water. Strain. Drink ½ to 1 cup (4 to 8 fl oz/125 to 250 ml) three to four times daily.

Herbal Decoction

2 tablespoons dried herbs, *or* 1½ cups (2 oz/60 g) fresh bark, roots, or stems, washed and dried well

2 cups (16 fl oz/500 ml) boiling water

Add the herbs to boiling water in an enamel saucepan, then simmer gently, without boiling, for 30 minutes. Strain, and drink ½ to 1 cup (4 to 8 fl oz/125 to 250 ml) three to four times daily.

Herbal Syrup

¼ cup (¾ oz/20 g) dried herbs, *or* 3 cups (4½ oz/140 g) packed fresh herbs, washed and dried well

1 quart (1 l) water

1–2 tablespoons honey

Combine the ingredients in an enamel saucepan. Bring to a boil and continue at a slow boil until the liquid is reduced by half. Add the honey, and store refrigerated for up to 1 month.

Herbal Compress

Follow the instructions for preparing an infusion or decoction, then soak a towel in the warm liquid. Wring it out and lay it upon the affected area, covering it with a dry towel. As the compress cools, replace it with a warm one. Continue treatment for 30 minutes or until the skin is flushed or tingly. A hot compress made with mustard, cayenne, garlic, or ginger will improve circulation and is good for treating nasal and chest congestion. Compresses prepared with herbs like comfrey or aloe are good for sprains and bruises.

Herbal Poultice

¼ cup (¾ oz/20 g) dried herbs, *or* 3cups (4½ oz/ 140 g) fresh herbs, washed, dried, and minced
4 cups (20 oz/600 g) oatmeal

Mix the herbs and oatmeal with enough hot water to form a paste. Place the paste directly on the skin and cover with a towel. As it cools, replace it with a warm one. Continue treatment for 30 minutes. Don't use hot, spicy herbs like mustard that may burn the skin. Poultices are used to draw out infection and relieve muscle aches.

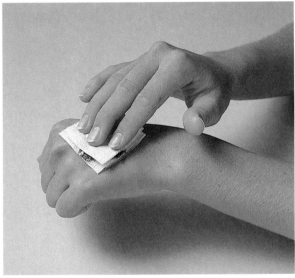

An herbal plaster is not applied directly onto the skin.

Herbal Plaster

Place dried or fresh herbs, or a paste (see the poultice recipe above) in the folds of a light towel or cheesecloth, then lay the plaster on injured area. Since the herbs don't contact the skin, you can use hot and spicy herbs. According to herbalists, plasters have antiseptic and healing properties.

Herbal Oil

¼ cup (¾ oz/20 g) dried herbs, *or* 3 cups (4½ oz/140 g) fresh herbs, washed and dried well
2 cups (16 fl oz/500 ml) olive or vegetable oil

Crush the herbs and add the oil. Let steep for several days; strain, then bottle.

The equipment in this herbal apothecary is beautiful as well as functional. But all you really need to prepare simple herbal remedies is a few basic materials, including measuring spoons and clean containers.

Herbal Ointment

1–1½ oz (30–45 g) melted beeswax or rendered lard
Herbal oil

Mix together the beeswax or lard and herbal oil. Store in a cool place for 1 week.

Herbal Tincture

¾ cup (2 oz/60 g) powdered dried herb
2 cups (16 fl oz/500 ml) brandy, vodka, or gin

Mix together ingredients in a glass bottle and allow to steep, shaking occasionally, for several weeks. Strain and store.

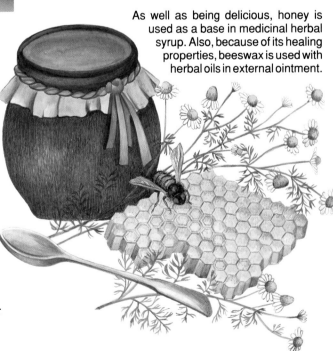

As well as being delicious, honey is used as a base in medicinal herbal syrup. Also, because of its healing properties, beeswax is used with herbal oils in external ointment.

Quick Guide to Medicinal Herbs

Use the following as a quick reference to some of the more common and beneficial medicinal herbs and their soothing and healing properties.

Aloe Apply the fresh transparent gel from the leaves externally to scalds and sunburn, blisters, scrapes, and acne to promote healing and prevent infection. Do not take internally.

Arnica Make a tincture from the flower heads and apply as a compress to soothe sore muscles and sprains. Do not take this herb internally.

valerian

horehound

garlic

peppermint

rosemary

Barberry Prepare a decoction from the roots and take 1 cup (8 fl oz/ 250 ml) daily before meals for antibacterial and laxative properties.

Calendula Make a compress from the flowers and apply to stings, bruises, scrapes, and burns.

Catnip Make an infusion from the flowers and leaves and drink 1 cup (8 fl oz/250 ml) for a calming effect and to aid digestion.

Chamomile Make an infusion from the flowers and drink 1 cup (8 fl oz/250 ml) two to three times daily to relieve cramps and upset stomachs, and to aid digestion.

Comfrey Make a compress or poultice from the leaves and apply to bruises and sprains. Or make an ointment to treat burns and abrasions.

Dandelion Make an infusion from the leaves or a decoction from the roots. Drink 1 cup (8 fl oz/250 ml) up to three times daily as a diuretic and laxative.

Eucalypt Make an infusion from the leaves and inhale the vapors as a decongestant and to relieve other cold and flu symptoms.

Fennel Make an infusion from the seeds or leaves and drink 1 cup (8 fl oz/250 ml) up to three times daily to soothe an upset stomach and to relieve flatulence.

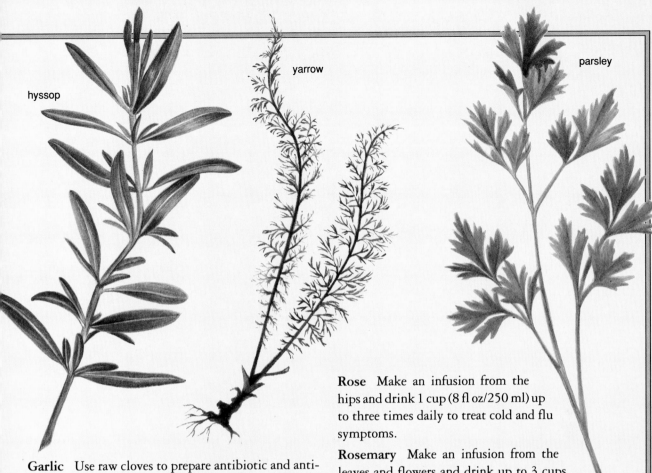

hyssop

yarrow

parsley

aloe

Garlic Use raw cloves to prepare antibiotic and antiseptic infusions, syrups, and plasters. (If you ingest raw garlic, chew a sprig of parsley afterwards to freshen your breath.)

Hops Make an infusion from the fresh "cones" and drink 1 cup (8 fl oz/250 ml) up to three times daily to calm nerves and settle an upset stomach.

Horehound Make an infusion from the leaves and drink 1 cup (8 fl oz/250 ml) up to three times daily as an expectorant. Make a syrup from the leaves and take ½ to 1 teaspoon up to three times daily for coughs, colds, sore throats, and bronchitis.

Hyssop Make an infusion from the leaves and tops and drink up to 2 cups (16 fl oz/500 ml) per day as a cold and flu remedy. Add honey to disguise hyssop's bitter taste.

Marsh Mallow Make a decoction from the roots and drink 1 cup (8 fl oz/250 ml) up to three times daily to soothe sore throats and calm upset stomachs.

Parsley Make an infusion from the leaves or seeds and drink 1 cup (8 fl oz/250 ml) two to three times daily as a diuretic and mild laxative.

Passionflower Make an infusion from the leaves and drink 1 cup (8 fl oz/250 ml) up to three times daily to relieve nervous tension, aid digestion, and ease menstrual discomfort.

Peppermint Make an infusion from the leaves and drink 1 cup (8 fl oz/250 ml) up to three times daily as a decongestant, or for an upset stomach.

Rose Make an infusion from the hips and drink 1 cup (8 fl oz/250 ml) up to three times daily to treat cold and flu symptoms.

Rosemary Make an infusion from the leaves and flowers and drink up to 3 cups (24 fl oz/750 ml) daily as an antiseptic, or for stomach upsets.

Sage Make an infusion from the leaves and drink as needed, up to 3 cups (24 fl oz/750 ml) daily, for cold symptoms and stomach upsets, and to aid digestion.

Thyme Make an infusion from the leaves and stems and drink up to 3 cups (24 fl oz/750 ml) daily for cold and flu symptoms.

Valerian Make an infusion from the roots and drink about ½ cup (4 fl oz/125 ml) once or twice daily to calm the nerves and relieve insomnia, headaches, and menstrual discomfort.

Witch Hazel Make a decoction from the leaves or the bark and use it as a compress for aching joints, sore muscles, cuts, bruises, and insect bites.

Yarrow Make an infusion from the flowers and leaves and drink 1 cup (8 fl oz/250 ml) up to three times daily for indigestion and to relieve menstrual cramps.

Herb Crafts

Fragrances from the garden can lift the spirits or refresh the air, as well as evoking memories and recreating experiences long forgotten. You can enjoy the aromas of herbs, whether sweet, spicy, or pungent, all year round in the form of aromatic oils, potpourris, sachets, and herbal arrangements.

Essential Oils

Essential oils are used in many kinds of herbal crafts. You can purchase essential oils in most craft and health food stores, or prepare your own at home. You'll need a lot of plant materials, since the amount of oil in most herbs is minute. Use the oils in potpourris, candles, soaps, and perfumes.

Extracting with Oil Pack an enamel or glass pan with the herb or herbal blend of your choice, then cover with vegetable oil. Let it steep for at least a day, strain away the herbs, and repeat the procedure using fresh herbs and the same oil. Follow this procedure five or more times. Store the oil in a tightly sealed glass bottle or jar. You can use the oil for making potpourris, candles, or soaps.

Extracting with Alcohol Follow the same procedure as above, using undenatured ethyl alcohol or vodka in place of the oil. Do not use rubbing alcohol. You can use these extracts for perfume bases.

Potpourris

Potpourris are long-lasting, fragrant mixtures of dried herbs and other crushed plant material. Making a potpourri preserves your favorite summer fragrances in a jar—just lift the lid and remember your garden's perfume. You may choose from recipes in herbal craft books, or create your own custom blends at home using plants you've grown in your garden or purchased at herb shops or craft fairs. Either way, potpourris are simple to make from flowers and spice and everything nice.

You will need a nonmetallic bowl, a wooden spoon, about 1 quart (1 l) of base (or main ingredient), several drops of essential oils, and 1 tablespoon each of powdered spice and a fixative. The recipe can end there, or you can add other plant materials to modify the scent and appearance.

Base Materials To start, collect about 1 quart (1 l) of fragrant, dried materials to form the base of the potpourri. Rose petals, lavender flowers, pine needles, ground cedarwood, scented geranium leaves, and other aromatic foliage or flowers in plentiful supply are good choices. To capture the essence of the culinary herb garden, use dried leaves, flowers, and seedpods of basil, thyme, or mint. For a "masculine" scent, start with a base of mint, pine, or lemon balm.

Harvest fragrant petals and leaves on a sunny day, just after the morning dew dries. To catch flowers at their peak fragrance, snip them off with scissors just after they've opened. To quickly strip leaves from stems, hold the stem upright with one hand while gently pulling downward along the stem with the other hand.

Spread the clean materials on a screen, and leave them to dry in a warm, dark, well-ventilated room (attics and barns are good choices in the summer) for several days to 2 weeks. Stir the materials occasionally, for uniform drying. Plants retain the most volatile oils when dried quickly. If your climate is humid, a dehumidifier may be necessary to hasten drying. You may gather and dry base materials throughout the season, then store them in air-tight containers until you are ready to use them. Just be sure that all ingredients are thoroughly dry.

Fixatives To preserve the fragrance of your potpourri, you will need to add a fixative to the base. Fixatives of animal origin, like ambergris, civet, and musk, are expensive and hard to find. Plant-derived fixatives like orris root, vetiver root, rose attar, dried rosemary, sweet flag, or tonka beans are less expensive

potpourri

and more readily available (usually from a pharmacist or craft store) and work just as well. Stir in 1 tablespoon of fixative for each quart (l) of dried base.

Make your own fixative if you grow your own orris root (*Iris* x *germanica* var. *florentina*). Dig the roots, scrub them well, then split them into small pieces. Spread the pieces on paper or on a screen to dry, then grind them to a powder in an old blender, or use the fine mesh of a food grater. It's easier if you do it while the pieces are still slightly moist. Store the powder in a dark glass container.

Spice For a hint of the exotic, add 1 tablespoon of finely ground spices to each quart (l) of potpourri base. Make your own spice mix with equal parts of cinnamon, cloves, nutmeg, and allspice. Or mix together equal parts of anise, cardamom, and coriander.

Aromatic Oils and Seeds To enhance the natural fragrance of your potpourri, add 3 or 4 drops of an aromatic oil. Choose from rose, citrus, jasmine, sweet woodruff, vanilla, sandalwood, and other essential oils available in specialty shops, or learn how to make your own by reading "Essential Oils" on page 92. Add vanilla or tonka beans, or other whole spices. To use orange or lemon peel, scrape away the white inner membrane before drying, then break the peel into tiny fragments that will dry quickly. Your goal is to create a unique fragrance unlike any of the individual ingredients. As you experiment, make notes so that you may duplicate especially pleasing combinations.

Interesting Extras Finally, add colorful plant materials of various shapes and textures for an interesting appearance. Include crushed or whole herb leaves like mint, basil, rosemary, lemon verbena, or betony. Include whole or crushed air-dried flowers like yarrow, statice, or strawflowers.

Enjoying Your Potpourri Store your potpourri in tightly sealed jars (canning jars with rubber seals work well) in a dark, cool spot. Let it rest for at least 1 month

Herb craft projects make delightful gifts.

before using it. Put it in ornamental jars or pots and open them for brief periods to expose the potpourri inside when you desire a hint of scent.

Herb Sachets

These fragrant sachets are great projects for children. Gather together squares of colorful cotton fabric cut in any shape or size; use pinking shears along the edges for a pretty border. Place several tablespoons of crushed potpourri in the center of each fabric square, gather together the edges, and tie with a length of ribbon; you can also add lace and other special effects. Use sachets to scent drawers, closets, linen chests, or luggage, or toss them in the clothes dryer to scent your clothing. When they begin to lose their scent, gather several in a glass jar and sprinkle them lightly with essential oils. Cover and let them sit for 1 week before reusing them.

Herbal Hotpads

Set hot casserole dishes upon these pads to release the fragrance of the herbs inside. Cut two 8-inch (20 cm) squares of prequilted fabric, place them with right sides together, then stitch them together on three sides. Turn inside out, then hem the open side. If you like, add press studs or buttons to fasten the open side. Make a second pillow of muslin, stuffing it loosely with potpourri before sealing. Slip the herbal pillow inside the open edge of the hotpad. You can refresh the herb scent with a few drops of essential oils.

Stove-top Simmers

Here is yet another way to enjoy a potpourri or spice blend. These mixtures are especially good if you plan to spend the day in the kitchen. Just set them in a saucepan toward the back of the stove where the gentle heat will release the oils, or use a commercial potpourri pot. Add ½ cup (1½ oz/45 g) dried herbs to 2 cups (16 fl oz/500 ml) of water. Use any potpourri, or make a spicy mix with equal parts of allspice, star anise, cinnamon sticks, gingerroot, whole cloves, and citrus peel. You can add a few drops of essential oils to accent the aroma. Keep an eye on the mixture to make sure all of the water doesn't simmer away, or the herbs may burn.

Add color to your potpourri with rose petals.

Herbal Pillows

Herb-scented pillows were originally a medical treatment for inducing sleep when stress prevented a restful night. It was thought that the fragrance of herbs such as hyssop would send you to sleep quickly. You can fill herbal pillows with whatever herbal blend suits you. Cut two pieces of fabric 8 inches (20 cm) square and stitch them, right sides together, along three sides. Turn them inside out, and stuff the pocket loosely with potpourri or any mixture of dried herbs (without the stems), then stitch closed. Slip the pillow inside your pillowcase for a soothing sleep.

Herbal Soaps

Once you learn how simple it is to make your own scented soap, you'll want to make plenty to keep for yourself and to give as gifts. For the strongest aroma, use herbs like rosemary, lavender, and thyme—their oils seem to linger on skin the longest.

thyme

Soft Herbal Soap

1½ cups (4½ oz/140 g) dried herbs
1½ quarts (1.5 l) water
　2 cups (16 oz/500 g) shredded pure soap
　½ cup (4 oz/125 g) borax

In an enamel saucepan, combine the herbs and water and bring to a boil. Simmer for 30 minutes to release the oils. Reheat slowly and add the shredded soap and borax while stirring. Boil gently for 3 minutes, then cool. Pour the soft soap into covered containers.

Hard Herbal Soap

2　teaspoons dried herbs *or* 2 tablespoons fresh herbs
¼　cup (2 fl oz/60 ml) water
　Several drops essential oil
2　cups (16 oz/500 g) shredded pure soap

In an enamel saucepan, combine the herbs, water, and oil and bring to a boil. Simmer for 30 minutes, and then add the shredded soap, mixing thoroughly. Allow to cool for 15 minutes, then mix with your hands. Divide into six parts and roll each into a ball. Place the soaps on waxed paper to dry for several days.

If you are a good sewer, you can add little extras like lace, frills, beautiful materials, and fine stitching to herb pillows to create special gifts.

Herbal Baths

The soothing relaxation of herbal baths is hard to beat. Warm water slowly releases the fragrant oils that rise with the steam. For the most soothing bath, keep the water temperature around 96 to 98°F (35 to 36°C). A hotter bath will dry your skin and make you sleepy. To soften your skin, use chamomile or calendula blossoms, lemon balm leaves, or marsh mallow root. The most relaxing herbal baths are made with catnip, hyssop, scented geranium, or valerian root.

To soothe dry skin, common during cold weather, use your own scented bath oil (see instructions below). Herbal bath bags are wonderful for massaging strained and tired muscles.

Herbal Bath Bag

½ cup (1½ oz/45 g) dried herbs, *or* 3 cups (4½ oz 140 g) packed fresh herbs
1 8-inch (20 cm) square of muslin or cheesecloth

Center the herbs in the fabric, bring the edges together, and secure tightly with string. To soften the water, you can add dried milk powder or a few teaspoons of oatmeal. Allow the bag to float in the water as the bath fills.

Enjoy the fragrances of your herb garden all year round by using herbs in your craft projects. This is a fun and practical way to get constant use out of your herbs.

pennyroyal

Herbal Bath Oil

1 part essential herb oil
3 parts vegetable oil

Shake the ingredients together. Store in a glass bottle away from light. Use about 1 tablespoon.

Herbal Massage Oil

½ teaspoon essential herb oil
½ cup (4 fl oz/125 ml) sweet almond oil

Shake the ingredients together. Store in a glass bottle away from light. Use just a small amount to massage weary muscles.

Insect Repellents for People

Herbs were one of the first pest controls used by our earliest ancestors. Herbs work safely to control pests, and they're easily recycled through the compost pile. Use herbs to help control pests on clothing and people with the following remedies.

Insect Repellent for Clothing

½ cup (1½ oz/45 g) cedar shavings
¼ cup (¾ oz/20 g) each of at least four of: dried lemon verbena, lavender, pennyroyal, mint, rue, rosemary, santolina, southernwood, tansy, or wormwood
2 tablespoons each of at least two of: whole cloves, cinnamon, nutmeg, lemon peel, peppercorns, or bay leaves
5–10 drops essential oil of cedar, lemon, lavender, or pine
2 tablespoons orris root

Mix all of the ingredients together and allow the mixture to stand in a covered jar for 1 week. Cut scraps of fabric at least 8 inches (20 cm) square. Place at least ½ cup (3 oz/90 g) of the mix in the center of the fabric, gather the edges together, and tie securely with string or ribbon. You can hang the repellent sachets in closets, or place them in stored luggage or linens to chase away the moths that like a meal of cotton or wool. Replace the sachets each season.

Insect Repellent for Skin

1 teaspoon each of: essential oils of pennyroyal,
   citronella, eucalypt, rosemary, and tansy
1 cup (8 fl oz/250 ml) vegetable oil

Shake ingredients together and store away from
light. To repel outdoor insect pests, rub a small
amount between the palms of your hands, then
apply to any exposed skin. Avoid applications to
the face to prevent contact with your eyes. Reapply
as necessary. If a rash develops, discontinue use.

Insect Repellents for Pets

Use one or both of the following herbal insect repellents
for your pets, depending on the extent of the problem.

Herbal Dip

2 cups (3 oz/90 g) packed fresh peppermint,
   pennyroyal, or rosemary
1 quart (1 l) boiling water
4 quarts (4 l) warm water

Prepare an infusion by pouring the boiling water
over the herbs, and allow it to steep for 30
minutes. Strain the liquid and dilute with the
warm water. Saturate the animal's coat thoroughly with the solution, allowing it to air-
dry. Use at the first sign of flea activity.

Herbal Bedding

Sew together small pillows of muslin or
other cotton fabric. Stuff loosely with dried
pennyroyal, cedar, rue, tansy, pine shavings, or rosemary. Seal the bags and place in
the folds of your pet's bedding. Refresh the
dried materials weekly. Use at the first sign of
flea activity.

Tussie-mussies

Miniature herbal bouquets were a special way of com-
municating long before the days of telephones, comput-
ers, and facsimile machines. They're still a subtle way to
get your message across. Tussie-mussies are composed
of herbs and flowers with different meanings that vary
from region to region. Since they were held to the nose
to mask offensive odors in the days of poor sanitation,
they were often called nosegays.

Select herbs and flowers that express your thoughts,
and pick them in the morning just after the dew has
dried. Place the herb representing the most important
sentiment in the center, and surround it with sprigs or
bunches of herbs that denote related thoughts in groups

of three. Surround the tiny bouquet with fresh greens
like geranium leaves or tansy, then secure the stems
with a small rubber band. Cut an X in a doily and insert
the stems, wrapping the doily to support the bouquet.
You can place the arrangement in a vase with water. If
your tussie-mussie will be traveling, wrap the stems
with cotton soaked in water, then with aluminum foil.
Attach several lengths of narrow ribbon, and a card
explaining the meaning of each plant. You can preserve
the bouquet in silica gel, which absorbs moisture, or air-
dry it and then sprinkle with fine orris root.

Herbal Wreaths

Wreaths are an attractive and fragrant way to display
your own homegrown herbs and flowers. Start with a
wreath frame of straw or wire, and sufficient quantities
of a dried or fresh base herb like southernwood or wormwood to cover the frame. Make small bunches of the
base herb and wrap the cut end of each with florist's
wire, then insert them into the frame or wrap them onto
the frame with
some florist's
wire.

tussie-mussie

Continue adding the
base herb until the
entire wreath form is
covered. If you began
with fresh material, hang the wreath to dry in a dark
place for several weeks. You can attach contrasting
herb bunches, dried flowers, or ribbon-wrapped bundles of spices with more wire, or use a glue gun. Create
different themes to suit the occasion or mood. Add

small packets of herb seeds for your gardening friends. Or design a wreath for the kitchen covered with bunches of your favorite culinary herbs. Store the wreath in a box to preserve it for up to several years between displays.

Dried Herbal Arrangements

1 wicker basket
Dried southernwood base material
Assorted dried herb bunches and flowers
Ribbons or bundles of spices

Pack the bottom of the basket with southernwood, then insert stems of herbs and flowers. Create contrast with silver and green foliage. Add ribbons or bundles of spices like cinnamon sticks or vanilla beans. Fragrant arrangements will help to relieve the winter doldrums.

Herb-scented Candles

Scented candles can help to create a refreshing or a tranquil atmosphere, and they are easy to make in the home. Make them as strongly scented as you like, and leave in the plant materials—they will add extra color and texture and make your candle prettier and more interesting. You can use any of the herbal scents you'd like to evoke indoors. Lavender is a favorite, along with rosemary and southernwood. Mix your own blends using materials you've grown in your herb garden.

Herb-scented Candles

2 lb (1 kg) paraffin wax, broken into small pieces
2 cups (6 oz/185 g) dried herbs, *or* 4 cups (6 oz/ 185 g) packed fresh herb leaves, blossoms, or woody stems, *or* 1 fl oz (30 ml) essential oil
2 wax crayons or candle colorant
Sufficient candle wicking to reach the lengths of your candle molds
Several candle molds or recycled tin cans
Petroleum jelly
Pencils

Melt the wax slowly in a bowl placed over a saucepan of hot water, then stir in the coloring. Remove from heat; as it cools, add the plant materials or oil. Coat the molds with petroleum jelly. Drop a length of wicking to the bottom of each mold, wrapping the opposite end around a pencil resting across the top of the mold to keep the wick centered while you pour in wax. When the wax resembles a gel, pour it into the molds. Allow the candles to set overnight, then remove carefully.

Violet flowers can mean modesty or devotion.

Herbal Dyes

Natural fibers like cotton, linen, silk, and wool are simple to dye at home using your own herbs, vegetables, flowers, and wild plant materials. You can create your own unique, subtle, earthy tones.

The following instructions are for dyeing wool, since it's the easiest material for beginners to work with. Before you begin, read through the procedure and assemble the tools and supplies you'll need.

Fiber You can dye 1 pound (500 g) of wool yarn with the instructions below. Tie the skeins loosely with cotton thread to hold them together while you work. Before dyeing, gently wash the wool with mild soap to clean any traces of soil or oil that may cause the fiber to color unevenly.

Water Use "soft" water for dyeing. Collect rainwater in a clean bucket, or add 1 tablespoon of washing soda or water softener if your water is hard.

Pots and Utensils Use stainless steel or enamel pots that won't react with the chemicals, and that will hold at least 4½ gallons (18 l) of water, plus the wool. Aluminum pots will brighten the color, copper pots add a greenish shade, and iron kettles tend to darken the colors. *Some dyeing chemicals are poisonous. Do not prepare food in any pot that has been used for dyeing.* For stirring, use glass rods or enamel or wooden spoons. You'll also need glass or enamel measuring spoons and cups, a scale that registers ounces (grams), a thermometer that goes up to 212°F (100°C), cheesecloth or an enamel colander, several buckets for rinsing, and rubber gloves.

Plant Materials Harvest leaves, flowers, stems, bark, roots, seeds, or nuts at their peak color. You'll need about 8 quarts (8 l) of light plant materials (leaves, blossoms, and small seeds) for each pound (500 g) of wool, *or* ½ to 1 pound (250 to 500 g) of heavy materials (nuts, large seeds, roots, stems, and bark). Getting the right hue will take some experimenting, since parts of the same plant combined with different mordants (see below) will create different colors.

Mordants Mordants help to set the colors and prevent fading and bleeding. Wear rubber gloves when handling mordants, in particular chrome, copper, and tin, as these materials can harm your skin.

Alum: The most common mordant. For each pound (500 g) of wool, use 4 oz (125 g) alum and 1 oz (30 g) cream of tartar to 4 gallons (16 l) of water.

Chrome (potassium dichromate): Use for deepening yellows and golds. It's light-sensitive, so keep the lid on the pot while dyeing. It is also very poisonous. For each 1 pound (500 g) of wool, use ½ oz (15 g) of chrome and ½ oz (15 g) cream of tartar to 4 gallons (16 l) of water.

Copper (cupric sulfate): Helps rid greens of yellowness. For each pound (500 g) of wool, use ½ oz (15 g) copper and 1 oz (30 g) cream of tartar to 4 gallons (16 l) of water. Or use a copper pot.

Iron (ferrous sulfate): Darkens most colors. For each pound (500 g) of wool, use ¼ to ½ oz (8 to 15 g) iron and 1 oz (30 g) cream of tartar to 4 gallons (16 l) of water. Or use an iron pot.

Tin (stannous chloride): Brightens most colors. For each pound (500 g) of wool, use ¼ to ½ oz (8 to 15 g) tin and 1 oz (30 g) cream of tartar to 4 gallons (16 l) of water.

Use herbal dyes to make your own uniquely colored garments. Natural fibers are simple to dye at home, and wool is the easiest material for beginners to try first.

Experiment with different materials to create varied colors.

Directions

1. Add the mordant and cream of tartar to a small amount of water, mixing well, then add 4 gallons (16 l) of water. Heat to lukewarm and add the dry or freshly washed wool. Heat to boiling, then lower the temperature and allow to simmer for 1 hour. Let the bath cool slowly, then remove the wool. Squeeze it dry and roll in towels to absorb excess moisture. (You can pause here if you like, and continue the dyeing process another day. Just tag the skeins with the type of mordant and date, and allow them to dry.)

2. Chop or break apart the plant materials you've collected. Soak heavier materials in water overnight. Mix plant materials with 4 gallons (16 l) of water, allow to simmer for 1 hour, then strain. This solution is the dye bath. Make it as light or dark as you like.

3. Place the prepared wool in the dye bath and slowly raise the temperature to simmer, poking the wool occasionally for a uniform color, for 1 hour. You can continue simmering for up to 2 hours if you want a stronger color. Pull the wool from the bath occasionally to check. When you've finished, remove the wool. You can add another pound (500 g) of wool to the bath, but this second lot will have a lighter shade than the first.

Use enamel or stainless steel pots when making dyes.

4. Rinse the wool in water of the same temperature, and continue rinsing with fresh water that is progressively cooler. Rinse until the water is clear, then rinse once more in a mixture of ¼ cup (2 fl oz/60 ml) vinegar in 1 gallon (4 l) water to set the color. Squeeze the water out of the wool, then hang the skein to dry.

PLANT BY PLANT GUIDE

All you need to know about planting, maintaining, and harvesting a wide variety of herbs is found in this "Plant by Plant Guide." And to make matters easier, the guide is arranged in an easy-to-use, quick-reference format. (See "How to Use This Book" on page 10 for details on how to use the "Plant by Plant Guide.")

The Plant by Plant Guide will ensure that you have success with your herb garden. Herbs are listed in alphabetical order by common name. Each herb is illustrated with a color photograph for easy identification, and each entry supplies specific cultivation details.

The entries include information on climatic zones—where the plant grows and whether it prefers sun or shade. Refer to the USDA Plant Hardiness Zone Map on page 154 to find out which zone you live in, since it is important to choose plants that grow in your Zone.

There is also information on the ideal soil conditions for each plant, including the ideal pH range (a measurement of the soil's acidity or alkalinity). Also see "Soil" on page 20 to find out how to adjust the pH of your soil.

The Growing Guidelines tell you when to sow seed, at what stage to transplant the herbs into the garden, when to feed and mulch, and when and how much to water your herbs.

The entries also tell you how to deal with pests and diseases using organic methods. They also list information about common problems. Having knowledge of the common problems of each herb is helpful in preventing pests and diseases.

In addition, there is information on how many days the herb takes to reach maturity and how to harvest and store each herb. "Special Tips" covers many topics such as companion planting and how to get a second harvest from your herbs. There are many other details about each herb that make this a complete guide for happy and successful herb growing.

Opposite: Chicory is a hardy perennial that prefers full sun and grows in average to poor soil. It grows to between 3 and 5 feet (90–150 cm) and is little bothered by pests and diseases. (See page 115 for more details on this herb.)

Agrimonia eupatoria   Rosaceae

AGRIMONY

Beginning herb growers will appreciate this easy-to-grow, aromatic perennial herb with dark green, downy foliage and yellow blossoms. Its most common use is as a tea, but it is also used as a gargle for sore throats and as a cleanser for wounds.

BEST CLIMATE AND SITE: Zones 6–9. Full sun to partial shade.

IDEAL SOIL CONDITIONS: Light soil with good drainage; pH 6.0–7.0.

GROWING GUIDELINES: Sow seed outdoors in early spring and thin to 6 inches (15 cm). Agrimony self-sows each year. Or divide older plants in spring. Thrives with little attention.

GROWING HABIT: Height to 5 feet (1.5 m).

FLOWERING TIME: July to August; tall spikes with small, yellow flowers.

PEST AND DISEASE PREVENTION: Keep foliage dry to prevent powdery mildew.

HARVESTING AND STORING: Collect and dry foliage just before blooming. Strip the leaves and spread them to dry, or hang in bunches.

SPECIAL TIPS: Adds height to rock gardens.

Aloe barbadensis {A. vera}   Liliaceae

ALOE

For color and textural contrast, grow several of the more than 300 perennial species of succulent aloe. The long, tapering leaves are ornamented with soft spines and contain a medicinal as well as cosmetic gel.

BEST CLIMATE AND SITE: Zones 9–10. Prefers full sun but tolerates light shade.

IDEAL SOIL CONDITIONS: Well-drained soil low in organic matter; pH 6.7–7.3.

GROWING GUIDELINES: Separate new shoots from established plants. In cool climates, plant in pots and move them indoors in winter. Aloes thrive with little attention. Indoors, avoid overwatering and mix coarse sand with potting soil to facilitate good drainage.

GROWING HABIT: Variable height; stemless rosette of spiny, tapered leaves.

FLOWERING TIME: Rarely flowers in cool climates; drooping, tubular, yellow to red blossoms atop a tall stalk.

PEST AND DISEASE PREVENTION: Spray with insecticidal soap to control mealybugs, or purchase biological controls like mealybug destroyers or green lacewings. Control insect pests before bringing pots indoors.

HARVESTING AND STORING: Cut leaves for gel as needed; remove outer leaves first.

SPECIAL TIPS: Grow on sunny windowsills in the kitchen and bathroom.

PRECAUTIONS: Unsafe to use internally.

OTHER COMMON NAMES: First-aid herb, healing herb, medicine plant.

Angelica archangelica   Umbelliferae

ANGELICA, EUROPEAN

This tall, sweet-scented herb resembles its close relatives parsley and coriander. Leaf stems can be candied and used as cake decorations, or seeds and the dry root can be infused and taken as a tea. The seeds are also used to flavor drinks, especially gin.

BEST CLIMATE AND SITE: Zones 4–9. Partial shade.

IDEAL SOIL CONDITIONS: Cool, damp garden soil; pH 6.0–6.7.

GROWING GUIDELINES: Angelica seed needs light to germinate, so sow uncovered. Indoors, sow seed in early spring in peat pots placed in plastic bags in the refrigerator; in 6–8 weeks, place in bright, indirect light at 60°F (15°C). Or sow seed outdoors in late summer, preferably where they will grow, as angelica transplants poorly. Thin to 3 feet (90 cm) apart. Grows well in deep pots.

GROWING HABIT: Hardy biennial; height 5–8 feet (1.5–2.4 m); stout, hollow stems with broad, lobed leaves.

FLOWERING TIME: Blooms the second or third year in June or July, then dies; honey-scented, green flowers resembling fennel.

PEST AND DISEASE PREVENTION: Wash aphids from seed heads with a spray of water. Avoid growing in hot climates to prevent crown rot.

HARVESTING AND STORING: Collect small stems the first summer, then harvest roots in fall. Pick stems and leaves in spring of the second year; harvest the ripe seeds before they shatter, dry them, and store them in air-tight containers in the refrigerator.

SPECIAL TIPS: In potpourris, seeds act as a fixative.

American angelica grows wild in North America in wet areas such as damp meadows and riverbanks. It is similar in appearance to European angelica, except that it has a purple root; it is used the same way.

PRECAUTIONS: Some scientists say that angelica is a suspected carcinogen, while others say it contains an anticancer compound. Research is continuing.

OTHER COMMON NAMES: Wild celery, wild parsnip.

OTHER SPECIES:

AMERICAN ANGELICA (*A. atropurpurea*): Height to 6 feet (1.8 m); tiny white flowers in umbels 10 inches (25 cm) in diameter.

Pimpinella anisum   Umbelliferae

ANISE

Agastache foeniculum   Labiatae

ANISE HYSSOP

Use these licorice-scented leaves and seeds in salads, especially when combined with apples. The crushed, aromatic seeds enhance the fragrance of homemade potpourris.

BEST CLIMATE AND SITE: Zones 4–9. Full sun.

IDEAL SOIL CONDITIONS: Poor, light, well-drained soil; pH 6.0–6.7.

GROWING GUIDELINES: Sow seed outdoors in spring where plants will stand, then thin to 1 foot (30 cm) apart. Or sow several seeds in peat pots several months before the last frost in a warm (70°F/21°C) room. Transplants poorly. Stake or grow in clumps to prevent sprawling.

GROWING HABIT: Annual; height to 2 feet (60 cm); lacy foliage resembles Queen Anne's lace.

FLOWERING TIME: Summer; dainty white blossoms in umbels.

PEST AND DISEASE PREVENTION: Anise oil is said to have insect-repellent properties; few pests bother this plant.

HARVESTING AND STORING: Seeds are ready to harvest when they fall easily from the head. Dry seeds on paper for several sunny days outdoors, then pasteurize in oven at 100°F (38°C) for 15 minutes and store in air-tight containers. Snip foliage as needed.

SPECIAL TIPS: Enhances the growth of coriander. Anise was once used as a bait in mousetraps. It is the base of some alcoholic drinks.

Anise hyssop has the appearance of a mint with square stems and attractive lavender blossoms, but the leaves have a distinctive licorice scent and flavor.

BEST CLIMATE AND SITE: Zones 5–9. Prefers full sun but tolerates partial shade.

IDEAL SOIL CONDITIONS: Rich, well-drained garden soil; pH 6.0–7.0.

GROWING GUIDELINES: Sow seed shallowly in spring indoors or outdoors, thinning to 1 foot (30 cm); transplants very well. The tall plants occasionally require staking.

GROWING HABIT: Perennial; height to 3 feet (90 cm); tall and branched at the top.

FLOWERING TIME: Late summer to fall; topped with spikes of lavender flowers.

PEST AND DISEASE PREVENTION: Usually free from pests and diseases.

HARVESTING AND STORING: Harvest fresh leaves as necessary throughout the summer. The best time to collect foliage for drying is just before blooming; hang bunches to dry. Or cut whole plants after blooming, hanging them to dry for both foliage and dried flowers.

OTHER COMMON NAMES: Licorice mint, anise mint, Korean mint.

Arnica montana   Compositae

ARNICA

Arnica is a perennial with several flower stalks. An ointment to soothe aching muscles can be made using the flowers.

BEST CLIMATE AND SITE: Zones 6–9. Prefers full sun but tolerates light shade.

IDEAL SOIL CONDITIONS: Dry, sandy soil with some humus; pH 4.0–6.5.

GROWING GUIDELINES: Sow seed indoors in early spring, transplanting outdoors after danger of frost. Propagate by dividing the whole plant in spring.

GROWING HABIT: Height to 2 feet (60 cm); bright green leaves.

FLOWERING TIME: Midsummer; yellow-orange daisy-like blossoms 2–3 inches (5–7.5 cm) across.

PEST AND DISEASE PREVENTION: Occasionally bothered by aphids. To control the pests, spray tops and bottoms of leaves with water. Dust or spray severe infestations with a botanical insecticide like pyrethrin or rotenone.

HARVESTING AND STORING: Cut flowers from the stalk after they've dried. In fall, dig roots after the leaves have died. Mix flowers with some vegetable oil or lard to make an ointment for aching muscles.

PRECAUTIONS: Poisonous when taken internally. Use externally only; can cause dermatitis in allergy-prone individuals.

OTHER COMMON NAMES: Leopard's bane, mountain tobacco.

Berberis vulgaris   Berberidaceae

BARBERRY

This woody ornamental shrub makes an excellent hedge, and is easily trained to twist and turn in knot gardens.

BEST CLIMATE AND SITE: Zones 4–8. Full sun to partial shade.

IDEAL SOIL CONDITIONS: Moist, fertile, well-drained soil; pH 6.0–7.0.

GROWING GUIDELINES: Sow seed indoors or outdoors in spring, or plant fresh seeds outdoors in fall. Take cuttings and root suckers in fall. Prune and thin branches after flowering, or in late winter. If barberry becomes overgrown, cut all growth to 1 foot (30 cm). Provide wind shelter in winter.

GROWING HABIT: Height to 8 feet (2.4 m); deciduous, perennial, shrubby ornamental with spines.

FLOWERING TIME: Spring; hanging yellow petals are followed by orange-red berries.

PEST AND DISEASE PREVENTION: Usually free from pests and diseases. Provide well-drained soil to prevent weakening of the shrub.

HARVESTING AND STORING: Collect berries in fall. Dig the roots in summer or fall; shave to slices. Shave bark from stems anytime, then dry the bark thoroughly. Use roots and bark for yellow dye and berries to make jellies, jams, and a gargle for sore throats.

SPECIAL TIPS: Barberry quickly becomes overgrown if neglected. Prune in fall to guide its growth.

OTHER COMMON NAMES: Jaundice berry, piprage.

Ocimum basilicum   Labiatae

Basil, Sweet

Sweet basil is one of the most popular herbs in home gardens, mainly due to its strong flavor (with hints of licorice and pepper), which is so useful in the kitchen.

BEST CLIMATE AND SITE: Zones 4–10. Thrives on heat and full sun.

IDEAL SOIL CONDITIONS: Accepts a wide range of soil textures; likes rich, moist soil; pH 5.5–7.5.

GROWING GUIDELINES: Sow seed outdoors after all danger of frost, to a depth of ⅛ inch (3 mm), then thin to 6 inches (15 cm). Or sow indoors in flats (seedling trays) under lights 6 weeks before last frost, then transplant to trays or small pots before setting outdoors. Mulch with compost to retain soil moisture, and prune away flowers to maintain best foliage flavor. Side-dress with compost in midseason to enhance production. Basil is easily damaged by cold temperatures. In fall, cover with plastic to prolong the season and protect from the earliest frosts.

GROWING HABIT: Annual; height 1–2 feet (30–60 cm), width 18 inches (45 cm).

FLOWERING TIME: Continuous beginning in mid-summer; white blooms, carried on green spikes at terminal buds.

PEST AND DISEASE PREVENTION: Plant away from mint to prevent damage from plant bugs.

HARVESTING AND STORING: Harvest leaves every week, pinching terminal buds first to encourage branching. Leaves can be used fresh or dried. Dried foliage loses color and flavor but can be used as a tea to aid digestion; use about 1 teaspoon of leaf per

The purple-red heads and white flowers of anise basil form a striking contrast in the flower garden. Use the fresh leaves in teas, salads, juices, and fruit dishes.

cup of water. Best preserved chopped and frozen, or as pesto. If freezing pesto, leave out the garlic until you're ready to use it, as garlic has a tendency to become bitter after a few months. Basil keeps well in a glass jar covered with olive oil.

OTHER COMMON NAMES: St. Josephwort.

SPECIAL TIPS: Plant near tomatoes and peppers to enhance their growth. Some gardeners plant a second crop to ensure a plentiful supply when older plants become woody.

CULTIVARS: The many different cultivars range widely in foliage size, color, aroma, and plant habit.

ANISE BASIL (*O. basilicum* 'Anise'): Height to 4 feet (1.2 m); leaves have a sweet licorice scent; seed heads are a medium purple-red; easy to grow.

BUSH BASIL (*O. basilicum* 'Minimum'): Dwarf, bushy, compact, globe-like form; white flowers and tiny green leaves; grows well in pots.

DARK OPAL BASIL (*O. basilicum* 'Purpurascens'): Lavender blossoms and deep purple, shiny foliage; poor germination.

LEMON BASIL (*O. basilicum* 'Citriodorum'): Flowers and foliage with a strong lemony fragrance; whole plant and leaves smaller and more compact than sweet basil. Unlike sweet basil, lemon basil successfully reseeds itself each season if left in the garden to flower and produce seed.

PURPLE RUFFLES BASIL (*O. basilicum* 'Purple Ruffles'):

BAY, SWEET

Dark opal basil has a gingery aroma and adds an exotic flavor and decorative air to any salad. Grow it near silver foliage in the flower garden as a contrast plant.

Bay leaf garlands represent victory and accomplishment. Use leaves for flavor in stews and soups, and as an aromatic addition to potpourri and herbal wreaths.

Slow-growing, delicate seedlings. Plant early indoors in peat pots to minimize disturbance; do not overwater seedlings. Best preserved in salad vinegars. Several types offer a range of color and leaf texture.

BEST CLIMATE AND SITE: Zones 8–9. Native to Mediterranean region. Full sun to partial shade.

IDEAL SOIL CONDITIONS: Rich, well-drained soil; pH 6.0–7.0.

GROWING GUIDELINES: Take cuttings from fresh green shoots in fall and keep the soil in which you plant them moist, since rooting may take 3–9 months. In warm climates, sow seed outdoors; germination may require 6–12 months. Grows well in the North in pots if moved indoors for the winter; survives light frost. Trim away roots from large, pot-bound plants and add sterilized compost to stimulate new growth.

GROWING HABIT: Evergreen, perennial shrub; height to 60 feet (18 m) where native; height to 6 feet (1.8 m) in pots.

FLOWERING TIME: Spring; inconspicuous, yellowish flowers; rarely flowers in pots.

PEST AND DISEASE PREVENTION: Watch for signs of scale and wipe them away with alcohol swabs. Dried leaves sprinkled throughout kitchen cupboards are said to repel storage pests.

HARVESTING AND STORING: Collect and dry the leathery leaves as needed; store in air-tight jars.

SPECIAL TIPS: Add whole leaves to soups and stews at the beginning of recipes, since bay holds its flavor a long time in cooking. Remove before serving.

OTHER COMMON NAMES: True laurel.

Purple ruffles basil is excellent in vinegar and as a garnish. It is also a striking ornamental.

Arctostaphylos uva-ursi	Ericaceae	*Monarda didyma*	Labiatae

BEARBERRY

BEE BALM

Prostrate, creeping shrub with 1-inch (2.5 cm) long shiny leaves, pink or white flowers, and red berries that are said to appeal to bears.

This North American native has a citrusy fragrance and brilliant blooms in a range of colors. Wild varieties grow readily in sandy locations.

BEST CLIMATE AND SITE: Zones 2–6. Full sun to partial shade.

IDEAL SOIL CONDITIONS: Well-drained soil with plenty of organic matter; pH 4.5–5.5.

GROWING GUIDELINES: Sow seed outdoors in spring or fall, or take cuttings from new growth in fall. Runners may be layered in pots set close to the mother plant; snip the runner once the new plant has rooted. Bearberry needs little care except for pinching away young plant tops to encourage sideshoots.

GROWING HABIT: Height to 3 inches (7.5 cm); low-growing, creeping, perennial shrub with leathery, shiny leaves.

FLOWERING TIME: Spring to early summer; flowers white or pink, waxy, and drooping.

PEST AND DISEASE PREVENTION: Usually free from pests and diseases.

HARVESTING AND STORING: Gather fresh green leaves during sunny fall weather, in the morning; dry in the sun or shade and store in air-tight containers. Use the leaves to make a medicinal, diuretic tea to treat bladder infections.

SPECIAL TIPS: Folklore recommends an infusion of bearberry to stop the spread of poison ivy rashes.

OTHER COMMON NAMES: Mealberry, hog cranberry, mountain box, bear's grape, uva ursi.

BEST CLIMATE AND SITE: Zones 4–9. Likes full sun but tolerates partial shade.

IDEAL SOIL CONDITIONS: Rich, moist, humusy soil; pH 6.0–6.7.

GROWING GUIDELINES: Grow from seed, cuttings, or division. Plants grown from seed flower second year. Spreads quickly; divide established plants every 3 years and discard old growth. For fall blooms, prune stems to 1 inch (2.5 cm) after first flowering.

GROWING HABIT: Perennial; height 3–4 feet (90–120 cm), width 16 inches (40 cm); grows in quickly spreading clumps.

FLOWERING TIME: Midsummer for several weeks; tubular flowers clustered together in bracts range in color from red and pink to lavender and white.

PEST AND DISEASE PREVENTION: Plant away from mint, since it attracts the same insect pests. Prune after flowering to discourage foliage diseases.

HARVESTING AND STORING: Harvest leaves for tea just before blooming and dry them quickly for best flavor. Pull individual flowers for a fresh salad garnish. Dry flowers with stems in bunches of five or six, then add to wreaths and arrangements.

SPECIAL TIPS: Plant near tomatoes or peppers to enhance their growth, or near a window to enjoy the hummingbirds this herb attracts.

OTHER COMMON NAMES: Bergamot, Indian nettle, Oswego tea.

BETONY

Dotted mint has long, lance-shaped, purple-green leaves and striking yellow flowers. Both bee balm and dotted mint contain the antiseptic called thymol, which pharmacists add to ointments and powders.

OTHER SPECIES:

> DOTTED MINT (*M. punctata*): Annual, biennial, or perennial; height to 3 feet (90 cm); also called horsemint.
>
> LEMON MINT (*M. citriodora*): Annual or biennial; height to 2 feet (60 cm); 2-inch (5 cm) long, lance-shaped leaves; flowers spring to summer.

Place betony, an attractive perennial, between tall herbs and border plants that flower in midsummer, for a pretty garden arrangement. In the Middle Ages, people believed that betony kept away evil spirits.

BEST CLIMATE AND SITE: Zones 4–8. Full sun to partial shade.

IDEAL SOIL CONDITIONS: Average soil with good drainage; pH 5.5–7.0.

GROWING GUIDELINES: Easily started from seed sown outdoors in early spring. Cuttings will quickly root. Or divide established root systems for new plants. Control summer weeds. Every 3–4 years, dig up the plant and divide to several new clumps, adding compost or rotted manure to the hole.

GROWING HABIT: Height to 3 feet (90 cm); erect, rosette-forming, with square stems.

FLOWERING TIME: July to August; red to purple flowers along a terminal spike.

PEST AND DISEASE PREVENTION: Usually free from pests and diseases.

HARVESTING AND STORING: Collect leaves in July or just before blooming; dry them quickly and store in an air-tight container. Use the leaves to make a pleasant tea and a chartreuse dye.

SPECIAL TIPS: Gargle tea made from the astringent leaves to treat throat irritations, or drink the tea to treat diarrhea.

PRECAUTIONS: Excessive internal use irritates the stomach.

Betula spp.   Betulaceae

BIRCH

The twigs and inner bark and sometimes the sap of birch trees are used as the main ingredient in birch beer, and the leaves can be used to make tea.

BEST CLIMATE AND SITE: Zones 4–8. Full sun to partial shade.

IDEAL SOIL CONDITIONS: Fertile, sandy soil with good drainage; pH 5.0–6.0.

GROWING GUIDELINES: Collect and dry ripe catkins, then sow seed in late summer or fall. Indoors, sow thickly in trays, cover only lightly, and keep moist. Transplant seedlings when 1 year old. Staking may be necessary to maintain upright growth.

GROWING HABIT: Height 40–90 feet (12–27 m); perennial, deciduous trees that live for 50 years.

FLOWERING TIME: Spring; on the same tree, female catkins are cone-shaped and male catkins are pendulous.

PEST AND DISEASE PREVENTION: Provide ample water during the summer months, to keep birch trees free from pests and diseases. Watch for borers on young, sappy limbs.

HARVESTING AND STORING: In spring, collect the sap by boring holes in the trunk, inserting a tube, and collecting the liquid in a container. Collect leaves in spring and use them fresh, or dry and store them in an air-tight container. Collect bark as it peels off the tree; dry the bark and twigs in a cool, dry area; store in air-tight containers; keeps well.

Borago officinalis   Boraginaceae

BORAGE

This silvery green, sprawling mound contrasts nicely with dark greens in the garden. The drooping clusters of blossoms attract honeybees, and the leaves have a cucumber flavor.

BEST CLIMATE AND SITE: Zones 3–9. Prefers full sun but tolerates partial shade.

IDEAL SOIL CONDITIONS: Fairly rich, moist soil with good drainage; pH 6.0–7.0.

GROWING GUIDELINES: Sow seed ½ inch (1 cm) deep outdoors after danger of heavy frost. Indoors, plant in peat pots to avoid disturbing the sensitive taproot when transplanting. Control weeds to reduce competition for moisture. To promote blooming, go easy on the nitrogen. Self-sows well. Tall plants may need support.

GROWING HABIT: Annual; height 2–3 feet (60–90 cm), width 16 inches (40 cm), with broad, hairy leaves arising from a central stalk.

FLOWERING TIME: Continuously from midsummer until first frost; star-shaped circles of pink, purple, lavender, or blue, with black centers.

PEST AND DISEASE PREVENTION: Mulch with light materials like straw to keep foliage off soil and prevent rot. Japanese beetles will attack this plant if their preferred food sources are scarce.

HARVESTING AND STORING: Harvest foliage anytime and use raw, steamed, or sautéed. Snip blossoms just after they open and candy, toss fresh in a salad, or dry with silica gel for flower arrangements.

PRECAUTIONS: Some sources suggest that borage is toxic when consumed in large quantities over long periods of time.

| *Arctium lappa* | Compositae | *Calendula officinalis* | Compositae |

BURDOCK

CALENDULA

This biennial or short-lived perennial has large, wooly leaves, purplish red thistle-like daisy flowers, and a long, edible root.

BEST CLIMATE AND SITE: Zones 2–10. Full sun to partial shade.

IDEAL SOIL CONDITIONS: Deep, loose, moist soil; pH 5.0–8.5.

GROWING GUIDELINES: Sow seed shallowly in early spring outdoors or indoors. Burdock's deep tap-root makes transplanting difficult. Thrives despite neglect.

GROWING HABIT: Height 1½–12 feet (45–300 cm). A biennial grown as an annual, burdock is stocky but branched at the top.

FLOWERING TIME: Summer; individual purple to red blossoms mature to burr-like seed heads that cling to passersby.

PEST AND DISEASE PREVENTION: Usually free from pests and diseases.

HARVESTING AND STORING: At the end of the first season, dig up roots, scrub them, and slice to dry on paper in the sun. Store thoroughly dried roots in air-tight containers and use for tea.

SPECIAL TIPS: Use the root fresh in salads or soups, or steam or sauté the roots or young leaves.

OTHER COMMON NAMES: Cuckold, harlock; often confused with many similar relatives.

Calendula are cheery, dependable bloomers in the garden. Plant enough to make long-lasting fresh and dried bouquets.

BEST CLIMATE AND SITE: Zones 3–9. Full sun to partial shade.

IDEAL SOIL CONDITIONS: Average garden soil with good drainage; pH 6.0–7.0.

GROWING GUIDELINES: In the North, start seeds indoors in spring, setting them out as soon as the soil can be worked. In the South, sow seed outdoors in fall; thin to 10–18 inches (25–45 cm). Work in compost or aged manure before planting. Pinch away old blooms for continuous flowering.

GROWING HABIT: Height 1–2 feet (30–60 cm); annual with branched stem, leaves with fine hairs.

FLOWERING TIME: Summer; yellow to orange ray flowers.

PEST AND DISEASE PREVENTION: Provide good air circulation and drainage to prevent foliage diseases like powdery mildew and leafspot. When aphids, whiteflies, or leafhoppers appear, dislodge them with a spray of water, or use insecticidal soap for persistent pests. Keep mulch away from stems to prevent stem rot and discourage slugs.

HARVESTING AND STORING: Dry petals in shade on paper to prevent sticking; store in moisture-proof jars. Preserve whole flowers in salad vinegar. Use dried and ground calendula flowers as a substitute for saffron.

SPECIAL TIPS: Plant calendula seed in pots in July for indoor fall color.

OTHER COMMON NAMES: Pot marigold.

| *Carum carvi* | Umbelliferae | *Rhamnus purshiana* | Rhamnaceae |

CARAWAY

CASCARA SAGRADA

The seeds of this annual or biennial have been used for 5,000 years for flavoring and for their carminative effect. The seeds are also aromatic and can be used in potpourris.

In Spanish, "cascara sagrada" means "sacred bark." It yields an extract that is an active ingredient in several commercial laxatives, for both people and their pets.

BEST CLIMATE AND SITE: Zones 3–7. Full sun to light shade.

IDEAL SOIL CONDITIONS: Fertile, light garden soil; pH 6.0–7.0.

GROWING GUIDELINES: Sow seed shallowly outdoors as early as the soil can be worked, or indoors in peat pots; thin to 6–12 inches (15–30 cm). In fall, take cuttings from new growth, or sow seed outdoors for early spring plants. Don't allow seedlings to dry out. A large taproot makes transplanting difficult.

GROWING HABIT: Height 1–2 feet (30–60 cm); glossy, fine foliage resembling the carrot plant.

FLOWERING TIME: Spring and early summer of the second year; white to pink flowers in umbels on stalks.

PEST AND DISEASE PREVENTION: Watch for pests in dried, stored seeds.

HARVESTING AND STORING: Snip tender leaves in spring and use fresh in salads, soups, and stews. After blooming, cut plants when seeds are brown and almost loose, then hang them upside down in paper bags to dry. Collect seeds and dry a few more days in the sun; store in a tightly sealed container.

SPECIAL TIPS: Excessive pruning during the first year weakens the plant.

BEST CLIMATE AND SITE: Zones 7–8. Full sun to partial shade.

IDEAL SOIL CONDITIONS: Fertile, moist garden soil; pH 6.0–6.7.

GROWING GUIDELINES: Propagate by seed, layering, or cuttings from new growth.

GROWING HABIT: Height 5–25 feet (1.5–7.5 m); deciduous shrub with reddish gray bark and thin, elliptical leaves.

FLOWERING TIME: Spring; tiny greenish yellow flowers in clusters, followed by small red berries that blacken when ripe.

PEST AND DISEASE PREVENTION: Usually free from pests and diseases.

HARVESTING AND STORING: In spring and fall, strip bark from wood. Dry well before storing.

PRECAUTIONS: The bark must be aged for at least 1 year before use. Infusions made from fresh bark tend to cause intestinal cramping.

OTHER COMMON NAMES: Bearberry.

Nepeta cataria   Labiatae

CATNIP

Catnip is closely related to mint and is similarly hardy. Look for it growing wild among the weeds near homes, in gardens, or in fields.

BEST CLIMATE AND SITE: Zones 4–9. Full sun to partial shade.

IDEAL SOIL CONDITIONS: Dry, sandy garden soil; pH 7.0–8.0.

GROWING GUIDELINES: Sow seed outdoors in early spring; thin to 18 inches (45 cm). Take cuttings in spring only. Self-sows freely. Grows like a weed under most conditions but transplants poorly.

GROWING HABIT: Height 1–3 feet (30–90 cm); new stems each season from a perennial root; heart-shaped, toothed, grayish green leaves.

FLOWERING TIME: Continuous summer bloomer; white flowers in spikes.

PEST AND DISEASE PREVENTION: Usually free from pests and diseases.

HARVESTING AND STORING: In late summer, strip topmost leaves from stems and spread them to dry on a screen in the shade, or hang bunches upside down. Store in tightly sealed containers. Make a tea from the dried leaves to use as a carminative, tonic, and mild sedative. Use fresh leaves in salads.

SPECIAL TIPS: Grow enough to share with your cat, since the bruised foliage releases a scent that turns cats into playful kittens.

OTHER COMMON NAMES: Catnep, catmint.

Capsicum annuum   Solanaceae

CAYENNE PEPPER

Peppers are heat-lovers, so be patient in the spring and don't set plants out too early. Surprisingly, they often withstand light frosts in the fall.

BEST CLIMATE AND SITE: Perennial in Zone 10, annual in cooler zones. Full sun.

IDEAL SOIL CONDITIONS: Well-fertilized, moist soil; pH 6.0–7.0.

GROWING GUIDELINES: Sow seed indoors like sweet peppers; set young plants outdoors several weeks after last frost. Plant 12–18 inches (30–45 cm) apart in 30-inch (75 cm) rows. Water-loving peppers should be mulched if summers are dry.

GROWING HABIT: Height 1–2 feet (30–60 cm); shrubby tropical perennial, grown as an annual.

FLOWERING TIME: Midsummer; flowers followed by red, orange, or yellow fruit.

PEST AND DISEASE PREVENTION: Pests tend to avoid these spicy plants.

HARVESTING AND STORING: When fruits are uniformly red, cut them from the plant, leaving at least ½ inch (1 cm) of stem. Dry immediately on screens, or string them together using a needle and heavy thread. Or pull and hang the whole plant to dry. Store peppers whole or ground in tightly sealed containers.

SPECIAL TIPS: For a bountiful harvest, pinch off the earliest blossoms.

Chamaemelum nobile   Compositae

CHAMOMILE, ROMAN

Herb gardens of yesterday often included a lush lawn of chamomile that released a sweet, apple-like scent when walked upon. The tea is relaxing after a stressful day.

BEST CLIMATE AND SITE: Zones 3–8. Full sun to partial shade.

IDEAL SOIL CONDITIONS: Light, moist garden soil; pH 6.7–7.3.

GROWING GUIDELINES: Sow seed indoors or outdoors at a soil temperature of 55–65°F (13–18°C); thin to 6 inches (15 cm). Once established, it self-sows. Divide older plants in early spring. In the first year, clip to prevent flowering and encourage vegetative growth while it becomes established. Chamomile is a poor competitor, so weed often. Established lawns can be mowed like grass.

GROWING HABIT: Height 6–9 inches (15–23 cm); low-growing perennial with aromatic lacy foliage.

FLOWERING TIME: Summer; tiny, white daisy-like rays with yellow centers.

PEST AND DISEASE PREVENTION: Cover flowers with cheesecloth while drying, to prevent the arrival of potential storage pests.

HARVESTING AND STORING: Collect flowers at full bloom and dry on screens or paper. Store in tightly sealed containers.

OTHER COMMON NAMES: Garden chamomile, ground apple, Russian chamomile.

OTHER SPECIES:

GERMAN CHAMOMILE (*Matricaria recutita*): Annual; reseeds itself readily and prefers full sun; height to 18 inches (45 cm).

Anthriscus cerefolium   Umbelliferae

CHERVIL

Chervil grows best when temperatures are cool, in spring and fall. Grow this lacy, delicate-looking plant for medicinal, culinary, and craft uses.

BEST CLIMATE AND SITE: Zones 3–7. Partial shade.

IDEAL SOIL CONDITIONS: Moist, humusy garden soil; pH 6.0–6.7.

GROWING GUIDELINES: Sow fresh seed shallowly outdoors in early spring or fall; thin to 9–12 inches (23–30 cm); keep seedlings moist. Sow again at 2-week intervals until mid-July for continuous harvest. Transplants poorly. Mulch to protect fall-sown seeds. Once established, chervil reseeds itself each year if flowers are left to mature in the garden.

GROWING HABIT: Annual; height 1–2 feet (30–60 cm); fern-like leaves resemble carrot tops.

FLOWERING TIME: May to July; small umbrella-like, white flowers.

PEST AND DISEASE PREVENTION: Keep mulch away from plants to prevent earwig damage (plants defoliated overnight).

HARVESTING AND STORING: Snip leaves continuously after 6–8 weeks; best used fresh.

SPECIAL TIPS: Loses flavor quickly when heated, so add to recipes at the end.

OTHER COMMON NAMES: Salad chervil.

Cichorium intybus   Compositae

CHICORY

Look for chicory's bright blue flowers along field edges and highways. This hardy wild plant thrives under a variety of harsh conditions.

BEST CLIMATE AND SITE: Zones 3–7. Full sun.

IDEAL SOIL CONDITIONS: Average to poor, deeply tilled, well-drained garden soil; pH 6.0–6.7.

GROWING GUIDELINES: Sow seed outdoors in early spring, thinning to 1 foot (30 cm). Side-dress in midsummer with compost or rotted manure, but avoid heavy nitrogen applications. Keep weeded and moist. In the fall, plants can be "forced" indoors away from light to produce the salad delicacy called Belgian endive. To do this, plant roots trimmed to 8–9 inches (20–23 cm) long in deep containers and keep away from light. Within about 3 weeks, 6-inch (15 cm) long cone-shaped heads of leaves are ready to be sliced off and used. Discard the root and start again with a new one.

GROWING HABIT: Height 3–5 feet (90–150 cm); deep-rooted perennial with bristly, branched stem.

FLOWERING TIME: Early spring to fall; bright blue flowers open and close each morning and evening, even when cut for arrangements.

PEST AND DISEASE PREVENTION: Few pests bother this fast-grower.

HARVESTING AND STORING: Use leaves fresh in salads or cook like spinach. Chicory does not dry or freeze well. Collect the roots in fall, and dry and grind them for a coffee substitute.

OTHER COMMON NAMES: Blue-sailors, succory, witloof, Belgian endive.

Allium schoenoprasum   Liliaceae

CHIVES

The graceful leaves and blossoms have a mild onion flavor, especially when used fresh. Use the leaves in cooking and toss the flowers in salads or use them as a garnish.

BEST CLIMATE AND SITE: Zones 3–9. Full sun.

IDEAL SOIL CONDITIONS: Rich, well-drained soil; pH 6.0–7.0.

GROWING GUIDELINES: Sow seed indoors in late winter, covering seed lightly and keeping the soil moist; transplant in clumps in early spring; space 5–8 inches (12–20 cm) apart. Divide older clumps in the early spring every 3 years, and freshen with compost or rotted manure.

GROWING HABIT: Height 6–12 inches (15–30 cm); perennial bulb with green, tubular leaves.

FLOWERING TIME: June; pink or lavender to purple globular blossoms.

PEST AND DISEASE PREVENTION: Avoid wet areas that encourage stem and bulb diseases.

HARVESTING AND STORING: Use fresh leaf tips all summer once plants are 6 inches (15 cm) tall; leave at least 2 inches (5 cm) remaining. Best used fresh; or chop and dry. Freezes poorly.

SPECIAL TIPS: Chives are recommended companion plants for carrots, grapes, roses, and tomatoes.

OTHER SPECIES:

     GARLIC CHIVES (*A. tuberosum*): Same as above but flowers are white and leaves are flat and broad. They have a garlicky aroma and flavor. Also known as Chinese chives.

CLARY

Fresh clary has a bitter, warm aroma and flavor and makes an attractive flowering garden plant. Fresh and dried leaves are used for seasoning—it has the same culinary uses as sage.

BEST CLIMATE AND SITE: Zones 4–7. Full sun.

IDEAL SOIL CONDITIONS: Average, well-drained soil; pH 4.8 to 7.5.

GROWING GUIDELINES: Sow seed outdoors in spring; thin to 9 inches (23 cm). Or propagate by division of older plants in early spring or fall; divide every 3 years for best vigor. Mulch after the ground freezes in winter and remove gradually in spring to protect plants from heaving.

GROWING HABIT: Perennial; height 2–5 feet (60–150 cm); upright, branched, square stems with broad, oblong aromatic leaves.

FLOWERING TIME: June to July after first year; small pale blue to lavender blossoms resemble garden sage.

PEST AND DISEASE PREVENTION: Usually free from pests and diseases.

HARVESTING AND STORING: Snip leaves for fresh use. Strip leaves and dry them on screens for potpourri.

SPECIAL TIPS: Clary can be used as a substitute for garden sage.

OTHER COMMON NAMES: Clear eye.

COFFEE

In cool climates, coffee is grown as an ornamental in pots or planted in greenhouses. Coffee beans are actually the seeds, inside a pulpy fruit.

BEST CLIMATE AND SITE: Zone 10. Full sun.

IDEAL SOIL CONDITIONS: Humusy, well-drained soil; pH 6.0–7.0.

GROWING GUIDELINES: Sow seed shallowly in spring; germinates quickly. Does well indoors in pots, but requires regular misting with water to maintain humidity.

GROWING HABIT: Height 15–40 feet (4.5–12 m); shrubby perennial evergreen.

FLOWERING TIME: Late spring; white, star-shaped blooms in clusters followed by deep red berries.

PEST AND DISEASE PREVENTION: For healthy plants, keep coffee well watered during periods of dry weather.

HARVESTING AND STORING: Collect the berries when they are deep red, and extract and roast the seeds.

SPECIAL TIPS: Most commercial brands of coffee are actually a blend of several different types.

OTHER COMMON NAMES: Caffea.

Symphytum officinale   Boraginaceae

COMFREY

Comfrey is an attractive plant with blue-green, fleshy leaves. It has a colorful medicinal history, and was once thought to help repair broken bones.

BEST CLIMATE AND SITE: Zones 3–9. Full sun to partial shade.

IDEAL SOIL CONDITIONS: Rich, moist garden soil; pH 6.7–7.3.

GROWING GUIDELINES: Propagate by seed, division, or cuttings; space new plants 3 feet (90 cm) apart. Establishes easily and requires little care; remove dead leaves during fall cleanup. Divide every few years to prevent crowding.

GROWING HABIT: Height 3–5 feet (90–150 cm); new leaves sprout each spring from a perennial root; leaves lanceolate, large, deep green, and hairy.

FLOWERING TIME: May to early frost; terminal cluster of purple flowers.

PEST AND DISEASE PREVENTION: Occasionally visited by Japanese beetles; rarely threatened by other pests.

HARVESTING AND STORING: Pick the leaves and use fresh or dry. Leaves for drying are best picked in spring. Dig up the roots when the plant has died down in fall and dry; store leaves and roots in air-tight containers. Use roots and leaves to treat external bruises, wounds, and sores.

SPECIAL TIPS: Shaded plants will be smaller, with few blossoms.

PRECAUTIONS: Suspected carcinogen; do not take internally.

OTHER COMMON NAMES: Knitbone, slippery root.

Coriandrum sativum   Umbelliferae

CORIANDER

In seed catalogs, select types grown for either seed or foliage production. The seeds become more fragrant with age, and are popular ingredients in the kitchen and in potpourri.

BEST CLIMATE AND SITE: Zones 2–9. Full sun to partial shade.

IDEAL SOIL CONDITIONS: Rich, well-drained soil; pH 6.0–6.7.

GROWING GUIDELINES: Sow seed ½ inch (1 cm) deep outdoors after danger of frost, or in fall; thin to 4 inches (10 cm). Self-sows. Weed diligently to prevent delicate seedlings from being overcome by more vigorous weeds. To prevent sprawling, avoid heavy applications of nitrogen.

GROWING HABIT: Annual; height 1–3 feet (30–90 cm); graceful, glossy, lacy foliage resembles Queen Anne's lace.

FLOWERING TIME: Spring to late summer, depending on when sown; tiny white flowers in umbels.

PEST AND DISEASE PREVENTION: Usually free from pests and diseases.

HARVESTING AND STORING: Harvest foliage before seeds form and use fresh. Dried foliage is of lesser quality. Freezes poorly.

SPECIAL TIPS: Sow every 2–3 weeks for a continuous supply of fresh leaves.

OTHER COMMON NAMES: Chinese parsley, cilantro.

Chrysanthemum balsamita   Compositae

COSTMARY

In the summer, enjoy costmary's mint-scented leaves in your garden. In the fall, harvest whole stems for weaving into fragrant herb baskets.

BEST CLIMATE AND SITE: Zones 4–8. Full sun.

IDEAL SOIL CONDITIONS: Dry, fertile, loamy soil; pH 6.0–6.7.

GROWING GUIDELINES: Plants produce little or no seed, so propagate by dividing older plants in spring. Space at 2-foot (60 cm) intervals. Divide plants every 2–3 years, since they spread quickly. Avoid shade, since costmary will not flower without sun. For more foliage production, discourage flowering by pruning away buds.

GROWING HABIT: Height 1–3 feet (60–90 cm); perennial roots with gray-green, silvery, hairy foliage.

FLOWERING TIME: Late summer, but rarely blooms; ray flowers in loose clusters.

PEST AND DISEASE PREVENTION: Usually free from pests and diseases.

HARVESTING AND STORING: Collect leaves and dry as needed. To harvest foliage for baskets, harvest whole stems in late summer or fall and hang to dry.

SPECIAL TIPS: Add fresh leaves to salads for a minty flavor, or add dried leaves to homemade potpourri.

OTHER COMMON NAMES: Bible leaf, alecost, mace.

Taraxacum officinale   Compositae

DANDELION

Some of us have learned to appreciate this brightly colored lawn pest. If your thumb is other than green, try planting dandelions to boost your self-confidence in the garden!

BEST CLIMATE AND SITE: Zones 2–9. Full sun to partial shade.

IDEAL SOIL CONDITIONS: Any loose soil; pH 6.0–7.5.

GROWING GUIDELINES: Collect wild seed or buy it from specialty seed catalogs, and sow shallowly in early spring; transplants poorly. For large roots that are easy to dig, work in plenty of compost or rotted manure to loosen the soil.

GROWING HABIT: Perennial; height 6–12 inches (15–30 cm); leaves jagged, arising from a basal rosette.

FLOWERING TIME: Late spring; well-known golden yellow globes mature to puffballs of seeds.

PEST AND DISEASE PREVENTION: Usually free from pests and diseases.

HARVESTING AND STORING: Dig roots in fall, and cut or slice them to small pieces, then air dry or roast in a slow oven. Use dried, roasted, and ground roots to prepare a caffeine-free coffee substitute. Harvest young, fresh leaves for spring salads, soups, and wine.

Anethum graveolens Umbelliferae

DILL

Select dill varieties for either seed or foliage (called "dill weed") production. Dill's tall, graceful habit makes it an attractive background in flower beds.

BEST CLIMATE AND SITE: Zones 2–9. Full sun.

IDEAL SOIL CONDITIONS: Rich, well-drained soil; pH 5.5–6.7.

GROWING GUIDELINES: Sow seed shallowly in rows or in 5-inch (12 cm) bands outdoors in early spring after danger of frost; thin to 8–10 inches (20–25 cm); transplants poorly. Keep seedlings moist; weed diligently until plants shade the soil.

GROWING HABIT: Height 3 feet (90 cm); hardy annual resembling fennel.

FLOWERING TIME: Summer to fall; yellow-green to white flowers in umbels.

PEST AND DISEASE PREVENTION: Usually free from pests and diseases.

HARVESTING AND STORING: Clip fresh leaves at the stem as needed. Freeze whole leaves, or chop first; or dry foliage on nonmetallic screens. Collect flower heads before the seeds mature and shatter; hang in paper bags or dry on paper. Store dried foliage and seeds in an air-tight container. Fresh leaves can be refrigerated for 1 week.

SPECIAL TIPS: Sow seeds at 2- or 3-week intervals for a continuous harvest through fall.

Rumex spp. Polygonaceae

DOCK

Look for this common weed in pastures and hay fields. The seed stalks mature to a rusty color in late summer and fall. Only the roots of this plant are edible and are used in medicines.

BEST CLIMATE AND SITE: Zones 5–9. Full sun.

IDEAL SOIL CONDITIONS: Any soil with slightly acid pH (6.0–6.7).

GROWING GUIDELINES: Sow seed shallowly in spring, then thin to 6 inches (15 cm); transplants poorly. Weedy and hard to control, dock thrives despite neglect. Control its growth to prevent a future weed problem.

GROWING HABIT: Perennial; height 1–4 feet (30–120 cm); resembles garden rhubarb with long, lance-shaped, wavy leaves growing from a central point.

FLOWERING TIME: June to August; small greenish-yellow flowers in spreading panicles.

PEST AND DISEASE PREVENTION: Usually free from pests and diseases.

HARVESTING AND STORING: Dig roots in spring or fall; clean and slice them before drying in the sun or artificially. Store in a tightly sealed container. Use an infusion of dried, ground dock as a laxative, astringent tonic, and to treat skin problems.

SPECIAL TIPS: Grow sorrel, a cultivated cousin, for culinary uses (see the Sorrel entry on page 147).

Inula helenium   Compositae   *Eucalyptus* spp.   Myrtaceae

ELECAMPANE

EUCALYPT

Otherwise known as wild sunflower, elecampane is a tall perennial with hairy stems and bright yellow ray flowers.

BEST CLIMATE AND SITE: Zones 4–9. Full sun to light shade.

IDEAL SOIL CONDITIONS: Moderately fertile, moist soil; pH 6.5–7.0.

GROWING GUIDELINES: Sow seed outdoors in spring, or collect root cuttings from mature plants in fall; winter them indoors in pots, setting plants out in the garden the following spring after danger of frost.

GROWING HABIT: Height 4–6 feet (120–180 cm); branched perennial with large, elliptical basal leaves and smaller, oblong top leaves.

FLOWERING TIME: Summer months; sunflower-like yellow flowers 3–4 inches (7–10 cm) across.

PEST AND DISEASE PREVENTION: Watch for plant bugs that suck the juices from leaves. Control them with a botanical insecticide like pyrethrin or rotenone.

HARVESTING AND STORING: Collect roots for medicinal and culinary use in fall of the plant's second season, after several hard frosts. Dry them thoroughly before storing. Traditionally used as a remedy for chest ailments, the roots can also be candied and eaten as a sweet, or used as a flavoring for sweets.

OTHER COMMON NAMES: Wild sunflower, scabwort, velvet dock.

Eucalypts are evergreen trees well known for their pungent scent and silvery leaves.

BEST CLIMATE AND SITE: Zones 8–10. Full sun.

IDEAL SOIL CONDITIONS: Light loamy soils; tolerates wide range of soil pH.

GROWING GUIDELINES: Best to purchase young, potted trees.

GROWING HABIT: Over 500 species ranging from 5-foot (1.5 m) shrubs to 500-foot (150 m) trees. The blue gum is best known, with smooth blue-gray bark and silvery blue leathery leaves, both of which have a camphor-like fragrance.

FLOWERING TIME: Depends on species; most with umbel-like groups of flowers near leaf axils in white, cream, pink, yellow, orange, or red.

PEST AND DISEASE PREVENTION: Few severe pest problems.

HARVESTING AND STORING: Leaves, branches, and seedpods dry quickly for craft uses; oils are extracted from some species for medicinal and industrial use.

| *Foeniculum vulgare* | Umbelliferae | *Trigonella foenum-graecum* | Leguminosae |

FENNEL

FENUGREEK

Grow licorice-scented fennel as a tall ornamental in the flower garden, and for its culinary properties in the kitchen. Both leaves and seeds are used.

BEST CLIMATE AND SITE: Zones 6–9. Full sun.

IDEAL SOIL CONDITIONS: Humusy, well-drained soil; pH 6.0–6.7.

GROWING GUIDELINES: Sow seed shallowly outdoors in spring or fall and keep moist; thin to 6 inches (15 cm); transplants poorly.

GROWING HABIT: Semi-hardy perennial usually grown as an annual; height to 4 feet (1.2 m); leaves feathery, blue-green color.

FLOWERING TIME: July to October; small yellow flowers in umbels.

PEST AND DISEASE PREVENTION: Usually free from pests and diseases.

HARVESTING AND STORING: Snip leaves before blooming for fresh use; leaves can also be frozen. Collect seeds when dry but before they shatter, and dry them on paper.

SPECIAL TIPS: Fennel's delicate flavor is destroyed by heat, so add at the end of the recipe. Try the bronze-colored variety for foliage contrast outdoors, and on the dinner plate as a garnish.

Fenugreek is a member of the same family as beans and clover. The seeds are used as a substitute for maple flavoring in baked goods and to make a laxative tea.

BEST CLIMATE AND SITE: Zones 6–10. Full sun.

IDEAL SOIL CONDITIONS: Rich soil; pH 6.0–7.0.

GROWING GUIDELINES: When springtime soil temperatures reach 60°F (15°C), sow a thick band of seed outdoors, covering shallowly. Avoid growing in cold, wet soils since seeds will rot before germinating.

GROWING HABIT: Annual; height 1–2 feet (30–60 cm); clover-like stems and leaves.

FLOWERING TIME: Midsummer; white flowers that resemble garden pea blossoms.

PEST AND DISEASE PREVENTION: Handpick snails from new growth.

HARVESTING AND STORING: Harvest pods when ripe but before they shatter, like garden beans; leave seeds in the sun to dry, then store in an airtight container.

SPECIAL TIPS: Steep the seeds in boiling water and strain, for a substitute for maple syrup.

OTHER COMMON NAMES: Bird's foot, Greek hayseed.

FEVERFEW

Double-flowered feverfew makes an attractive border plant. Folklore states that it repels undesirable insects from the garden.

BEST CLIMATE AND SITE: Zones 5–7. Full sun to partial shade.

IDEAL SOIL CONDITIONS: Well-drained garden soil; pH 6.0–6.7.

GROWING GUIDELINES: Sow seed shallowly in late winter indoors, then transplant outdoors 9–12 inches (23–30 cm) apart 2 weeks after danger of frost; in mild areas, sow directly outdoors when danger of frost is past. Divide mature plants or take cuttings in spring or fall. Avoid planting in wet areas; for vigorous plants, pinch blossoms before seeds set; side-dress with compost or rotted manure in early spring.

GROWING HABIT: Biennial or perennial; height 2–3 feet (60–90 cm); erect stems and foliage resemble chamomile.

FLOWERING TIME: Midsummer to fall; daisy-like white rays with yellow center.

PEST AND DISEASE PREVENTION: Usually free from pests and diseases.

HARVESTING AND STORING: Cut and dry stems at full bloom for arrangements.

SPECIAL TIPS: Also known as *Matricaria parthenium; Tanacetum parthenium.*

GARLIC

Garlic is one of the most familiar herbs, used to flavor dishes from almost every ethnic group.

BEST CLIMATE AND SITE: Zones 5–10. Full sun to partial shade.

IDEAL SOIL CONDITIONS: Humusy, deep, well-drained soil; pH 4.5–8.3.

GROWING GUIDELINES: Separate individual cloves from the bulb immediately before planting, then plant, root down, in October for harvesting the following summer; space 6 inches (15 cm) apart and 2 inches (5 cm) deep. For largest bulbs, prune away flower stalks (or scapes) that shoot up in early summer; side-dress with compost in early spring; avoid planting after heavy applications of fresh manure.

GROWING HABIT: Biennial or perennial; height to 2 feet (60 cm); foliage resembles onions, iris, or tulips, depending on variety.

FLOWERING TIME: Early summer; small, white to pinkish blooms atop a tall, central stalk.

PEST AND DISEASE PREVENTION: Avoid wet soil to prevent bulb diseases.

HARVESTING AND STORING: Dig bulbs after tops have died down, and before bulb skins begin to decay underground; place in a single layer in a shaded spot to dry, then cut away tops leaving a 2-inch (5 cm) stem; or braid together the tops of freshly dug plants. Hang braids or loose bulbs in nets from the ceiling in a cool, humid, dark place.

SPECIAL TIPS: Check with local gardeners for home-grown bulbs that will do best in your area.

Pelargonium spp.   Geraniaceae

GERANIUM, SCENTED

Add the fragrant leaves of rose-scented geraniums to potpourri. The many cultivars offer a variety of flavors and scents.

Apple-scented geranium has an intense scent and, like the rose-scented geranium, is a source of geranium oil.

BEST CLIMATE AND SITE: Perennial in Zone 10, annual in cooler zones. Full sun.

IDEAL SOIL CONDITIONS: Rich, loamy, well-drained soil; pH 6.0–7.0.

GROWING GUIDELINES: Sow seed shallowly indoors 2 months before last frost date; germination is very slow. Grow scented geraniums in the garden as annuals. Cuttings root quickly and easily from new growth in spring or fall; take them in summer for winter blossoms indoors. Grows well in pots near a sunny window. Fertilize with a liquid plant-food, like fish emulsion or compost tea, but hold back on the nitrogen for the best fragrance. Plants more than 1 year old tend to grow poorly; take new cuttings and discard the old plants. Prune away dead foliage regularly.

GROWING HABIT: Height to 3 feet (90 cm), foliage and growth habit vary with species or cultivar; leaves frilly, variegated, ruffled, velvety, or smooth.

FLOWERING TIME: Usually within 3 months of rooting; usually inconspicuous.

PEST AND DISEASE PREVENTION: Vacuum whiteflies from foliage, or control with weekly sprays of insecticidal soap or a botanical insecticide. You can purchase parasitic wasps from suppliers of biological controls to control whiteflies indoors and in the garden. Include sand in potting mixes for good drainage; avoid overwatering.

HARVESTING AND STORING: Pick leaves throughout the summer and dry them, storing in an airtight container, to use in winter potpourris. Use fresh leaves in jellies and tea, or as an aromatic garnish.

OTHER SPECIES:

APPLE-SCENTED GERANIUM (*P. odoratissimum*): Apple-scented; sprawling growth habit; white flowers.

LEMON-SCENTED GERANIUM (*P. crispum*): Woody, lemon-scented plants; height to 3 feet (90 cm); leaves small, three-lobed, with crinkled margins; petals rose or rosy white.

ROSE-SCENTED GERANIUM (*P. graveolens*): Rose-scented; woody; height to 3 feet (90 cm); leaves softly hairy, five- to seven-lobed, toothed; petals rose-colored; also called sweet-scented geranium.

Teucrium chamaedrys Labiatae

GERMANDER

Germander is grown for its boxy ornamental shape, and is well suited to the formal herb garden. The foliage is lightly aromatic and has been traditionally used as a cure for gout, rheumatism, and other ailments.

BEST CLIMATE AND SITE: Zones 5–9. Full sun to partial shade.

IDEAL SOIL CONDITIONS: Well-drained garden soil; pH 6.0–6.7.

GROWING GUIDELINES: Best propagated by cuttings, layering, or division, since seeds require 30 days for germination. Plant 1 foot (30 cm) apart; does well in pots. Germander is called poor man's box, since it can be pruned and trained like a hedge in knot gardens. Protect with mulch or burlap in northern winters.

GROWING HABIT: Perennial; height to 2 feet (60 cm); leaves oval-shaped and hairy.

FLOWERING TIME: July to September; purple to purple-red on stalks.

PEST AND DISEASE PREVENTION: Usually free from pests and diseases.

HARVESTING AND STORING: Harvest the leaves during spring and early summer. Dry and store them in an air-tight container.

OTHER COMMON NAMES: Poor man's box.

Zingiber officinale Zingiberaceae

GINGER

Fresh ginger has a zing that the powdered spice lacks. Grow your own in pots placed outdoors during the warm season. It has the double advantage of being both spicy and kind to your digestive system.

BEST CLIMATE AND SITE: Zones 9–10. Partial shade.

IDEAL SOIL CONDITIONS: Fertile, moist, well-drained garden soil; pH 6.5–7.5.

GROWING GUIDELINES: Plant roots in pots in a mix containing peat, sand, and compost; keep indoors or in a greenhouse in winter, moving the pots outdoors in summer. Thrives in low ground in the tropics and subtropics.

GROWING HABIT: Tender perennial; height 2–4 feet (60–120 cm); leaves grass-like, 6–12 inches (15–30 cm) long.

FLOWERING TIME: Rarely flowers under cultivation; in the wild, dense cone-like spikes on a stalk have yellow-green flowers.

PEST AND DISEASE PREVENTION: Usually free from pests and diseases. For healthy growth, water well during the hot, summer months.

HARVESTING AND STORING: Pull plant after 1 year and remove leaf stalks, cutting away as much root as you need; replant the remaining root. Refrigerate harvested roots wrapped in paper toweling inside a plastic bag, for up to 1 month. Or dry shaved bits of root and store in an air-tight container.

Solidago spp.   Compositae   _Humulus lupulus_   Cannabaceae

GOLDENROD   # HOP

Look for over 130 species of goldenrod, some of which have medicinal properties, growing wild in open fields and along roadsides. Use the dried flowers for flower arrangements or to make a yellow dye.

A pillow stuffed with hops is said to relieve toothache and earache, and cure nervous conditions. Hop is an attractive vining perennial for arbors and screens, as well as an essential ingredient in beer.

BEST CLIMATE AND SITE: Zones 4–9. Full sun.

IDEAL SOIL CONDITIONS: Average to poor, well-drained garden soil; pH 5.5–7.0.

GROWING GUIDELINES: Easily grows from seed sown in early spring, or purchase plants from nurseries. Divide mature plants in spring or fall. Quickly becomes weedy if the soil is too rich, so hold off on the nitrogen.

GROWING HABIT: Height 3–7 feet (90–210 cm); unbranched perennial with simple leaves.

FLOWERING TIME: August to September; yellow blossoms the second year.

PEST AND DISEASE PREVENTION: Usually free from pests and diseases.

HARVESTING AND STORING: Collect foliage when flowering, and dry in bunches or on screens; quickly turns black without adequate air circulation. Store in air-tight containers. Use the leaves to make a tea to treat flatulence.

BEST CLIMATE AND SITE: Zones 3–7; will stand temperatures as low as –35°F (–37°C). Full sun.

IDEAL SOIL CONDITIONS: Well-fertilized, deep, rich soil; pH 6.0–7.0.

GROWING GUIDELINES: Take cuttings from perennial underground stems 1 year before planting out, then plant in clumps of three to five plants spaced 6 inches (15 cm) apart. Place poles for vines at the base of plants before growth begins; in fall, remove both poles and old growth. Dig in fresh compost or rotted manure each spring. Seeds are slow to germinate and grow so are not good for propagation.

GROWING HABIT: Height 20–30 feet (6–9 m) in one season; prickly, vining stems with dark green, lobed, grape-like leaves.

FLOWERING TIME: Mid- to late summer; bears male and female flowers on separate plants the third year; female flowers resemble cones.

PEST AND DISEASE PREVENTION: Encourage beneficial insects; control aphids and mites with strong water spray. Kill pests with insecticidal soap or a botanical insecticide like pyrethrin or rotenone. Spray or dust with sulfur to prevent fungal disease.

HARVESTING AND STORING: Collect female "cones" when they are brown- to amber-colored and immediately dry them in an oven at 125–150°F (50–65°C). Does not store well, so use promptly.

Marrubium vulgare   Labiatae

HOREHOUND

Plant this ornamental to attract bees to your garden. The menthol-flavored leaves are said to soothe coughs when taken as a syrup or decoction.

BEST CLIMATE AND SITE: Zones 4–8. Full sun to partial shade.

IDEAL SOIL CONDITIONS: Deep, well-drained garden soil; pH 6.7–7.3.

GROWING GUIDELINES: Sow seed ⅛ inch (3 mm) deep in early spring, thinning to 10–20 inches (25–50 cm). Horehound germinates slowly, then grows easily. Divide mature plants in early spring. Plant in a well-drained location, since horehound will die in winter in a damp soil.

GROWING HABIT: Perennial; height 2–3 feet (60–90 cm); branching, square stems with round, wooly leaves.

FLOWERING TIME: June to September; white blooms in dense whorls are produced at stem and leaf axils the second year.

PEST AND DISEASE PREVENTION: Usually free from pests and diseases.

HARVESTING AND STORING: The first year, cut foliage sparingly. The second year, harvest leaves at budding, chop and dry them, then store in air-tight containers.

PRECAUTIONS: Causes irregular heartbeat if over-used internally.

OTHER COMMON NAMES: White horehound.

Armoracia rusticana   Cruciferae

HORSERADISH

Horseradish is the white perennial root of a weedy herb. Folklore claims that horseradish should be planted near potatoes to protect them from disease.

BEST CLIMATE AND SITE: Zones 5–8. Full sun.

IDEAL SOIL CONDITIONS: Heavy, rich, moist soil; pH 6.0–7.0.

GROWING GUIDELINES: Plant straight, young roots 8–9 inches (20–22.5 cm) long and ½ inch (1 cm) wide so that crown or growing point is 3–5 inches (7.5–12.5 cm) below the soil surface, and plants are 12–18 inches (30–45 cm) apart. Plant at an angle to the horizontal. Till 18–24 inches (45–60 cm) deep before planting for easier harvest, adding plenty of compost or rotted manure. Replant after two seasons, removing the old roots to prevent volunteers.

GROWING HABIT: Second-year plants grow 2–3 feet (60–90 cm) tall; leaves are stalked and oblong.

FLOWERING TIME: Midsummer; small, white blossoms do not produce viable seed.

PEST AND DISEASE PREVENTION: Usually free from pests and diseases.

HARVESTING AND STORING: Harvest roots in late October or November, and scrub them before storing in the refrigerator, or pack in dry sand in the cellar for spring planting. Or leave roots in the soil and harvest the following spring.

SPECIAL TIPS: Harvest early for the most tender roots.

OTHER COMMON NAMES: Mountain radish.

| *Equisetum* spp. | Equisetaceae | *Hyssopus officinalis* | Labiatae |

HORSETAIL

HYSSOP

A primitive, spore-bearing, grass-like plant containing silica, horsetail has often been used as a pot-scrubber and for sanding wood. Look for it along low-lying edges of woods.

BEST CLIMATE AND SITE: Zones 4–9. Full sun to partial shade.

IDEAL SOIL CONDITIONS: Humusy, moist, or water-logged soils; acid to neutral pH.

GROWING GUIDELINES: Rarely cultivated, since it is difficult to eradicate once established. Plant in buckets in shallow ponds to prevent its spread. Propagate in the fall by division of mature plants.

GROWING HABIT: Perennial; height 4–18 inches (10–45 cm); primitive spore-bearing herbs, with hollow stems impregnated with silica.

FLOWERING TIME: April; spikes form atop stalks, and terminal cone-like structures release spores.

PEST AND DISEASE PREVENTION: Usually free from pests and diseases.

HARVESTING AND STORING: Cut stems just above the root, dry in the sun, and tie in bundles.

SPECIAL TIPS: Dried stems are said to act as a garden fungicide; steep the stems in warm water, strain, and spray on plants outdoors.

PRECAUTIONS: Horsetail is toxic when large doses are taken internally.

OTHER COMMON NAMES: Bottle brush, scouring rush.

The blossoms of this evergreen, shrubby plant attract honeybees and hummingbirds. The leaves add a minty aroma and flavor to salads and soups.

BEST CLIMATE AND SITE: Zones 3–9. Prefers full sun or partial shade.

IDEAL SOIL CONDITIONS: Light, well-drained soil; pH 6.0–7.0.

GROWING GUIDELINES: Sow seed ¼ inch (5 mm) deep in early spring, thinning to 1 foot (30 cm). Take cuttings or divide mature plants in spring or fall. Prune to 6 inches (15 cm) in spring and replenish the soil with fish emulsion or compost. Replace every 4–5 years.

GROWING HABIT: Height 1–2 feet (30–60 cm).

FLOWERING TIME: June to August; blue or violet, in whorls along the stem tops.

PEST AND DISEASE PREVENTION: Usually free from pests and diseases.

HARVESTING AND STORING: For medicinal use, harvest only green material and cut stems just before flowers open and hang bunches to dry; store in an air-tight container.

SPECIAL TIPS: Excellent border plant in knot gardens.

Galium verum   Rubiaceae

LADY'S BEDSTRAW

Lady's bedstraw needs little attention and readily spreads by seed. It is often grown as an ornamental. Herbalists seal the dried foliage in pillows that release a sleep-inducing scent when rested upon.

BEST CLIMATE AND SITE: Zones 3–7. Full sun to light shade.

IDEAL SOIL CONDITIONS: Deep, light, well-drained soil; pH 6.7–7.3.

GROWING GUIDELINES: Sow seed shallowly in spring or divide roots of mature plants; plant 2 feet (60 cm) apart. Self-sows; requires little attention.

GROWING HABIT: Height to 3 feet (90 cm); hardy perennial with slightly branched square stems and linear leaves.

FLOWERING TIME: July to August; small, bright yellow blossoms.

PEST AND DISEASE PREVENTION: Usually free from pests and diseases.

HARVESTING AND STORING: Harvest foliage and hang in small bunches for quick drying.

OTHER COMMON NAMES: Our Lady's bedstraw, maid's hair, cheese rennet.

Lavandula angustifolia   Labiatae

LAVENDER, ENGLISH

Most herb growers never have enough lavender, since this aromatic garden ornamental is also useful for crafts and cosmetics. The silvery foliage and purple blossoms are stunning in borders, and the blossoms attract bees.

BEST CLIMATE AND SITE: Zones 5–8. Full sun.

IDEAL SOIL CONDITIONS: Light, well-drained soil; pH 6.7–7.3.

GROWING GUIDELINES: As seeds do not always produce plants identical to the original, the best way to propagate is with cuttings 2–3 inches (5–7 cm) long taken from sideshoots in spring or fall; space 12–30 inches (30–75 cm) apart. Pinch away flowers on first-year plants to encourage vigorous growth. Provide shelter from winter winds; hardiness varies with species. Some growers find that plants weaken with age, requiring replacement every 5 years. Remove old plants each spring, and rejuvenate the soil with compost or well-aged manure before planting new, young plants.

GROWING HABIT: Perennial; height 2–3 feet (60–90 cm); shrubby with slender gray-green leaves.

FLOWERING TIME: June to July; lavender blossoms on tall spikes.

PEST AND DISEASE PREVENTION: Soils with plenty of sand will prevent waterlogging and discourage fungal diseases; handpick caterpillar pests, or spray with BT if populations are heavy.

HARVESTING AND STORING: Harvest foliage after the first year; pick flower spikes in the early blossom stage during dry weather. Hang in bunches away from sunlight.

LEMON BALM

French lavender has attractive, fern-like leaves and makes an interesting and fragrant pot plant.

Lemon balm has a fragrance much like lemon-flavored candy. Both foliage and flowers are attractive in flower beds.

OTHER SPECIES:

FRENCH LAVENDER (*L. dentata*): Less hardy than English lavender. Zones 8–9.

ITALIAN or SPANISH LAVENDER (*L. latifolia*): Produces more oil of lesser quality than English lavender; also called spike lavender.

BEST CLIMATE AND SITE: Zones 4–9. Full sun to partial shade.

IDEAL SOIL CONDITIONS: Any sandy, well-drained soil; pH 6.7–7.3.

GROWING GUIDELINES: Sow shallowly in spring, thinning to 18–24 inches (45–60 cm); readily self-sows. Take cuttings or divide older plants in spring or fall. Each fall, cut away old stalks.

GROWING HABIT: Perennial; height 1–2 feet (30–60 cm); stems square, branching, with oval, toothed, fragrant leaves.

FLOWERING TIME: June to October; greenish or white blossoms in bunches at leaf axils.

PEST AND DISEASE PREVENTION: Thin dense plantings for best air circulation, to prevent powdery mildew. Rarely bothered by insects.

HARVESTING AND STORING: Collect leaves in late summer and dry quickly to prevent them from turning black. Cut the entire plant, leaving about 2 inches (5 cm) of stem. Use leaves fresh in salads and for cooking, or dry them for making tea.

SPECIAL TIPS: The leaves lowest on the plant are said to be highest in essential oils. Lemon balm is said to repel insect pests.

OTHER COMMON NAMES: Sweet balm, bee balm.

Oil from Italian lavender is sometimes mixed with higher-quality lavender oil.

Cymbopogon citratus   Annonaceae   *Aloysia triphylla*   Verbenaceae

LEMONGRASS

LEMON VERBENA

Grassy foliage provides contrast with broad-leaved garden herbs. Use the dried foliage for teas, or add it to potpourri.

Grown for its strong lemon aroma and flavor used in teas and cosmetics, lemon verbena is well worth the extra care required.

BEST CLIMATE AND SITE: Zones 9–10. Full sun to partial shade.

IDEAL SOIL CONDITIONS: Well-drained garden soil enriched with organic matter; pH 6.5–7.3.

GROWING GUIDELINES: Propagate by division of older plants. Grow in pots in areas cooler than Zone 9, setting outdoors in a protected spot during summer. Trim the leaves to several inches before dividing.

GROWING HABIT: Tender perennial; height to 6 feet (1.8 m); forms dense clumps of grass-like leaves.

FLOWERING TIME: Seldom flowers.

PEST AND DISEASE PREVENTION: Usually free from pests and diseases.

HARVESTING AND STORING: Snip fresh foliage as needed. Harvest foliage anytime in summer; dry quickly for best flavor.

SPECIAL TIPS: Cultivated in Florida for its lemon-scented oil.

OTHER COMMON NAMES: Fevergrass, West Indian lemon.

BEST CLIMATE AND SITE: Zones 9–10. Full sun.

IDEAL SOIL CONDITIONS: Rich, moist garden soil; pH 6.0–6.7.

GROWING GUIDELINES: In cold climates, grow in pots placed outdoors in summer and indoors in winter. Keep the soil moist but not soggy; fertilize lightly with fish emulsion regularly, since lemon verbena is a heavy feeder. Pinch tips to encourage bushy growth. In fall, prune away old branches before bringing pots indoors; overwinter in a greenhouse kept at 55°F (13°C). Or cut back and store in a cool basement, watering infrequently.

GROWING HABIT: Height 5–10 feet (1.5–3 m); tender, perennial, deciduous, woody shrub with light green lance-like leaves in whorls.

FLOWERING TIME: Late summer to fall; tiny white to lavender blossoms on spikes from leaf axils.

PEST AND DISEASE PREVENTION: Wash mites from foliage with a spray of water directed at the undersides of leaves. For stubborn infestations, wipe infected areas with cotton soaked in alcohol, or spray with a botanical insecticide, like citrus oil, pyrethrin, or rotenone.

HARVESTING AND STORING: Snip sprigs of leaves all year. Or cut foliage back halfway in midsummer and again in fall. Dry foliage in a shady spot; store in an air-tight container.

SPECIAL TIPS: Can be trained as a standard.

Levisticum officinale Umbelliferae	*Catharanthus roseus* Apocynaceae

LOVAGE

MADAGASCAR PERIWINKLE

If you are unsuccessful growing celery, try this easy and flavorful substitute.

BEST CLIMATE AND SITE: Zones 5–8. Prefers full sun to partial shade.

IDEAL SOIL CONDITIONS: Fertile, moist, well-drained soil; pH 6.0–7.0.

GROWING GUIDELINES: Sow ripe seed shallowly in late summer or early fall; thin to 2–3 feet (60–90 cm) apart. Prune away flowers to encourage vegetative growth. Each spring, replenish the soil with compost or well-rotted manure. Replace plants every 4–5 years.

GROWING HABIT: Perennial; height to 6 feet (1.8 m); hollow, ribbed stems; glossy, dark green leaves.

FLOWERING TIME: June to July; tiny greenish yellow flowers in umbels.

PEST AND DISEASE PREVENTION: Watch for leafminers (small maggots that tunnel just under the leaf surface) and prune away infested foliage.

HARVESTING AND STORING: Once established, harvest leaves as needed for fresh use. In fall, bunch foliage and stems and hang to dry. Or blanch small bunches before freezing for winter use. Seeds are ripe and ready to harvest when the fruits begin to pop open. Dig roots in late fall, wash and slice into ½-inch (1 cm) pieces, and dry before storing.

SPECIAL TIPS: Sow seed thickly, as germination tends to be poor.

This tender perennial is often grown as a flowering annual. Grow this ornamental outdoors, or indoors in pots.

BEST CLIMATE AND SITE: Zones 9–10. Full sun to partial shade.

IDEAL SOIL CONDITIONS: Well-drained soil; pH 6.0–7.0.

GROWING GUIDELINES: Propagate by seed sown shallowly indoors several months before last frost date; plant outdoors after danger of frost; space at 10–12 inches (25–30 cm). In cool climates, bring potted plants indoors to overwinter. Pinch tops for best growth and shape.

GROWING HABIT: Height to 2 feet (60 cm); glossy evergreen leaves on a compact plant.

FLOWERING TIME: May to October; rosy pink to white blossoms.

PEST AND DISEASE PREVENTION: Usually free from pests and diseases.

HARVESTING AND STORAGE: Poisonous; use only as an ornamental.

Rubia tinctorum   Rubiaceae

MADDER

Madder needs space to sprawl, but will climb if planted beside a wooden fence.

BEST CLIMATE AND SITE: Zones 7–9. Thrives in full sun.

IDEAL SOIL CONDITIONS: Deep, well-drained soil; pH 6.7–7.0.

GROWING GUIDELINES: Sow seed shallowly indoors in spring, and set out in late spring or early fall 1 foot (30 cm) apart. New plants will spring up from roots.

GROWING HABIT: Perennial; height to 4 feet (1.2 m); reddish brown succulent root, with weak stems that lie along the ground.

FLOWERING TIME: June; loose spikes of green-white, starry flowers in second or third year.

PEST AND DISEASE PREVENTION: Usually free from pests and diseases.

HARVESTING AND STORING: Dig the roots of 2- to 3-year-old plants after flowering, or after growth slows in fall; use the roots fresh or dry to make red or orange dye. Madder root has also been used medicinally as a diuretic.

OTHER COMMON NAMES: Dyer's madder.

Origanum majorana   Labiatae

MARJORAM, SWEET

Some herb growers find this bushy aromatic plant with lush foliage an easy-to-grow substitute for oregano.

BEST CLIMATE AND SITE: Zones 9–10. Full sun.

IDEAL SOIL CONDITIONS: Light, well-drained soil; pH 6.7–7.0.

GROWING GUIDELINES: Sow seed shallowly indoors in spring; germinates slowly. Set plants out after danger of frost, spacing clumps of several plants 6–12 inches (15–30 cm) apart. Cut back severely just before blooming, to maintain vegetative growth. In fall divide roots and bring indoors in pots to a cool location, replanting outdoors in early spring.

GROWING HABIT: Height to 2 feet (60 cm); bushy, tender perennial.

FLOWERING TIME: August to September; white or pink blossoms.

PEST AND DISEASE PREVENTION: Usually free from pests and diseases.

HARVESTING AND STORING: Cut fresh leaves as needed for cooking; hang small bunches to dry, then store in air-tight containers.

OTHER COMMON NAMES: Annual marjoram, knotted marjoram.

Althaea officinalis   Malvaceae

MARSH MALLOW

Use leaves to add a fresh flavor to salads, or slice and cook the roots like potatoes. The roots were originally used to produce the consistency typical of the confection marshmallow.

BEST CLIMATE AND SITE: Zones 5–8. Full sun.

IDEAL SOIL CONDITIONS: Light soil that stays damp; pH 6.0–8.0.

GROWING GUIDELINES: Sow seed shallowly outdoors in spring, thinning to 2 feet (60 cm); divide rhizomes or take cuttings from foliage or roots in the fall.

GROWING HABIT: Height 4–5 feet (1.2–1.5 m); perennial roots; soft, gray, velvety foliage dies down in fall.

FLOWERING TIME: August to September; pink or white blossoms followed by circular seedpods called "cheeses."

PEST AND DISEASE PREVENTION: Usually free from pests and diseases.

HARVESTING AND STORING: Harvest leaves in fall just before flowering. Collect and dry flowers at their peak. Dig taproots in fall from plants at least 2 years old, scrub them, and cook them like potatoes or slice before drying.

OTHER COMMON NAMES: White mallow.

Mentha spp.   Labiatae

MINT

The mints are attractive perennials that thrive in most locations. Fresh and dried foliage provide flavoring for both sweet and savory dishes.

BEST CLIMATE AND SITE: Zones 5–9. Full sun or partial shade.

IDEAL SOIL CONDITIONS: Rich, moist, well-drained soil; pH 6.0–7.0.

GROWING GUIDELINES: Propagate from new plants that spring up along roots, or by cuttings in spring or fall. Allow 12–18 inches (30–45 cm) between plants. Mint is a rampant spreader. To control, plant in bottomless cans 10 inches (25 cm) deep, or in pots placed on cement. Cut frequently and severely, or the plant becomes woody after several years. Large areas can be mowed frequently, like lawns. Top-dress with compost or well-rotted manure in fall.

GROWING HABIT: Height to 30 inches (75 cm); square stems with smooth lance-like leaves.

FLOWERING TIME: July to August; tiny purple or pink blossoms in whorls on spikes.

PEST AND DISEASE PREVENTION: Thin crowded clumps for good air circulation to prevent root and foliage diseases. Watch for aphids, which stipple leaves; control them with a strong spray of water or with a botanical insecticide, like pyrethrin or rotenone.

HARVESTING AND STORING: Harvest fresh leaves as needed. Just before blooming, cut the stalks and hang in bunches to dry; store in air-tight containers.

MINT—*Continued*

MUGWORT

Eau-de-cologne mint has the sweetest-smelling scent and is the mint most often used in perfumes and soaps. This mint also makes a pleasant, citrusy tea.

SPECIAL TIPS: Mints are said to do well when planted where water drips, such as near outdoor faucets that are used often in summer.

SPECIES:

APPLE MINT (*M. suaveolens*): Apple-scented, round, and hairy leaves; a variegated cultivar is sometimes called pineapple mint.

CORSICAN MINT (*M. requienii*): Creeping growth habit, good as a groundcover but less hardy than most mints; tiny, bright green leaves with a strong peppermint flavor; also called crème-de-menthe plant, or menthella.

EAU-DE-COLOGNE MINT (*M. x piperita* var. *citrata*): Crushed leaves give off lemony aroma; also called bergamot mint or lemon mint.

JAPANESE MINT (*M. arvensis* var. *piperescens*): Large, green leaves with hairy stems and strong peppermint flavor; major source of menthol in Japan; also called field mint.

PEPPERMINT (*M. x piperita*): Leaves smooth, lance-like; smooth, purple stems; height 2–4 feet (60–120 cm); strong peppermint flavor; rampant grower; likes lots of water; rarely bears fertile seeds; must be started by cuttings or division; also called brandy mint.

SPEARMINT (*M. spicata*): Lance-shaped, serrated leaves with spearmint flavor.

Mugwort is an attractive ornamental both in the garden and as part of dried arrangements or for making wreaths. The leaves have a sage-like smell and are said to repel insects.

BEST CLIMATE AND SITE: Zones 4–9. Full sun.

IDEAL SOIL CONDITIONS: Well-drained garden soil enriched with organic matter; pH 6.0–7.0.

GROWING GUIDELINES: Sow seed shallowly indoors at 55°F (13°C), then transfer outdoors after danger of frost. In spring or fall, divide older plants.

GROWING HABIT: Perennial; height 3–6 feet (90–180 cm); purple stem with deeply cut dark green leaves, soft and cottony below.

FLOWERING TIME: Late summer; reddish brown or yellow ball-shaped flower heads in panicles.

PEST AND DISEASE PREVENTION: Usually free from pests and diseases.

HARVESTING AND STORING: Collect leaves in August; dry in shade; store in air-tight containers.

PRECAUTIONS: Unsafe when taken internally.

OTHER COMMON NAMES: St. John's plant, felon herb.

| *Brassica* spp. | Cruciferae | *Tropaeolum majus* | Tropaeolaceae |

MUSTARD

NASTURTIUM

Most mustards are annuals or biennials. Some are "winter annuals" that remain green even when buried in snow.

Nasturtiums are a favorite of both gardeners and chefs. The blossoms are a reliable source of color all summer long.

BEST CLIMATE AND SITE: Zones 2–9. Full sun.

IDEAL SOIL CONDITIONS: Rich, well-drained soil; pH 4.2–6.0.

GROWING GUIDELINES: Easily grows from seed sown shallowly outdoors from early spring until fall; thin to 9 inches (23 cm). Self-sows. Prepare beds with compost or well-rotted manure, but avoid excessive applications of manure, as this could damage the roots.

GROWING HABIT: Very hardy; height 4–6 feet (1.2–1.8 m); leaves various shapes.

FLOWERING TIME: Early summer; four-petaled greenish flowers in terminal racemes.

PEST AND DISEASE PREVENTION: Attracts the same pests as its close relatives in the cabbage family. Cover with fabric row covers at planting for pest prevention, removing them when the plant flowers. Spray or dust with BT to control common caterpillar pests in summer.

HARVESTING AND STORING: Collect and dry seeds when ripe.

SPECIES:

BLACK MUSTARD (*B. nigra*): Much-branched annual; height to 6 feet (1.8 m); cultivated as the main source of pungent table mustard.

WHITE MUSTARD (*B. hirta*): Annual; height to 4 feet (1.2 m); cultivated for greens, and mustard- and oil-producing seeds.

BEST CLIMATE AND SITE: Zones 3–9. Blooms best in full sun.

IDEAL SOIL CONDITIONS: Average, moist, well-drained, nutrient-poor soil; pH 6.0–8.0.

GROWING GUIDELINES: Sow seed outdoors ½–¾ inch (1–2 cm) deep as soon as soil is warm in spring; thin plants to 6–9 inches (15–23 cm). For bushels of blooms, hold back the nitrogen. Also does well as a potted annual. Nasturtiums often survive several light frosts in fall.

GROWING HABIT: Annual; height 1–2 feet (30–60 cm), or a low-growing 6-foot (1.8 m) vine; leaves umbrella-like.

FLOWERING TIME: Summer; a rainbow of funnel-shaped, sweet-smelling blossoms.

PEST AND DISEASE PREVENTION: Wash away aphids with a spray of water. For persistent populations, spray with insecticidal soap.

HARVESTING AND STORING: Snip young, fresh leaves and blossoms all summer as needed for salads. In fall, pickle the unopened buds for a homemade version of capers.

SPECIAL TIPS: Look for dwarf, vining, and variegated types in seed catalogs.

OTHER COMMON NAMES: Indian cress.

Urtica dioica   Urticaceae

NETTLE

A noxious pest to farmers, nettle is high in vitamin C and is used by practitioners of homeopathic medicine. The fibers have been used to make cloth.

BEST CLIMATE AND SITE: Zones 5–9. Full sun to partial shade.

IDEAL SOIL CONDITIONS: Most garden soil; pH 5.0–8.0.

GROWING GUIDELINES: Sow seed shallowly outdoors in early spring; self-sows readily. Nettle is a common garden weed that quickly multiplies.

GROWING HABIT: Hardy perennial; height 2–6 feet (60–180 cm); whole plant has stinging hairs.

FLOWERING TIME: June to September; greenish male flowers in loose sprays; female flowers more densely clustered together.

PEST AND DISEASE PREVENTION: Usually free from pests and diseases.

HARVESTING AND STORING: Harvest whole plant above the root, just before flowering; hang in bunches to dry. Cook fresh greens like spinach. Collect seeds and dry on paper. Wear heavy gloves when harvesting, since the hairs will cause skin to swell and sting for several hours.

PRECAUTIONS: Avoid skin contact with stinging hairs. Rub dock leaves onto stings to soothe them.

OTHER COMMON NAMES: Stinging nettle.

Ceanothus americanus   Rhamnaceae

NEW JERSEY TEA

This plant has small, sparse leaves, small white flowers, and seedpods resembling acorns with horns. An astringent tea made from the leaves has been used as a gargle for sore throats.

BEST CLIMATE AND SITE: Zones 4–8. Full sun to partial shade.

IDEAL SOIL CONDITIONS: Light, well-drained soil; pH 6.0–7.0.

GROWING GUIDELINES: Snip cuttings from new growth in spring or fall. The roots are tough and difficult to divide. Plants tend to be short-lived and may need replacement every few years. Prune severely each winter to control growth.

GROWING HABIT: Height 2–3 feet (60–90 cm); straggly, deciduous shrubs with downy, dark green leaves.

FLOWERING TIME: September; small white blossoms on long stalks.

PEST AND DISEASE PREVENTION: Usually free from pests and diseases.

HARVESTING AND STORING: Collect leaves anytime; use fresh or dried for tea.

OTHER COMMON NAMES: Redroot, mountain-sweet, wild snowball.

Origanum vulgare Labiatae

OREGANO

Experiment with several types to find the flavor you like most. Sprigs with small, rounded leaves and miniature blossoms make an attractive garnish.

BEST CLIMATE AND SITE: Zones 5–9. Full sun to light shade.

IDEAL SOIL CONDITIONS: Well-drained, average garden soil; pH 6.0–7.0.

GROWING GUIDELINES: Sow seed shallowly indoors in winter for best germination; sow outdoors if soil temperature is above 45°F (7°C). Plant in clumps 1 foot (30 cm) apart. Prune regularly for best shape. Since seedlings will not always produce the same flavor as the original plants, take cuttings or divide roots in early spring or fall for best results. Replenish the soil each spring with compost or well-rotted manure. Some varieties may not overwinter outdoors in cold climates.

GROWING HABIT: Perennial; height 12–30 inches (30–75 cm); herbaceous and shrubby.

FLOWERING TIME: July to September; tubular, rose to white blossoms.

PEST AND DISEASE PREVENTION: Plant in sandy soil to provide drainage and prevent root diseases. Wash away mites and aphids with a spray of water; spray with a botanical insecticide, like pyrethrin, for stubborn infestations.

HARVESTING AND STORING: Snip fresh sprigs as needed all summer; cut whole plant in June and again in late August; hang foliage in bunches to dry.

OTHER COMMON NAMES: Wild marjoram, pot marjoram.

Iris x *germanica* var. *florentina* Iridaceae

ORRIS

A fan-like spray of green blade-like leaves sprouts from an aromatic root. The dried root may be used as a fixative for potpourri and has a strong violet fragrance.

BEST CLIMATE AND SITE: Zones 5–7. Full sun.

IDEAL SOIL CONDITIONS: Deep, rich, well-drained soil; pH 6.7–7.3.

GROWING GUIDELINES: Plant rhizomes in early spring, leaving half of each rhizome above the surface to prevent rot. Divide every 3 years. Takes 2–3 years to reach maturity.

GROWING HABIT: Height to 30 inches (75 cm); perennial with sword-shaped leaves, overlapping at the base.

FLOWERING TIME: May to June; blossoms white with blue or purple.

PEST AND DISEASE PREVENTION: Usually free from pests and diseases.

HARVESTING AND STORING: Harvest the roots at maturity. Wash and split them, then cut or grind into small pieces before drying on paper.

SPECIAL TIPS: The strength of this fixative increases with age.

Petroselinum crispum var. *crispum* Umbelliferae

PARSLEY, CURLED

Kitchen gardens always include parsley, since it is required in so many recipes. The delicate, dark green foliage makes it an excellent plant for borders or growing on windowsills.

BEST CLIMATE AND SITE: Zones 5–9. Full sun to partial shade.

IDEAL SOIL CONDITIONS: Moderately rich, well-drained soil; pH 5.5–6.7.

GROWING GUIDELINES: Sow seed shallowly outdoors in early spring when soil reaches 50°F (10°C), thinning to 8 inches (20 cm) apart; germinates slowly. Or soak seeds overnight in warm water before sowing in peat pots indoors in early spring; transplants poorly. Remove all flower stalks that form, and prune away dead leaves. For productive plants, side-dress with compost in midseason. May survive the winter, but quickly goes to seed in spring. Plants may be grown in pots to bring indoors for winter harvests.

GROWING HABIT: Biennial grown as an annual; height 8–12 inches (20–30 cm); leaves are finely divided, on a long stalk.

FLOWERING TIME: Early spring of second year; tiny, greenish yellow umbels.

PEST AND DISEASE PREVENTION: Follow proper spacing guidelines for best air circulation to prevent diseases. Rarely bothered by insect pests.

HARVESTING AND STORING: Cut leaf stalks at the base for fresh foliage all summer. Hang in bunches to dry in shade, or freeze whole or chopped.

SPECIAL TIPS: Will go to seed prematurely if taproot is damaged during transplanting or weeding.

Passiflora incarnata Passifloraceae

PASSIONFLOWER

This wild, vining perennial with yellow, edible fruit has medicinal uses, but is usually grown as an ornamental for its unusual blossoms.

BEST CLIMATE AND SITE: Zones 7–9. Partial shade.

IDEAL SOIL CONDITIONS: Deep, fertile, well-drained soil; pH 6.0–6.7.

GROWING GUIDELINES: Propagate by seed or cuttings. Freshen the soil each spring by scratching in a new layer of compost. Prune away old growth in winter or early spring.

GROWING HABIT: Height 25–30 feet (7.5–9 m); leaves are finely toothed.

FLOWERING TIME: Early to late summer; sweet-scented, white or lavender petals.

PEST AND DISEASE PREVENTION: Watch for leaf speckling or streaks caused by minute thrips. Control them with a light oil spray during cloudy weather, or spray with insecticidal soap or botanical insecticide, like pyrethrin or rotenone. Avoid planting where parasitic nematodes are a problem.

HARVESTING AND STORING: Collect the fruit in summer when ripe. It is best eaten fresh. The leaves and flowers are used medicinally but should not be taken without professional advice.

OTHER COMMON NAMES: Maypop, apricot vine.

Mentha pulegium   Labiatae   _Chimaphila umbellata_   Pyrolaceae

PENNYROYAL, ENGLISH   # PIPSISSEWA

An attractive and low-maintenance groundcover that has a pleasant, mint-like fragrance and repels insects.

A prostrate evergreen, used for making root beer. Native Americans used pipsissewa as a medicine.

BEST CLIMATE AND SITE: Zones 5–9. Full sun.

IDEAL SOIL CONDITIONS: Moist, loamy garden soil; pH 6.0–7.0.

GROWING GUIDELINES: Sow seed shallowly and thickly outdoors in early spring; thin to 6 inches (15 cm). Or take cuttings from stems, which easily root at joints. Divide old plants in spring or fall.

GROWING HABIT: Perennial; height 1 foot (30 cm); stems prostrate.

FLOWERING TIME: July to August; reddish purple to lilac blossoms in clusters at the nodes.

PEST AND DISEASE PREVENTION: Usually free from pests and diseases; reported to repel insects.

HARVESTING AND STORING: Harvest foliage just before blooming, then hang in bunches to dry; store in an air-tight container.

SPECIAL TIPS: Crush the leaves and rub on your skin to repel insects while you work in the garden.

PRECAUTIONS: Unsafe when taken internally.

OTHER SPECIES:
   AMERICAN PENNYROYAL (_Hedeoma pulegioides_): Height 12–15 inches (30–38 cm); annual; purple-blue flowers; prefers dry soil.

BEST CLIMATE AND SITE: Zones 4–6. Partial shade.

IDEAL SOIL CONDITIONS: Rich but sandy soil; pH 4.8–6.5.

GROWING GUIDELINES: Propagate by division of older plants, or take root cuttings in spring or fall. Slow-grower. Mulch with pine needles to maintain acid pH and soil moisture.

GROWING HABIT: Height to 10 inches (25 cm); low-growing evergreen with thick, glossy leaves.

FLOWERING TIME: May to August; lavender, pink, or white petals in terminal clusters.

PEST AND DISEASE PREVENTION: Usually free from pests and diseases.

HARVESTING AND STORING: Harvest leaves for medicinal and culinary uses in late summer or early fall; store in an air-tight container. Tea made with pipsissewa leaves has a good reputation as a remedy for kidney problems.

OTHER COMMON NAMES: Wintergreen, waxflower, ground holly.

Plantago major Plantaginaceae

PLANTAIN

Plantain is a common weed found in lawns, hay fields, and pastures. Try its tender, young leaves in salads, or steam and eat them like spinach.

BEST CLIMATE AND SITE: Zones 2–9. Full sun to partial shade.

IDEAL SOIL CONDITIONS: Grows in any well-drained soil; pH 5.0–8.0.

GROWING GUIDELINES: Sow seed shallowly outdoors in early spring or fall.

GROWING HABIT: Perennial; height 6–18 inches (15–45 cm); broad leaves grow from a basal rosette.

FLOWERING TIME: June to September; tall spikes with purplish green flowers.

PEST AND DISEASE PREVENTION: Usually free from pests and diseases.

HARVESTING AND STORING: Use fresh leaves in salads, or for medicinal purposes such as treating bee stings and insect bites. Dig roots in fall, scrub them well, and allow to dry until brittle. Chew the root to relieve toothache, or use with the rest of the plant to make a gold or camel-colored dye.

OTHER COMMON NAMES: Waybread, broad-leaved plantain.

Trifolium pratense Leguminosae

RED CLOVER

Red clover is a member of the legume family. With the aid of microscopic soil organisms, legumes add nitrogen, an important element for all plant growth, to the soil.

BEST CLIMATE AND SITE: Zones 5–9. Full sun to partial shade.

IDEAL SOIL CONDITIONS: Light, sandy garden soil; pH 6.0–6.7.

GROWING GUIDELINES: Broadcast seed shallowly in early spring for a cover crop. Where legumes have not been grown before, use the appropriate inoculant to help the clover to take atmospheric nitrogen into the soil.

GROWING HABIT: Perennial; height 1–2 feet (30–60 cm); leaflets oval, hairy.

FLOWERING TIME: Mid- to late summer; red to purple, fragrant, globe-like heads.

PEST AND DISEASE PREVENTION: Usually free from pests and diseases.

HARVESTING AND STORING: Collect flowers at full bloom and dry on paper in the shade; store in airtight containers. Use to make a slightly sweet tea that is said to purify the blood, relieve irritating coughs, and be a mild sedative.

SPECIAL TIPS: Sow as a cover crop to renew the soil between demanding crops or use as a permanent groundcover.

OTHER COMMON NAMES: Trefoil, purple clover.

Rosmarinus officinalis   Labiatae

ROSEMARY, UPRIGHT

Rosemary is a highly scented herb used to season meat, poultry, and fish (particularly when roasted), bread, and desserts. Use both the flowers and leaves for cooking and garnishing.

White-flowered rosemary is an aromatic and ornamental herb with glossy green, needle-like leaves. Use it in cooking as you would other types of rosemary.

BEST CLIMATE AND SITE: Zones 8–10. Grown outdoors where temperatures remain above 10°F (-12°C). Full sun to partial shade.

IDEAL SOIL CONDITIONS: Light, well-drained soil; pH 6.0–6.7.

GROWING GUIDELINES: Sow seed shallowly indoors in early spring, then transplant to pots outdoors; plant out to garden for second season, spacing 3 feet (90 cm) apart. Or take cuttings from new growth in fall, or layer the stems during summer. Overwintering success varies with local conditions and cultivar; larger plants may overwinter better outdoors than small ones. Potted plants may be brought into a sunny greenhouse for the winter; or keep them at 45°F (7°C) in a sunny garage or enclosed porch, watering infrequently.

GROWING HABIT: Height 2–6 feet (60–180 cm); tender perennial with scaly bark and aromatic, needle-like leaves.

FLOWERING TIME: Varies according to climate and cultivar; small pale blue to pink clusters.

PEST AND DISEASE PREVENTION: Indoors, watch for scale pests and wipe them from foliage with cotton soaked with rubbing alcohol.

HARVESTING AND STORING: Snip fresh foliage as needed all year.

SPECIAL TIPS: In warm climates, rosemary makes an attractive shrub.

OTHER SPECIES AND VARIETIES:

PROSTRATE ROSEMARY (*R. prostratus*): Some cultivars have deep blue flowers almost all year; good for rock gardens, hanging baskets; not very winter-hardy.

WHITE-FLOWERED ROSEMARY (*R. officinalis* var. *alba*): Showy blossoms; said to be the hardiest variety.

ROSES

Roses can be a challenge to grow successfully. These shrubs have aromatic blossoms used for making perfume.

BEST CLIMATE AND SITE: Zones 4–8. Full sun to partial shade.

IDEAL SOIL CONDITIONS: Well-drained, clayey soil; pH 6.0–7.5.

GROWING GUIDELINES: Propagate from seed, cuttings, or buddings. Purchase nursery stock for best results. Work in plenty of compost or well-rotted manure when planting, and renew at the surface each spring. Plant approximately 30 inches (75 cm) apart in beds, and provide support for climbing types. Roses will be injured by standing in water, and need at least half a day of sunshine along with frequent watering and feeding. Prune in winter to maintain shape, and remove dead or damaged stems.

GROWING HABIT: Perennial; height varies with species; stems thorned and upright, creeping, or vining.

FLOWERING TIME: May to frost; single or clustered flowers with berry-like hips ripening in fall.

PEST AND DISEASE PREVENTION: Space correctly, provide adequate sunshine, and water in early morning, when foliage will dry quickly, to prevent foliage and root diseases. Knock aphids and mites from leaves with a spray of water. Handpick large pests like Japanese beetles and rose chafers daily.

HARVESTING AND STORING: Gather the petals before completely open and dry them quickly on screens or paper. Collect rosehips in fall and dry them, or make vinegars and preserves.

RUE

Rue has a pungent, skunk-like odor. Its green, delicate foliage has a blue tint that contrasts well with the usual garden greens.

BEST CLIMATE AND SITE: Zones 4–9. Full sun.

IDEAL SOIL CONDITIONS: Poor, well-drained soil; pH 6.0–7.0.

GROWING GUIDELINES: Sow seed shallowly indoors in late winter, transplanting outdoors in late spring 18–24 inches (45–60 cm) apart. Or take cuttings from new growth, or divide older plants. Grows well in a pot, and continues growing when wintered indoors by a sunny window. Renew with compost or well-rotted manure each spring, and prune away dead stems.

GROWING HABIT: Perennial; height 2–3 feet (60–90 cm); woody stems with greenish blue foliage.

FLOWERING TIME: June to August; yellow-green blossoms in clusters.

PEST AND DISEASE PREVENTION: Prevent root diseases with good drainage.

HARVESTING AND STORING: Harvest several times each season, bunching foliage to dry. Use the dried seedpods and leaves for flower arrangements.

SPECIAL TIPS: According to folklore, rue slows the growth of basil, sage, and members of the cabbage family.

PRECAUTIONS: Can be toxic when used internally; often causes irritation on contact with skin.

OTHER COMMON NAMES: Herbgrass, common rue, garden rue, herb of grace.

SAFFLOWER

SAFFRON

The dried flowers of safflower are used for yellow and red dyes. The plant yields a popular cooking oil.

Saffron is the source of a yellow dye and valuable spice used in cooking seafoods, meats, rice, and poultry dishes.

BEST CLIMATE AND SITE: Zones 3–9. Full sun.

IDEAL SOIL CONDITIONS: Dry soil enriched with organic matter; pH 6.0–7.0.

GROWING GUIDELINES: Sow seed shallowly outdoors in early spring; thin to 6 inches (15 cm). Transplants poorly.

GROWING HABIT: Annual; height 2–3 feet (60–90 cm); upright stems branch at the top; leaves spiny.

FLOWERING TIME: Summer; orange to yellow thistle-like flowers.

PEST AND DISEASE PREVENTION: Handpick snails and slugs from seedlings. Usually free from other pests and diseases.

HARVESTING AND STORING: Collect flowers when fully opened and dry on paper in the shade.

OTHER COMMON NAMES: American saffron, fake saffron.

BEST CLIMATE AND SITE: Zones 6–9. Full sun to light shade.

IDEAL SOIL CONDITIONS: Light, well-drained soil; pH 6.5–7.5.

GROWING GUIDELINES: Plant corms 3–4 inches (7.5–10 cm) deep, rooting side down, in fall or spring at 6-inch (15 cm) intervals. Lift and divide corms every 2–3 years, after foliage has died down in spring or fall. Self-propagates. Cover with a light mulch, like straw, in severe winters.

GROWING HABIT: Perennial; height 12 inches (30 cm); grass-like leaves.

FLOWERING TIME: September; flowers arise from soil without stems.

PEST AND DISEASE PREVENTION: Usually free from pests and diseases.

HARVESTING AND STORING: Collect individual dark yellow stigmata; dry on paper away from breezes; store in an air-tight container in a cool place.

SAGE

Sage is an easy-to-grow, shrubby perennial with aromatic foliage used most often with poultry. A tea of sage is said to settle the stomach.

BEST CLIMATE AND SITE: Zones 4–8. Full sun to partial shade.

IDEAL SOIL CONDITIONS: Well-drained garden soil; pH 6.0–6.7.

GROWING GUIDELINES: Sow seed shallowly outdoors in late spring or indoors in late winter; plant at 20–24-inch (50–60 cm) intervals. Take cuttings or divide older plants in spring or fall. Mulch during severe winters and prune severely in spring to prevent flowering. Grows easily for several years, then begins to decline. Other species or cultivars may not be as hardy.

GROWING HABIT: Height 1–2 feet (30–60 cm); woody stems have wrinkled gray-green foliage.

FLOWERING TIME: Spring; tubular pink to purple flowers in whorls.

PEST AND DISEASE PREVENTION: Plant in a sandy location at the proper spacing for best drainage and air circulation necessary for preventing disease and slug problems. Rarely bothered by other pests.

HARVESTING AND STORING: Snip fresh leaves as needed, or bunch them and hang to dry for use during winter months. Refrain from harvesting the first year.

OTHER SPECIES AND CULTIVARS:

GOLDEN SAGE (*S. officinalis* 'Aurea'): Height 18 inches (45 cm); leaves variegated gold and green; excellent bushy border plant.

Purple sage is grown and used like common sage. Try it in stuffings, omelets, soups, and stews. Its purplish foliage adds interest to any garden.

PINEAPPLE SAGE (*S. elegans*): Height 24–42 inches (60–105 cm); dark green, pineapple-scented leaves; brilliant red tubular flowers bloom all summer; prefers full sun; pinch tops for bushier growth; grown as an annual; may need staking.

PURPLE SAGE (*S. officinalis* 'Purpurea'): Height 18 inches (45 cm); leaves reddish purple; grow and use like common sage.

TRICOLOR SAGE (*S. officinalis* 'Tricolor'): Height 2–3 feet (60–90 cm); leaves finely wrinkled with cream, purple, and green.

| *Santolina chamaecyparissus* | Compositae | *Sassafras albidum* | Lauraceae |

SANTOLINA

SASSAFRAS

A perennial evergreen with a lavender-like scent, santolina is actually a member of the daisy family.

BEST CLIMATE AND SITE: Zones 6–8. Full sun.

IDEAL SOIL CONDITIONS: Poor, well-drained soil; pH 7.0–8.0.

GROWING GUIDELINES: Sow seed shallowly outdoors in late spring; thin to 3 feet (90 cm). Germinates slowly. Take cuttings, layer, or divide older plants in spring. Grows poorly in wet soils.

GROWING HABIT: Height to 2 feet (60 cm); leaves are finely cut, gray.

FLOWERING TIME: June to July; clusters of yellow buttons.

PEST AND DISEASE PREVENTION: Usually free from pests and diseases. Cut back straggly, old plants each spring to promote new, healthy growth.

HARVESTING AND STORING: Harvest and bunch the top 8–10 inches (20–25 cm) of foliage in summer, and hang to dry. Use as a backing for making aromatic wreaths. Collect flowers with stem at full bloom; hang to dry.

OTHER COMMON NAMES: Lavender cotton.

Sassafras is a tall, deciduous tree that produces an oil once used as a flavoring for cold and hot beverages.

BEST CLIMATE AND SITE: Zones 5–9. Sun or shade.

IDEAL SOIL CONDITIONS: Well-drained garden soil; pH 6.7–7.3.

GROWING GUIDELINES: Propagate by seed, suckers, or root cuttings. Only very small, young trees transplant successfully.

GROWING HABIT: Height 20–60 feet (6–18 m); tree with smooth, orange-brown bark.

FLOWERING TIME: Spring; small, inconspicuous greenish yellow flowers.

PEST AND DISEASE PREVENTION: Usually free from pests and diseases.

HARVESTING AND STORING: Peel the bark off the tree as required or dry and store in an air-tight container. Use a decoction of the bark externally as an antiseptic on wounds and sores.

SPECIAL TIPS: Sassafras is now grown mostly as an ornamental, for its colorful fall foliage.

PRECAUTIONS: Do not take internally.

Satureja montana   Labiatae

SAVORY, WINTER

This aromatic, bushy, hardy perennial has a peppery flavor and has been used in cooking for 2,000 years.

BEST CLIMATE AND SITE: Zones 6–9. Full sun.

IDEAL SOIL CONDITIONS: Poor, well-drained soil; pH 6.7–7.3.

GROWING GUIDELINES: Sow seed shallowly outdoors in late spring, thinning to 1 foot (30 cm). Germinates slowly. Take cuttings, or divide older plants in spring or fall.

GROWING HABIT: Height 6–12 inches (15–30 cm); branched, woody stems; oblong, needle-like leaves.

FLOWERING TIME: June; pale purple blossoms.

PEST AND DISEASE PREVENTION: Usually free from pests and diseases.

HARVESTING AND STORING: Harvest fresh as needed, or cut and dry the foliage just before flowering. Use as a flavoring in a variety of dishes, teas, herb butters, and vinegars.

OTHER SPECIES:

SUMMER SAVORY (_S. hortensis_): Annual; prefers light, well-fertilized soil; transplants poorly; height 12–18 inches (30–45 cm); linear, downy leaves; pale lavender or white blossoms; used as an antiflatulent.

Saponaria officinalis   Caryophyllaceae

SOAPWORT

This hardy perennial is a common roadside weed, often found in old pastures and hay fields.

BEST CLIMATE AND SITE: Zones 3–8. Full sun to light shade.

IDEAL SOIL CONDITIONS: Average to poor, well-drained soil; pH 6.0–7.0.

GROWING GUIDELINES: Sow seed shallowly indoors in winter, spring, or fall; transplant outdoors the following spring. Once established, soapwort self-sows and spreads rapidly.

GROWING HABIT: Height 1–2 feet (30–60 cm); branching stem.

FLOWERING TIME: July to September; pink to white, five-petaled flowers in terminal clusters.

PEST AND DISEASE PREVENTION: Usually free from pests and diseases.

HARVESTING AND STORING: Harvest fresh roots and leaves as needed. Clean, chop, and boil the root to make a sudsy solution. Use the juice from fresh leaves to relieve itching skin conditions.

OTHER COMMON NAMES: Bouncing bet.

Rumex spp. Polygonaceae

SORREL

In the spring, use sorrel's tender new leaves to make a delicate soup or add them to salads.

BEST CLIMATE AND SITE: Zones 5–9. Full sun.

IDEAL SOIL CONDITIONS: Rich, moist garden soil; pH 5.5–6.0.

GROWING GUIDELINES: Sow seed shallowly outdoors in late spring, thinning to 18 inches (45 cm). Or divide older plants in early spring or fall.

GROWING HABIT: Hardy perennial; height 30–36 inches (75–90 cm); wavy, green leaves.

FLOWERING TIME: Midsummer; greenish yellow to red flowers.

PEST AND DISEASE PREVENTION: Handpick snails from new spring leaves.

HARVESTING AND STORING: Harvest the outside leaves regularly to promote new growth. Sorrel leaves are best eaten fresh, but may also be blanched and frozen.

SPECIES:
FRENCH SORREL (*R. scutatus*): Low-growing perennial; best-tasting flavor.
GARDEN SORREL (*R. acetosa*): Also called sour dock; has a very bitter flavor.

Artemisia abrotanum Compositae

SOUTHERNWOOD

This ornamental and hardy perennial was once used as an aphrodisiac and to stimulate the growth of men's beards.

BEST CLIMATE AND SITE: Zones 4–8. Full sun.

IDEAL SOIL CONDITIONS: Well-drained garden soil; pH 6.0–7.0.

GROWING GUIDELINES: Propagate by cuttings, or divide older plants in spring or fall, and space 2–4 feet (60–120 cm) apart. In spring, prune to shape.

GROWING HABIT: Height 3–6 feet (1–1.8 m); finely divided, gray-green leaves.

FLOWERING TIME: August; small, inconspicuous yellow-white blossoms (rarely blooms in northern climates).

PEST AND DISEASE PREVENTION: Usually free from pests and diseases.

HARVESTING AND STORING: Collect foliage anytime in summer and hang in bunches to dry. Use dried foliage to repel moths in stored clothing, or as an aromatic backing for herbal wreaths.

OTHER COMMON NAMES: Old-man.

| *Myrrhis odorata* | Umbelliferae | *Galium odoratum* | Rubiaceae |

SWEET CICELY

SWEET WOODRUFF

Sweet cicely has a scent like lovage and a sweet licorice taste. It is an ornamental and hardy perennial.

Sweet woodruff is a hardy perennial groundcover that grows well in full shade and smells like vanilla when dried.

BEST CLIMATE AND SITE: Zones 3–7. Partial shade.

IDEAL SOIL CONDITIONS: Rich, humusy, well-drained soil; pH 6.0–6.7.

GROWING GUIDELINES: Sow seed shallowly outdoors in late spring, thinning to 2 feet (60 cm); germination is very slow; self-sows. Divide older plants in spring or fall, leaving each new piece with a bud. Side-dress each spring with compost or well-rotted manure.

GROWING HABIT: Height to 3 feet (90 cm); leaves are fern-like, finely divided.

FLOWERING TIME: May to June; numerous white blossoms in umbels.

PEST AND DISEASE PREVENTION: Usually free from pests and diseases.

HARVESTING AND STORING: Use fresh leaves as needed all summer in salads and cooking. Collect seed heads and dry on paper in a shady spot; store in air-tight containers. Use the seeds in cakes and desserts. Dig roots after the first year, scrub them, and dry until brittle or use them fresh like parsnips.

OTHER COMMON NAMES: Myrrh, anise, sweet chervil.

BEST CLIMATE AND SITE: Zones 3–9. Prefers shade.

IDEAL SOIL CONDITIONS: Moist, humusy, well-drained, soil; pH 5.0–8.0.

GROWING GUIDELINES: Sow seed shallowly in fall outdoors; germination may take as long as 200 days. Purchase plants from nurseries, or divide established plants in the spring or fall.

GROWING HABIT: Height 8–12 inches (20–30 cm).

FLOWERING TIME: May to June; small, funnel-shaped, white blossoms.

PEST AND DISEASE PREVENTION: Usually free from pests and diseases; has insect-repellent properties.

HARVESTING AND STORING: Gather foliage anytime in summer, hanging bunches to dry. Use in potpourris and herbal wreaths and to make tan-colored dye.

PRECAUTIONS: May be toxic when taken internally.

Tanacetum vulgare Compositae	*Artemisia dracunculus* var. *sativa* Compositae

TANSY

TARRAGON, FRENCH

This easy-to-grow, aromatic, and attractive perennial has brilliant green foliage and yellow button-like flowers.

Tarragon's heavy licorice flavor holds well in cooking, making it an extremely useful herb in the kitchen.

BEST CLIMATE AND SITE: Zones 4–8. Full sun to partial shade.

IDEAL SOIL CONDITIONS: Well-drained garden soil; pH 6.0–7.0.

GROWING GUIDELINES: Sow seed shallowly in late winter indoors; transplant outdoors after danger of frost, 4 feet (1.2 m) apart. Divide established plants in spring or fall. Spreads easily. Prune vigorously in midsummer for lush growth in late fall. Plants may need support; they will stand upright when grown along fences.

GROWING HABIT: Height 3–4 feet (90–120 cm); erect, branched stems with fern-like, aromatic leaves.

FLOWERING TIME: July to September: button-like, yellow blossoms in terminal clusters.

PEST AND DISEASE PREVENTION: Usually free from pests and diseases. Aphids may be a problem in some northern locations; to control, dislodge them with a spray of water.

HARVESTING AND STORING: Collect foliage anytime during summer and hang in bunches to dry. Flowers dry well but lose their bright yellow color. Use leaves and flowers to make green-gold dye. Use flowers in dried flower arrangements.

SPECIAL TIPS: Tansy is said to repel certain pest insects, while attracting the beneficials.

PRECAUTIONS: May be toxic when taken internally.

OTHER COMMON NAMES: Golden buttons.

BEST CLIMATE AND SITE: Zones 4–8. Full sun to partial shade.

IDEAL SOIL CONDITIONS: Well-drained garden soil; pH 6.0–7.3.

GROWING GUIDELINES: Cannot be grown from seed. Take cuttings from new growth in fall, over-wintering the young plants indoors until the following spring. Or divide older plants in spring every 3 years; space 12–24 inches (30–60 cm) apart. Prune away flower stems each year, for most vigorous growth and best flavor. To grow indoors in winter, pot young plants in summer, cutting foliage to just above the soil. Seal pot in a plastic bag, and refrigerate to mimic winter. In fall, unwrap and place in a sunny window for winter harvests.

GROWING HABIT: Height to 2 feet (60 cm); hardy perennial with long, branched green stems.

FLOWERING TIME: Remove inconspicuous yellow-green blossoms to encourage growth of foliage.

PEST AND DISEASE PREVENTION: Plant in well-drained soil to prevent most root and stem diseases.

HARVESTING AND STORING: Clip foliage as needed all summer, or indoors in winter. Foliage may be harvested entirely twice each summer. Fresh foliage lasts several weeks in the refrigerator when wrapped in paper towels, then placed in a plastic bag. Bunch and hang to dry away from sunlight. May also be preserved in salad vinegars.

Thymus vulgaris Labiatae

THYME, GARDEN

Thyme is a favorite of chefs and gardeners, as it grows easily and there is at least one variety to suit every taste and location.

Creeping thyme, with its dense dark green leaves, makes an ideal groundcover.

BEST CLIMATE AND SITE: Zones 5–9. Full sun to partial shade.

IDEAL SOIL CONDITIONS: Sandy, well-drained soil; pH 6.0–6.7.

GROWING GUIDELINES: Sow seed shallowly in late winter indoors, keeping the soil at 70°F (21°C) for best germination. Plant outdoors in late spring in clumps, 1 foot (30 cm) apart. You can take cuttings, or divide older plants in spring. In winter, mulch with a light material like straw. Replace plants every 3–4 years to control woody growth.

GROWING HABIT: Height 6–15 inches (15–38 cm); hardy perennial; woody stems; tiny, aromatic leaves.

FLOWERING TIME: Midsummer; tubular lilac to pink blossoms in clusters.

PEST AND DISEASE PREVENTION: Plant in well-drained soil to prevent root and stem diseases.

HARVESTING AND STORING: Snip foliage as needed during the summer, or harvest entirely twice per season, leaving at least 3 inches (7.5 cm) of growth. Bunch together and hang to dry, or first strip the leaves and dry on a screen. Foliage freezes well in air-tight containers or bags.

SPECIAL TIPS: Thyme is said to benefit the growth of eggplant, potatoes, and tomatoes; it also repels cabbageworms and whiteflies.

RELATED PLANTS:

CREEPING THYME (*T. praecox* subsp. *arcticus*): Height to 4 inches (10 cm); forms a dense, dark green

groundcover; flower color (rose, purple, crimson, or white) varies with cultivar; also called mother-of-thyme.

LEMON THYME (*T.* x *citriodorus*): Height to 1 foot (30 cm); leaves are dark green or variegated, glossy, and lemon-scented; not grown from seed.

Lemon thyme is a small bush. Its lemon-scented leaves can be used in cooking, especially with fish or chicken.

Valeriana officinalis   Valerianaceae

VALERIAN

In the United States, valerian is best known as an ornamental perennial, although it does have sedative properties.

BEST CLIMATE AND SITE: Zones 4–7. Full sun to partial shade.

IDEAL SOIL CONDITIONS: Rich, moist garden soil; pH 5.0–8.0.

GROWING GUIDELINES: Sow seed shallowly outdoors in April, transplanting to the garden when small plants are established. Germinates poorly. Propagate by crown or runner division in spring or fall, spacing new plants 1 foot (30 cm) apart. Plants quickly become crowded, so dig and renew them every 3 years.

GROWING HABIT: Height 36–60 inches (1–1.5 m); herbaceous plant with fetid smell.

FLOWERING TIME: June; small, tubular pink to lavender blossoms.

PEST AND DISEASE PREVENTION: Usually free from pests and diseases.

HARVESTING AND STORING: Dig roots in fall or spring, before new shoots form; wash and dry quickly at 120°F (49°C) until brittle. Stores well. Prepare a soothing bath by adding a decoction made from valerian.

SPECIAL TIPS: The roots of valerian attract earthworms, so plant it in mixed borders and vegetable gardens.

OTHER COMMON NAMES: Garden heliotrope.

Verbena officinalis   Verbenaceae

VERVAIN, EUROPEAN

This ancient annual has a religious and medicinal history. Currently, it is grown as an ornamental.

BEST CLIMATE AND SITE: Zones 5–9. Common in tropical and subtropical North and South America. Prefers full sun.

IDEAL SOIL CONDITIONS: Rich, moist garden soil; pH 6.0–7.0.

GROWING GUIDELINES: Easily grows from seed sown outdoors; thin to 1 foot (30 cm). Take cuttings from the new growth of overwintered plants. Self-sows. In the North, plant as an annual. An organic mulch in spring will encourage better flowers and foliage.

GROWING HABIT: Height 1–3 feet (30–90 cm); loosely branched with oblong leaves.

FLOWERING TIME: Spring; small purple to white blossoms.

PEST AND DISEASE PREVENTION: Usually free from pests and diseases.

HARVESTING AND STORING: Legend instructs that vervain should be harvested when neither sun nor moon is in the sky, and that pieces of honeycomb should be left in exchange.

PRECAUTIONS: May be toxic when taken internally.

OTHER SPECIES:

AMERICAN VERVAIN (*V. hastata*): Height 4–5 feet (1.2–1.5 m); somewhat hardier; blue flowers; also called blue vervain.

Viola odorata Violaceae

VIOLET

Hamamelis virginiana Hamamelidaceae

WITCH HAZEL

Violets are early fragrant bloomers that grow well in shaded locations during cool weather.

BEST CLIMATE AND SITE: Zones 5–8. Partial shade.

IDEAL SOIL CONDITIONS: Rich, moist garden soil; pH 6.0–7.0.

GROWING GUIDELINES: Sow seed shallowly outdoors in fall; cover with burlap; thin to 1 foot (30 cm). Divide mature plants in winter or early spring.

GROWING HABIT: Perennial; height 4–6 inches (10–15 cm); stemless, kidney-shaped, downy leaves.

FLOWERING TIME: April to May; fragrant purple, violet, white, or pink blossoms.

PEST AND DISEASE PREVENTION: Control mites with a forceful spray of water directed at undersides of leaves, or spray with insecticidal soap or botanical insecticide, like pyrethrin or rotenone.

HARVESTING AND STORING: Thoroughly dry flowers for culinary use; store in air-tight containers. Petals may be candied, or added to jams, flans, and fruit salads.

OTHER COMMON NAMES: Sweet violet, garden violet, English violet, florist's violet.

Distilled witch hazel extract remains a popular astringent, despite the lack of proof that it works.

BEST CLIMATE AND SITE: Zones 4–8. Full sun to partial shade.

IDEAL SOIL CONDITIONS: Moist, rich garden soil; pH 6.0–7.0.

GROWING GUIDELINES: Store fresh seed in a warm room for 5 months, then at 40°F (4°C) for 3 months, before sowing. You can take cuttings or layerings from established plants.

GROWING HABIT: Height 8–15 feet (2.5–4.5 m); deciduous shrubs and small trees with smooth, gray to brown bark.

FLOWERING TIME: October to November; yellow thread-like petals followed by black nuts.

PEST AND DISEASE PREVENTION: Usually free from pests and diseases.

HARVESTING AND STORING: Collect leaves, twigs, and bark as needed without damaging the tree.

SPECIAL TIPS: The twigs of witch hazel are often used for water divining.

OTHER COMMON NAMES: Spotted alder, snapping hazelnut.

Artemisia absinthum   Compositae

WORMWOOD

Wormwood is an attractive, common, and hardy member of sand-dune communities, with gray-green foliage and bushy growth.

BEST CLIMATE AND SITE: Zones 4–6. Full sun to partial shade.

IDEAL SOIL CONDITIONS: Poor, well-drained soil; pH 6.0–6.7.

GROWING GUIDELINES: Sow seed shallowly outdoors in fall; or sow seed indoors in late winter, planting outdoors in late spring. Thin first-year plants to 15 inches (38 cm), then to 3 feet (90 cm) the second year. Take cuttings or divide established plants in early spring or early fall. Most plants last 7 years, with peak production during the second or third year.

GROWING HABIT: Height to 4 feet (1.2 m); hardy perennial with gray-green foliage.

FLOWERING TIME: July to August; green-yellow in panicle.

PEST AND DISEASE PREVENTION: Few pests. Wormwood is said to repel most insect and mammal pests.

HARVESTING AND STORING: Restrict harvests to the tops of plants when they flower after July. Hang in bunches to dry, then store in an air-tight container. Withstands two harvests per season. Use in sachets to repel insects, or make a tea to repel aphids in the garden.

PRECAUTIONS: Unsafe when taken internally.

OTHER COMMON NAMES: Absinthe.

Achillea millefolium   Compositae

YARROW

Yarrow displays light, delicate foliage and long-lasting flowers. It is hardy and very easy to grow from seed.

BEST CLIMATE AND SITE: Zones 2–8. Full sun.

IDEAL SOIL CONDITIONS: Moderately rich, well-drained soil; pH 6.0–6.7.

GROWING GUIDELINES: Sow seed shallowly indoors in late winter, or outdoors in late spring. Divide established plants in early spring or fall. To extend flowering, pick blossoms often. Some cultivars will bloom from seed the first year.

GROWING HABIT: Height to 3 feet (90 cm); a perennial with fern-like, finely divided leaves.

FLOWERING TIME: June to September; numerous tiny florets in clusters.

PEST AND DISEASE PREVENTION: Provide well-drained soil to avoid powdery mildew. Said to attract beneficial insects.

HARVESTING AND STORING: Pick flowers with plenty of stem, and strip foliage before hanging in bunches to dry; holds color well. Use in dried flower arrangements or to make yellow or olive-colored dye.

SPECIAL TIPS: Although wild yarrow usually has white blossoms, you can purchase seed for several colorful cultivars.

PRECAUTIONS: May cause allergic reactions when taken internally.

USDA
PLANT HARDINESS ZONE MAP

The map that follows shows the United States and Canada divided into 10 zones. Each zone is based on a 10°F (5.6°C) difference in average annual minimum temperature. Some areas are considered too high in elevation for plant cultivation and so are not assigned to any zone. There are also island zones that are warmer or cooler than surrounding areas because of differences in elevation; they have been given a zone different from the surrounding areas. Many large urban areas are in a warmer zone than the surrounding land.

Plants grow best within an optimum range of temperatures. The range may be wide for some species, narrow for others. Plants also differ in their ability to survive frost and their sun or shade requirements.

The zone ratings indicate conditions where designated plants will grow well, and not merely survive. Refer to the map to find out which zone you are in. In the "Plant by Plant Guide," starting on page 100, you'll find recommendations for the plants that grow best in your zone.

Many plants may survive in zones warmer or colder than their recommended zone range. Remember that other factors, including wind, soil type, soil moisture and drainage capability, humidity, snow, and winter sunshine, may have a great effect on growth.

Average annual minimum temperature (°F/°C)

Zone 1	Below -50°F/-45°C	
Zone 2	-40° to -50°F/-40° to -45°C	
Zone 3	-30° to -40°F/-34° to -40°C	
Zone 4	-20° to -30°F/-29° to -34°C	
Zone 5	-10° to -20°F/-23° to -29°C	
Zone 6	0° to -10°F/-18° to -23°C	
Zone 7	10° to 0°F/-12° to -18°C	
Zone 8	20° to 10°F/-7° to -12°C	
Zone 9	30° to 20°F/-1° to -7°C	
Zone 10	40° to 30°F/4° to -1°C	

INDEX

ACKNOWLEDGMENTS

Mulching chart, page 67: adapted from *Rodale's Illustrated Encyclopedia of Gardening and Landscaping Techniques*, © 1990 by Rodale Press, Inc. Permission granted by Rodale Press, Inc., Emmaus, PA 18098.

Weldon Russell would like to thank the following Australian companies and people for their assistance in the production of this book: June Bland; Colonial Cottage Nursery, Kenthurst; Common Scents Cottage, Dural; Duane Norris Garden Designers, Woollahra; Fragrant Garden, Erina; Henry Doubleday Research Association; Honeysuckle Garden Centre, Double Bay; Russell Lee; Di McDonald; McNaturals Nursery, Hazelbrook; Catherine Wallace.

Photo Credits

Ardea, London: pages 111 (left), 121 (right), 132 (left, photographer A.P. Paterson), and 136 (left).

Auscape/Jacana: page 133 (left, photographer Paul Nief).

A–Z Botanical Collection: pages 104 (left), and 137 (left).

Heather Angel: back cover (center), pages 24, 118 (right), 124 (right), 126 (right), and 145 (right).

Gillian Beckett: pages 17 and 19.

Bruce Coleman Ltd: photographers B & C Calhoun: page 119 (right); photographer Robert P. Carr: page 152 (right); photographer Eric Crichton: endpapers, opposite title page, pages 116 (left), 147 (left), and 148 (left); photographer Gerald Cubitt: page 97; photographer Halle Flygare: page 108 (left); photographer Rocco Longo: page 125 (right); photographer Marie Read: copyright page; photographer Hans Reinhard: title page, opposite contents, pages 11, 105 (left and right), 115 (left), 127 (left), and 129 (bottom left); photographer Norbert Rosing: page 56; photographer John Shaw: page 100; photographer Michel Viard: page 112 (left).

Earth Scenes: page 139 (right, photographer Richard Kolar).

Derek Fell: pages 12, 48, 58, and 71.

Steven Foster: pages 103 (right), 109 (left), and 136 (right).

Rowan Fotheringham (stylist Karen Byak): front cover.

The Garden Picture Library: pages 79 (top), 84 (left), and 85; photographer Brian Carter: pages 8, 15, 26, 46, 47, 54, 72, and 103 (left); photographer Michael Homes: page 44; photographer Anne Kelley: page 59 (top); photographer Gary Rogers: page 75 (left).

Denise Greig: pages 152 (left) and 153 (right).

Harry Smith Collection: pages 118 (left), 127 (right), 131 (left), and 151 (right).

Stirling Macoboy: pages 107 (left) and 114 (left).

Cheryl Maddocks: page 18.

Patricia S. Michalak: page 106 (right).

Jerry Pavia: page 112 (right).

Joanne Pavia: page 104 (right).

Photos Horticultural: pages 23, 25, 45, 59 (bottom), 64, 87 (top), 124 (left), and 143 (right).

Rodale Stock Images: back cover (bottom), half title page, pages 28, 40, 61 (top), 65, 82 (bottom), 84 (right), 89 (top and center), 94 (bottom left), 98, 107 (bottom left), 108 (right), 122 (right), 128 (right), 138 (right), 142 (right), and 148 (right).

Tony Rodd: back cover (top), pages 11, 94 (top), 107 (top right), 110 (left and right), 111 (right), 115 (right), 116 (right), 120 (left and right), 121 (left), 123 (left), 125 (left), 131 (right), 134 (left and right), 135 (right), 140 (right), 143 (left), 145 (left), and 146 (right).

Lorna Rose: page 16.

Weldon Russell: page 78 (top, photographer Carlo Cantini).

Weldon Trannies: pages 7, 75 (right), 84 (top), 86 (top), and 95 (top).

All other photographs by David Wallace.